Arduino Wearables

Tony Olsson

Apress®

Arduino Wearables

ISBN-13 (pbk): 978-1-4302-4359-5

ISBN-13 (electronic): 978-1-4302-4360-1

President and Publisher: Paul Manning
Acquisitions Editor: Michelle Lowman
Development Editor: Matthew Moodie
Technical Reviewer: Anne Niemetz
Editorial Board: Steve Anglin, Ewan Buckingham, Gary Cornell, Louise Corrigan, Morgan Ertel, Jonathan Gennick, Jonathan Hassell, Robert Hutchinson, Michelle Lowman, James Markham, Matthew Moodie, Jeff Olson, Jeffrey Pepper, Douglas Pundick, Ben Renow-Clarke, Dominic Shakeshaft, Gwenan Spearing, Matt Wade, Tom Welsh
Coordinating Editor: Jessica Belanger
Copy Editor: Kimberly Burton
Compositor: Bytheway Publishing Services
Indexer: SPi Global
Artist: SPi Global
Cover Designer: Anna Ishchenko

Distributed to the book trade worldwide by Springer Science+Business Media New York, 233 Spring Street, 6th Floor, New York, NY 10013. Phone 1-800-SPRINGER, fax (201) 348-4505, e-mail orders-ny@springer-sbm.com, or visit www.springeronline.com.

For information on translations, please e-mail rights@apress.com, or visit www.apress.com.

Apress and friends of ED books may be purchased in bulk for academic, corporate, or promotional use. eBook versions and licenses are also available for most titles. For more information, reference our Special Bulk Sales–eBook Licensing web page at www.apress.com/bulk-sales.

Any source code or other supplementary materials referenced by the author in this text is available to readers at www.apress.com. For detailed information about how to locate your book's source code, go to www.apress.com/source-code.

Contents at a Glance

To whomever it may concern
—Tony

Contents

About the Author

■ Tony Olsson is an Art and Communication (K3) adjunct professor at Malmö University in Sweden. He has worked in academia around the world, introducing technology as a design material beyond traditional engineering. Olsson also works as a digital designer and artist, and is one of the founding members of the design group 1scale1. His work outside the university involves projects and collaborations that intersect design, fashion, architecture, art, and technology.

Olsson is a firm believer in the open-source philosophy. He also believes that any worthwile experience is an educational one and that sharing knowledge is the best way to become better at what you do.

About the Technical Reviewer

Anne Niemetz is a senior lecturer in the Media Programme, School of Design, Victoria University of Wellington, New Zealand. Anne's research interests and work spans a variety of media, including video, audio, installation, physical computing, and performance design. She is particularly fascinated by areas that combine design and art with technology and science, and she pursues collaborative and cross-disciplinary projects.

Anne first became involved in the field of fashion and technology about ten years ago, when she was completing her master's degree in the Design|Media Arts department at the University of California, Los Angeles. Her experience led her to create the Wearable Technology course at Victoria University in 2009, which has been and continues to be a source of joy, learning, frustration, surprise, and success.

Her work has been exhibited internationally. For more information, visit www.adime.de.

Acknowledgments

First, thanks goes to David Cuartielles, my mentor and friend, for his knowledge and patience during the years. If I never met David, this book would probably never have been written.

Thanks to all of our lab assistants at K3, Malmö University for their efforts in the lab during the time I was working on this book, and to Andreas Göransson for his support.

Thanks goes to my mother and sister. Even though they do not always understand what I do, they have always supported it.

Special thanks goes to David Gaetano, Samson Wiklund, and Jonas Odhner for our past collaboration, which made this book possible.

Thanks to the Apress team, who made working on this book a pleasure.

Of course, thanks also goes to Massimo Banzi, Tom Igoe, Gianluca Martino, David Mellis, and Nicholas Zambetti for more than just their work with Arduino.

Finally, thanks to the community and the everyday user for making Arduino the amazing thing it is.

Preface

If this is your first time working with Arduino or wearables or both, I would like to congratulate you on all the fun times ahead. Breaking stuff has always been a passion of mine—just to look inside to see what makes things work. Later in life, I found a passion for creating and designing new objects.

The knowledge in the book you are holding is by no means all my own invention; a large part of the knowledge comes from what other "makers" have shared with me during the years. It's a collection of knowledge from many fields of interest, like design, computer science, fashion, architecture, art, and electronics, which have been molded into projects that teach how to begin making your own wearable technology.

When I am not making stuff, I teach others how to make stuff, and during my years doing so, I have learned one important lesson: anyone can learn how to do anything. The only thing you need is the will to do it.

With that in mind, learning anything is then just a matter of time. I hope you find that this book helps you with that aspect.

Who This Book Is For

This book is for those interested in combining electronics with fashion. You might already own an Arduino board and be familiar with the concept of wearable computing, or all of this is completely new to you. The goal of this book is that no matter where you are in your learning process, you find something useful. Through a series of practical projects, this book aims to take complete beginners of programming and electronics from the basics to a fairly advanced level.

How to Read This Book

This book was written with the intention that most of the information you need to carry out each project is presented in the project's chapter. The chapters introduce you, the reader, to different theories and methods as you move along each chapter. The book starts by explaining the Arduino software and hardware, and gives an introduction to useful tools and materials.

The first two projects are not based around the Arduino board, but aim to give the reader a softer start to building wearables that do not require any programming. The remaining chapters introduce programming and gradually become more complex in construction and code.

If you are new to the field of wearable computing, I recommend starting at the beginning of the book because it gradually builds upon the knowledge of each chapter. If you are already familiar with working with Arduino, each chapter should provide you with the necessary information needed to complete the project. If you feel the need, you can always backtrack.

What You Need to Know

The only preexisting knowledge needed is that you know how to operate a computer and know how to install programs. The book tries to provide you with the rest. This book, however, is based on very practical projects that require a lot of materials and tools. Some of these materials are very specialized and may be a bit difficult to find if you don't know where to look. At the end of Chapter 1, I provide a list of a few electronics and materials vendors.

Downloading the Code

The code for the examples shown in this book is available on the Apress web site, www.apress.com. A link can be found on the book's information page under the Source Code/Downloads tab. This tab is located underneath the Related Titles section of the page.

Contacting the Author

Should you have any questions or comments related to this book, you can contact the author at t.olsson@1scale1.com.

CHAPTER 1

Introduction

At a young age, I lived very close to my grandmothers and I used to visit them often. Both of my grandmothers were very skilled in textile handcrafts and, along with my mother, were firm believers that sewing is one of those basic skills that everyone should know. One grandmother was amazing at crocheting and needlepoint, and the other one was very skilled in weaving and loved quilting. I've been very interested in everything practical and artistic since I was young, and my grandmothers were patient enough to teach me their skills.

I would never have thought that these faded skills would come in handy years later as I became more interested in other artistic areas. It was not long after I first saw an Arduino board that I realized that there was such a thing as combining electronics and textiles. Not long afterward, I got the chance to teach others about this amazing piece of technology in a course that focused on fashion and technology.

The product of all my time spent working with and teaching with the Arduino is what you now hold in your hands. This book is a practical introduction to the wonderful world of wearables; it mixes theory with a hands-on approach.

Since you made it as far as picking up this book, you are already half way there. The biggest challenge you face starting out with electronics and programming is the fear that these things are hard to learn. If you still have your doubts, dispel them. Even if part of the learning process is tricky, I can't think of a more fun way to learn electronics and programming than through making your own wearable project.

Rather than just explaining each step of the construction process, the projects in this book include a lot of theory behind how they actually work—so that you can build a deeper understanding of wearables. The goal is to build your skills and inspire you to develop upon the projects in this book to create new projects beyond it. Maybe in the future you will show me how it is done.

Wearables

Fashion and technology, wearable computing, techno fashion, embedded technology, e-textiles, wearable tech, or just plain "wearables." The list of names is long, but they all share the same principle of combining technology with textiles. This book serves as a practical introduction on how you can start experimenting within these areas.

As all of the names suggest, this book is about making technology wearable. The idea might sound new to some, but people have been wearing technology for centuries if you think about it. Eyeglasses are technology worn on your face to enhance sight; the first pair were made in Italy in the eleventh century. Watches are devices that are constructed to calculate time; we have been wearing them since the sixteenth century, but the idea for pocket watches has been recorded much earlier.

Today, tech is all around us. We carry computers in bags custom-made to fit them. We wear the technology to operate MP3 players on our heads as a fashion statement. I can't remember the last time I met someone without a mobile phone. And phones are not just phones any more; they are a combination of technologies—computers, phones, cameras, and GPS technology—that fit in our pockets. Portable computers are all around us.

It was not until 1961 that we started to talk about wearable computers. Edward Thorp and Claude Shannon developed what is considered to be the first wearable computer. Shannon is probably more known for his contributions to information theory and Thorp as the inventor of card counting in blackjack. It was Thorp's area of interest that inspired them to create the first wearable computer. Thorp and Shannon were mathematicians that developed a system for calculating the speed of a roulette ball to predict where it would stop. Their system included a shoe with hidden microswitches used to calculate speed, and this information was sent to a small computer that transferred it into a musical signal sent over radio to a miniature speaker hidden in a collaborator's ear.

Thorp and Shannon's system was not revealed until 1966 in one of Thorp's books, in which he admitted that the system was tested in Las Vegas. He also said that the system never worked beyond one trial run due to problems with the microphone, but popular theories and speculations indicate otherwise, due to the fact that it took the men five years to reveal the project.

Thorp and Shannon may have created the first wearable computer, but today wearable computing is synonymous with one man in particular: Steve Mann. In 1981, Mann began to develop a wearable computer; he has been wearing it since. The story I have been told is that it all started one day when Mann was out walking. As a photographer, he often found that when he saw a good moment to take a photo, the moment had passed by the time he had his camera ready. So his first wearable computer was a backpack-mounted system that constantly recorded everything he could see.

Since then, Mann has continued developing his system and today his entire computer fits into a pair of sunglasses with the full functionality of a normal computer.

Although a lot of wearable computers are based on the notion of extending the functions of the human body, technology has always been a subject for fashion. Even in the early stages of the development of eyeglasses and pocket watches, these objects became subject for personal expression and for projecting status.

Mann's wearable system also became a victim of fashion. While living his life wearing his computer, he often felt alienated due to the fact that his physical presence confused people. He felt limited by this. His system was meant to enhance his life, but to be constantly treated differently because of the way he looked interfered with his creative vision. So he began to develop his system in a more seamless way by trying to hide much of the technology and make his system look more like an object a person would normally wear. You might say that he was forced to become fashionable.

Yet it is not until the past ten years that technology has rooted itself within the field of fashion. Likely the best known reason for this is Hussein Chalayan's 2007 spring/summer collection, which presented an historical interpretation of engineering with dresses that seamlessly combined technology and textiles in a way that made them look magical. The dresses bended, twisted, and moved all by themselves, which gave the illusion that the garments had a life of their own. There were similar creations prior to Chalayan's show, but none really illustrated the endless possibility of combining computers, electronics, and textiles.

In 2005, something happened that I think had a direct impact on the recent increase in interest in wearable computing. That thing also happens to be the basis for this book.

World, Say Hello to Arduino

In 2005, David Cuartielles met Massimo Banzi in the Italian city of Ivrea. Banzi was teaching electronics to university students, and Cuartielles, a university electronics teacher in Sweden, was in Italy to work on a project. Both men felt that electronics should not be limited to engineers but should also be used as a material for design students. At the time, however, they had a major problem: the tools available for working with electronics were not aimed at students with no prior knowledge of electronics—and they were very expensive. Most universities could not buy tools for each student; they needed to be shared among the students. And most universities would not consider investing in such tools outside the engineering departments.

Cuartielles and Banzi both believed that students need full access to the tools they are supposed to use and it's the university's responsibility to provide the students with the tools. The two men couldn't solve the money problem, so they began developing a tool that students could buy by on their own and was easy enough to be used without prior knowledge of electronics. Tom Igoe, a New York City–based teacher, and David Mellis, his former student, joined the project. Later, Gianluca Martino joined the project as a main producer. Today these five are known as "the Arduino team" and what they created was the Arduino board and software. An early Arduino board is shown in Figure 1-1.

Figure 1-1. Early version of the Arduino serial board

Arduino is a microprocessor board that lets you connect the physical world to the world of computers. The idea behind the Arduino board was not unique in any way. On the contrary, there were other very similar boards available at the time; but what made Arduino unique was the Arduino team's approach to the project. The first board was released under an open-source licensing model, which was very uncommon for hardware at the time.

Open-source licensing means that the design of the board was available for anyone to copy, reproduce, and modify in any way. Most technology companies make their money developing hardware; they don't tell anyone how they make their products and they take out patents to prevent others from copying.

But making a lot of money was never the goal with Arduino; the team wanted to create a tool that propagates learning. This also opened development for others to make improvements and contributions to the project, which in turn meant that they could cut development costs—which in another turn kept the price of the Arduino low.

Another reason for their success is their "punk rock approach" to learning. If you know three basic chords, it's enough to write a song, and one song is enough to make a band. There is no reason to wait before getting started. The Arduino team took the same approach to electronics. You don't need to be an engineer or know math, physics, or a whole lot about computers to get started working with electronics and microcontrollers. In fact, you don't really need to know anything to start building stuff. You learn by doing it.

A few years after the first version of the Arduino board was created, Leah Buechley, a professor at MIT, had an idea for a new design of the board. There had been redesigns of the standard board, but Buechley's design was aimed at being sewn into fabrics and became known as the LilyPad. In 2012, Limor Fried, an electronics designer, came out with another sewable, an Arduino software–compatible board called the Flora.

Sharing is Caring

A large portion of the open-source community is dedicated to the sharing of knowledge and, as Otto von Busch has pointed out in his research, fashion and open source share a lot of the same ideas. Busch is a fashion theorist and designer. He has devoted part of his work to explaining hacking through the creation of new garments from old ones.

Hacking is often wrongfully considered to be illegal activities performed on computers, in which a person breaks into a system and steals information. The truth is, most hackers do not do anything illegal. Hacking is more the learning method where you take existing technology and modify it in different ways just for the fun of learning how it works. Fashion works in a similar sense: you borrow inspiration from other creations. In the same sense that you might borrow a pattern from a friend for a dress and modify that pattern to fit your measurements, the open-source community shares code and hardware designs, which they then modify to fit their needs.

This is also a philosophy shared within the Arduino community. Special acknowledgment goes out to this community; without their shared knowledge, I would have never gained the knowledge that became this book. I urge all readers of this book to share their knowledge. Sharing is caring about what you do, and by sharing your insights, you learn even more.

A good starting point for sharing your ideas or finding inspiration from others' ideas is the Arduino Playground (www.arduino.cc/playground/) and the Fashioning Technology (www.fashioningtech.com) web sites. The Arduino Playground features everything Arduino-related and has a strong and active community of users. Fashioning Technology is a blog with updates on wearables-related projects; it also features tutorials and a user forum. Two forums that are not strictly focused on wearables but are great resources in general are the Instructables (www.instructables.com) web site and the MAKE blog (blog.makezine.com). Both sites are devoted to anything related to DIY.

Talking the Talk

The progression of the field of wearable computing has forced the need for special terminology. If you are new to the field, this section offers quick definitions of some of the terminology you might come across while working with wearables.

Wearables

Wearables is a collective name that has to do with anything combining fashion and technology. It usually refers to technology-enhanced garments or a piece of technology that can be worn on the body. Wearables comes from the term "wearable computing." It does not need to include a computer or other computational device. Even garments with a minimal number of electronics are considered wearables. It's a term made popular by media to describe both the field of wearable computing and fashion and technology.

Wearable Computing

Wearable computing refers to a small computer that can be either worn on the body—inside or placed onto clothing. Thorp and Shannon are still considered to be the predecessors to the field of wearable computing, but the field itself was mostly defined by the work of Steve Mann. Wearable computing investigates the intersection between the user and the computer, where interaction is based on no conventional interaction devices. Mann's wearable systems, for example, do not include a screen; instead, images are projected straight onto his eye. Other common interactions with wearable computers are voice commands and movement gestures. According to Mann's definition of a wearable system, other key features are that they are never turned off and have the ability to multitask.

Everyday use of the term is not strict, and includes areas of research in health care, mobile phones, service management, electronic textiles, and fashion, among others.

Most of the progression in the field is made within the context of military use, where the US Army has lead the progress with their Land Warrior and Future Force Warrior systems.

Since its start, key issues for wearable computing have been wireless communication and energy sources. Power is always a problem when it comes to objects designed to move around; it is even a bigger problem when it comes to embedding power sources into materials like fabrics.

Inflatables

Inflatables are a subcategory within the field of fashion and technology. The term is used in relation to garments that fully or partially inflate. Air pumps are the most common technology used, but there are projects that have experimented with the gas inflation of garments. Common issues with inflatables regard the bulkiness of the technology and the noise. As in many other cases, power is often an issue since air pumps and other technologies require a lot of power to operate. Great examples of inflatables include the "space dress" by designer Teresa Almeida; Yael Mer's "evacuation" dress; and the "inflatable dress" by Diana Eng and Emily Albinski.

Moveables

As the term suggests, garments in the moveables category move in one way or another. Common technologies used to generate movement are motors and vibrators. Projects that are more complex use what is known as "smart wires" or "muscle wires." These metal wires have functionality that allows them to remember positions or decrease in size when electricity is applied to them. Hussein Chalayan is a designer that has experimented with movables in several of his collections.

Haptics

Haptics refers more to the communication between the wearer of a garment and the actual garment. Small vibrators are typically used for indicating types of information in different locations of the body. There is a lot of research using haptics in relation to health care; particularly, haptics are used as a substitute for other senses. The "tacit" is a good example of a haptic device. Created by Steve Hoefer, it's a wrist-mounted digital walking cane for the visually impaired that senses distance and feeds back this information to the user via vibrators. Some designers take an artistic approach to haptics, like Norwegian artist Stahl Stenslie with his "sense memory" and "psychoplastic" projects.

Embedded Technology

In contrast to personal computers that do many things, *embedded technology* is a complete, specific device that combines software, hardware, and mechanical parts. Normally you use the term to describe technology objects like MP3 players or even traffic lights. Most wearables become embedded technologies by default since everything is included in the wearable object itself. Some wearables have wireless communication with another object, and the definition becomes blurred.

E-textile

E-textiles or electronic textiles are also known as smart textiles. These textiles have nothing to do with intelligence, but "smart" refers to the fact that these materials have more than one state that they can switch between. In combination with other electronic components, usually microprocessors, they become e-textiles. E-textiles combine ordinary garments with technology to extend functionality or simply for esthetic purposes. The difference between e-textiles and wearable computing is that e-textiles focus more on the seamless integration of electronics into textiles. The term is used to describe technologically enhanced fabrics that can be worn and washed like any other fabric.

Conductive Materials

A lot of materials are conductive; but when it comes to wearables, there are two types of materials you hear mentioned most often: conductive fabric and conductive thread. They are both alternatives to using wires and have the capacity to transfer electricity. Other conductive materials include conductive paints suitable for painting on your body.

Hacking

There are many definitions of the word, which is used to describe a subculture of people interested in computers and electronics. The most common use of it describes someone breaking into a computer system, but the more proper use of the term would be to describe people who learn by inspecting and modifying existing technology. Otto von Busch explains the term using sewing analogies; modifying an old T-shirt into a dress is, in a sense, hacking.

Prototyping

People coming into the field of wearables from a fashion perspective are probably familiar with the concept but not the term. *Prototyping* refers to the practice of physically visualizing an idea. It's not about designing a finished product, but making an idea for a physical object. In a sense, fashion runway shows are an exhibition of prototypes. The fashions are not designed as finished products available for store purchase, but more as an expression of an idea. The idea is similar to how sewers make muslins (toiles) to check that a pattern fits before making an investment in expensive fabrics. Electronic prototyping is similar in that you make something to see if it works, and then you improve upon it. Not all prototypes are electronic. They can be made from any material; even drawings are considered early prototypes.

Techno Fashion

Techno fashion is a term used to describe a subcategory within fashion that doesn't necessarily include any technology at all. A lot of techno fashion does include technology, but in essence, it's more about finding inspiration in technology. For example, a garment could use the concept of complex functionality in technology and transfer that into fashion. A good example of this is Mandarina Duck's "jackpack," a backpack that unfolds into a jacket. By being transformable in construction, such garments offer the possibility of being more than one object.

Some techno fashion uses technology more for its added esthetic value, like Anouk Wipprecht's "pseudomorphs" self-painting dress.

Techno fashion is also simply referred to as "fashion and tech."

Interactivity

The term *interactivity* is used in a lot of fields in different ways, but when it comes to electronics and computers, it often refers to software or hardware that accepts and responds to inputs. Or, if you like, technology that does something when you do something to it. Some of the projects in this book are interactive and some are not. Some have very minimal interaction, like simply pushing a button. Some of the projects are not interactive in the sense that they still have functionality, but they will do things independent of the user. A wearable that reacts to its environment may also be considered interactive.

DIY

DIY is short for do-it-yourself. It is even considered a subculture. It simply refers to the act of creating something by yourself. It is also used as a teaching methodology that promotes the idea that knowledge comes from practical experience. DIY also promotes the idea that anyone can do anything. There are thousands of DIY books on any subject, even as complex as building your own mobile phone. Right now you are holding a DIY guide book. If you read it, I think we agree that you can do these projects yourself.

High and Low Tech

Normally *high tech* refers to complex technologies and *low tech* refers to simpler technologies or nondigital technology. In some cases the terms are used to describe prototypes; most projects in this book could be considered prototypes. They are not finished products, but rather examples of how products look. You might also say that the projects are a mix between high and low tech. Usually materials like paper and cardboard are used to make low-tech prototypes, and materials like wood or fabrics together with electronics are considered high tech. For someone that is not familiar with wearable computing, most projects in this book might seem high–tech, but I would not go as far as to call them this.

Critical Design

A lot of wearables fall under the category of critical design. *Critical design* is a design theory made popular by Anthony Dunne and Fiona Raby. It's based on the idea of using designed objects as critique or commentary that causes reflection. It is hard to avoid this when creating wearables, even if this is not your intention. When you decide to add electronics into a context that you usually don't find them raises the question "why?"

The solar-power glow-in-the-dark bag project in this book, for example, was inspired by another project that I worked on with the 1scale1 design studio in collaboration with artist Alicia Framis and the Spanish fashion house Purificación García. The project, known as "Thinking of Dallipur," raised awareness about sustainability in Dallipur, a village in India, where a glow-in-the-dark handbag (see Figure 1-2) acted as a symbol for creating a more sustainable society when designing everyday objects.

It is hard to avoid making a statement by changing or adding functionality to wearable objects. It also changes how we look at these objects.

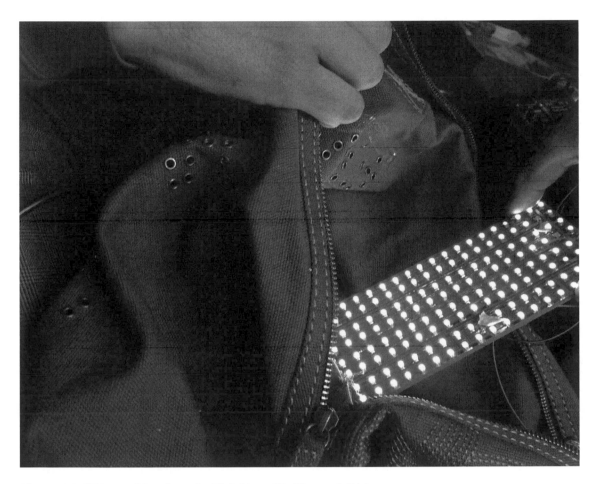

Figure 1-2. LED panel bag from the Thinking of Dallipur exhibition

Physical Computing

The term *physical computing* is used to describe designing with hardware and software that responds to the physical world. It is not true, however, that all physical computing objects respond to the analog world. The term is also used to describe a subcategory of interaction design that focuses on the relationships between users and digital objects; traditional nondigital objects are used and modified with electronics to explore this relationship. Wearables are also considered to be a part of physical computing as well as interactive art and design.

A classic example of physical computing is Daniel Rozin's work using mirrors. Rozin is an artist and educator who made a series of mirrors that project a mirror image in different materials, including wood, metal, and even trash.

Work Process

Everyone's work processes differ, and the process of making wearables usually depends on the project itself. Not all the projects in the book follow the same path. When working on a project, it is sometimes a good idea to pause and think it through first. Until you have found your own work process, it is good to follow the process of others.

This section includes some of the keystones that I think should be included in your process.

The Idea

When it comes to wearable computing or any physical computing, the idea is always a bit of a "the chicken or the egg" problem. To inspire ideas about what to do with wearables you need to know a bit about electronics and programming. At the same time, the best way to learn about electronics is to program and make things.

There is a misconception that you need to know a lot about electronics before you get started. Simple components, like the one shown in Figure 1-3, are enough to get started. There are tons of projects that can be made if you know how a LED works and know how to sew (I cover LEDs early in the book). Creating the projects in this book is a good starting point, and you will soon find that the more you learn through creating, the more ideas you have on other things to make. You should allow yourself the freedom of creativity to explore any ideas you have—and be certain to store them. Ideas are a bit strange that way; you can study and learn tons of things that help you generate good ideas, but in some cases, they just happen. Even if you don't have any ideas on what to do, I recommend you still do something.

I think it is true in any field of design: all good ideas start with pen and paper.

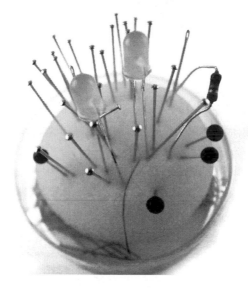

Figure 1-3. Combining what you already know with new information helps generate new ideas

Researching

This book is a good starting point, but one book will not make you an expert. You need to conduct your own research and keep an eye out for what is happening in the field of wearables. Besides learning new things, this will also help you generate better ideas for your own projects. Designers borrow ideas from one another, and you should find inspiration in the work of others. But if you plan to pass an idea off as your own, be sure not to copy a design in every detail. Instead, find areas in the design where you can make your own contributions. Always give proper credit if you borrow an idea or two from someone else.

Design

Design is what you do from the moment you start thinking about wearables until you finish your project. Having a clear plan helps a lot, but more often than not, a design plan is not as clear as you might want it. It is still a good thing. I'm a firm believer of iterative design, where you take steps in your design process and take time between each step to evaluate. The most important part is to not be afraid to change your designs. A plan is good, but it's hard to foresee every possibility, and believe me when I say a lot of your designs will not turn out as you thought they would.

Embrace failing as a part of your design process; this is when you learn the most. Designers fail from time to time, even if they don't tell you about it.

Building and Testing

A good rule is to test everything you make as you make it. If you solder a component, check that it works as soon as you are done; if you are programming, once in a while check that your program works. Again, iterating is key to making wearables. It's for the same reasons you would check that a dress fits the model before you stitch everything up. If you make wearables without testing things out in steps, it's harder to locate the problem when your completed wearable doesn't work.

Where to Buy Stuff

Knowing about the materials available is very important when it comes to building wearables. It's hard to learn anything if you can't try it out for yourself while following along. But if you are new to wearables and electronics, you might not know where to start looking. So I have included a list of vendors. The following list includes vendors I personally recommend. It also includes the places where you can find all the electronics and materials used in this book. Internet searches might also be a good idea to see if there are vendors closer to you or that offer better prices.

SparkFun Electronics

SparkFun Electronics (www.sparkfun.com) has one of the best selections of electronic components and materials in the world. Many of the components used in this book can be found here. The web site includes good descriptions and tutorials. Ships worldwide.

Adafruit Industries

Adafruit Industries (www.adafruit.com) carries a great selection of components and materials, and has excellent tutorials on different subjects. The company also produces an alternative to the LilyPad called Flora, another Arduino clone aimed at wearables.

RS Components

RS Components (www.rs-components.com) has a nice selection of standard Arduino components and ships worldwide.

Farnell

Farnell (www.farnell.com) has a nice selection of standard Arduino components, as well as traditional electronics tools. Ships worldwide.

Robot Italy

Robot Italy (www.robot-italy.com) has a good selection of Arduino boards and electronic components for hobbyists. The company also carries specialized components like the flexible solar panel used in this book. It is a SparkFun Electronics reseller. Ships worldwide.

PlugHouse

PlugHouse (www.plughouse.co.kr) is a Korea-based shop with a selection of the most common Arduino models and one of the most beautiful Arduino starter kit packages.

Seeed Studio

Seeed Studio (www.seeedstudio.com) is based in China and has a great selection of useful tools and materials. The company also produces a very small and the only flexible Arduino board clone in the world; it is called Seeeduino Film. Ships worldwide.

Squarebit

Squarebit (www.squarebit.com.au) is an online store based in Australia that caters to students, hobbyists, and hackers. The company has a good selection of components.

electro:kit

electro:kit (www.electrokit.com) is based in Sweden. The company features a great selection of components for both hobbyists and professionals. It also carries SparkFun products. Caters mainly to northern Europe.

Arduino Store

Arduino Store (`www.store.arduino.cc`) is the official Arduino store, carrying all official Arduino boards. Ships worldwide.

LessEMF

LessEMF (`www.lessemf.com`) features a large selection of conductive fabrics and thread. Ships worldwide.

Further Reading

The field of wearables is an intersection between electronics, programming, fashion, and traditional handcraft. This makes it impossible to cover every single aspect in one book. So in combination with this practical approach to wearables, you might find some of the following books good add-ons to your studies. The list includes both theoretical and practical titles.

Antonio Guerrero, Jose. *New Fashion and Design Technologies*. London, UK: A&C Black Publishers, 2010.

Igoe, Tom. *Making Things Talk*. Sebastopol, CA: O'Reilly Media, 2011.

Lee, Suzanne. *Fashioning the Future*. London, UK: Thames and Hudson, 2005.

Lewis, Alison. *Switch Craft*. New York: Potter Craft, 2008.

Olsson, Tony, et al. *Open Softwear*. Blushing Boy Publishing. 2011.

Pakhchyan, Syuzi. *Fashioning Technology*. Sebastopol, CA: O'Reilly Media, 2008.

Quinn, Bradley. *Techno Fashion*. London, UK: Berg Publishers, 2002.

San Martin, Macarena. *Future Fashion*. Barcelona, Spain: Promopress, 2010.

Seymour, Sabine. *Fashionable Technology*. New York: Springer Vienna Architecture, 2008.

CHAPTER 2

Software

Today, most people don't need to know how computers work. It is possible to interact with mobile phones, computers, and other technology by simply pushing buttons, sweeping a finger over a screen, or even speaking to the device. For most people, this knowledge of interacting with technology is enough; and for the everyday use of computers, this is what the average person needs to know. But if you are reading this book, my guess is that you are not like most people.

You are probably more like me in the sense that I don't want to be limited to using a computer as someone else thinks I should use it. I want to use a computer the way that fit my needs.

To make a computer do what we want, we need software.

In this chapter, we will start by covering how to install the Arduino IDE on your computer. Later, I will give a short introduction on software, the basic structure of code, and how to write programs for the Arduino.

Installing the IDE

The Arduino IDE is the software we need to put on our computer. The Arduino IDE is where you will write your programs (called *sketches*) and transfer them from your computer to the Arduino board. In other words, it is a program that helps us to write code and send it to the Arduino from the computer.

■ **Note** IDE stands for Integrated Development Environment.

An IDE is similar to a word processing program, but specialized for computers. The Arduino IDE borrowed its looks from another open-source programming environment called Processing. Processing was also designed for newcomers unfamiliar to software development.

The Arduino IDE supports all the official Arduino boards; so if you are working with an Arduino board clone, you might need to refer to the official documentation of that board. All supported boards can be found on the Arduino web site at http://arduino.cc/en/Main/Hardware.

To get started, you need to download the Arduino IDE; the best place to find it is on the Arduino web site at http://arduino.cc/en/Main/Software. Make sure that you download the software that corresponds to your operating system; also select the correct installation guide.

In this book, we cover how to install the Arduino Uno. To use older Arduino standard boards or the LilyPad with USB-to-serial adapter, you will need to install the additional FTDI driver. To do this, please refer to the Arduino web site at http://arduino.cc/en/Main/Hardware, though I'll briefly cover it in this chapter. If you are using a LilyPad with the Arduino serial light adapter, the installation instructions are the same as the Arduino Uno's.

■ **Note** For the projects in this book, we will use the Arduino Uno, the Arduino LilyPad, the Arduino LilyPad Simple, and the Arduino Mini, depending on the project.

Installing the IDE on Windows

Once you have downloaded the Arduino IDE, you need to unpack the file. If you are new to using the IDE, I suggest you unpack and place the folder on your desktop. When the Arduino IDE is installed onto your computer and you open it, you will find the Arduino launch application (see Figure 2-1).

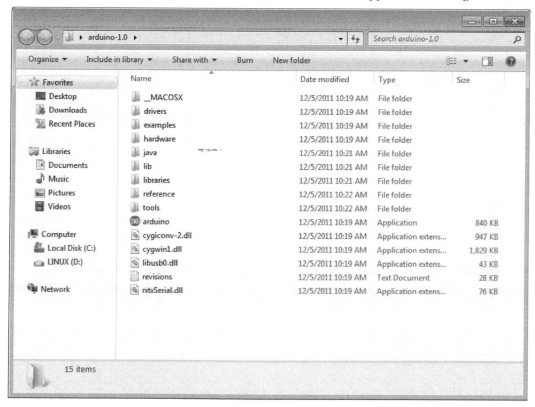

Figure 2-1. *Arduino folder on Windows*

Next, you will need to install the drivers for your Arduino board. To do this, you simply connect your Arduino board to your computer using a USB cable. Once you do this, Windows will try to install the drivers and it will fail. Sometimes this takes some time, so be patient. When it fails to install the drivers, do the following:

1. Open your search box (in the Start menu), type "device manager", and hit Enter. The device manager will pop up.

2. Under Ports you should see that it says Arduino Uno (it might also appear as Unknown Device in Other Devices).

3. Right-click on Arduino Uno and choose Update Driver Software.

4. This will open a new window and you should choose the step that says Browse My Computer for Drivers.

5. Navigate to your Arduino IDE folder. Inside the Arduino folder, you will find the drivers folder, which you should mark. Do not mark the FTDI USB Driver folder since the drivers for Arduino Uno are not inside this one. The driver update screen should now look like Figure 2-2.

■ **Note** For the most up-to-date installation instructions, have a look at http://arduino.cc/en/Guide/Windows.

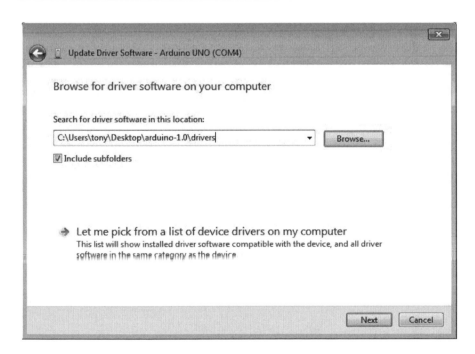

Figure 2-2. Windows driver installation

6. Press Next until Windows finishes the installation.

Installing the FTDI Driver on Windows

To install the FTDI driver on Windows, follow the previous guide for the Uno; but in step 5, choose the FTDI USB Driver. You have to repeat this process twice since there are two drivers that need to be installed.

Installing the IDE on Mac OS X

Once you download the Arduino IDE and mount the disk image by double-clicking on it, the desktop should look like Figure 2-3.

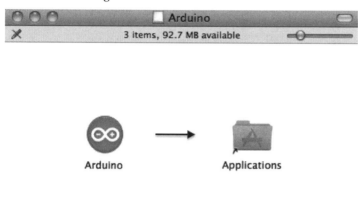

Figure 2-3. Arduino.dmg

Simply drag the Arduino icon to your Applications folder and the installation is done. You will then find your installed Arduino IDE under Applications.

Installing the FTDI Driver on OS X

To install the FTDI driver on OS X, click the icon that says FTDIUSBSerialDriver in Figure 2-3. This will start the installation program; you just have to follow the on-screen instructions. Note that this installation will force you to restart the computer, so make sure to save all files you may have opened before you started the installation.

Running the IDE

If you start your IDE, it should look something like Figure 2-4.

Figure 2-4. *The Arduino IDE launched*

The entire white area is where you will actually write your code, and the black area at the bottom is used to output information that the IDE thinks you should know about, such as errors. But before we get started with writing a sketch, let's have a look at a few important things inside the IDE.

Examining the File Menu

First we have the File menu, as shown in Figure 2-5.

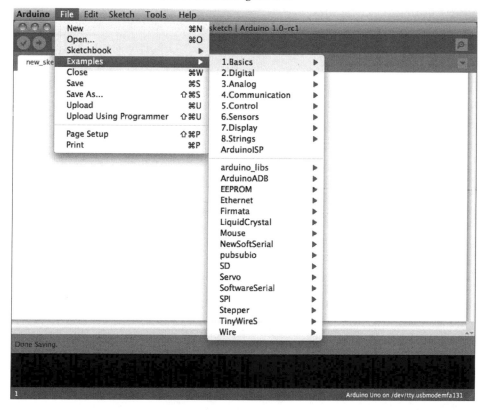

Figure 2-5. *The File menu*

In the File menu, you can open a new sketch, save sketches, and open old ones you already have saved. Saved sketches can also be found in the Sketchbook drop down. You will also find a collection of pre-made example sketches in the drop-down Examples menu. The first part has standard examples and the other part has example sketches that are included in libraries. Libraries are a collection of code that can be included in the standard Arduino IDE. Usually when someone figures out how to do something complicated that requires a lot of code, they make it into a library to make it easier to use the code. Another reason to make a library is to share code with others who may want to use it.

Examining the Edit Menu

Under the Edit menu you will find standard commands like Copy, Paste, and Select All, as well as their shortcut key commands.

Examining the Tools Menu

The Tools menu is probably the most important one to keep track of. Because of the large variety of Arduino boards, you always have to set the IDE to compile for your type of board. Inside the Tools menu under Board, you will find all boards that are supported by the official Arduino IDE, as shown in Figure 2-6.

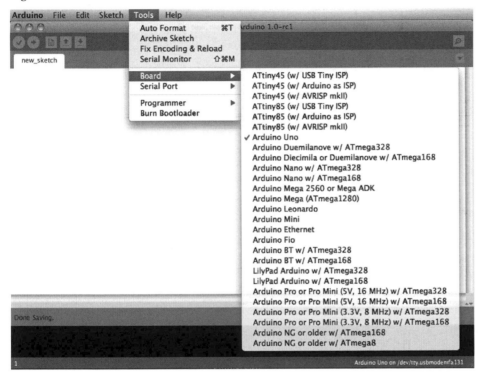

Figure 2-6. The Tools menu

Next to the Board drop-down menu, you will find the Serial Port menu. Besides setting the IDE to compile for your type of Arduino, you also need to set the IDE to upload over the right board USB port on your computer. On a Windows computer, every USB device you connect will be assigned a COM number; and if you open the Serial Port menu, you will find a list of COM ports with different numbers, such as COM 4, COM 7, or COM 23. If more than one COM port shows up, the easiest way to determine which of them is your Arduino board is to unplug the Arduino board and re-open the menu. The COM port that is missing will be your Arduino board. In Windows that particular board will always keep that COM number. If you connect a new Arduino board, that board will be assigned a different COM number.

In OS X, your Arduino board will show up as /dev/tty.usbXXX. The part after usb might be different depending on which board you are using, but that's usually the first one to show up in the list.

Examining the IDE Buttons

Inside the IDE you will find a few buttons, as shown in Figure 2-7.

Figure 2-7. Arduino IDE buttons

The first button is the Verify button. This button makes a logical check of your code to make sure you don't have any syntax errors or misspelled commands. If the code passes verification, the IDE will try to compile your code. If everything goes as planned, white text that reads "Binary sketch size" should appear in the black window of the IDE. The actual size of your sketch and the amount of available memory on your particular Arduino should also appear.

If something is wrong in your code, red text indicating the problem appears in the black window. If you are new to programming with the Arduino, these messages might be a bit cryptic; however, the IDE usually highlights in yellow the line of code it thinks contains the problem. Sometimes this is not the actual line with the problem; it could be the line before or after. Often, the problem is that you are missing a semicolon or one of the curly brackets. You should never feel stupid if you make small mistakes like this because it happens to the best of us. Even though I often write code, I make mistakes like that all the time; you should take comfort that you will get better at spotting these mistakes as you progress.

The second button is the Upload button, which is used to send the sketch from your computer to your Arduino board. This button also verifies your code and if it checks out, it compiles it and then sends the compiled code from the IDE to the board. While you are working with your sketch, you don't want to send it to the board every time, you just want to check that the code is correct; so, there is a separate Verify button for this.

The last three buttons on the left side are quick buttons for New Sketch, Open Sketch, and Save Sketch.

■ **Note** Older versions (less than 1.0) of the IDE have a different layout, but I recommend downloading the most recent version from the Arduino web site.

There is one button remaining on the right side of the IDE, the Serial Monitor. If you press this button, it opens a new window where any information sent from the Arduino board over the USB cable will appear. By default, if you open the Serial Monitor while the Arduino board is connected, nothing will happen since you have to initiate serial communication in your sketch to make the Arduino board send information.

Figure 2-8 shows what the Arduino IDE looks like when the Serial Monitor is open.

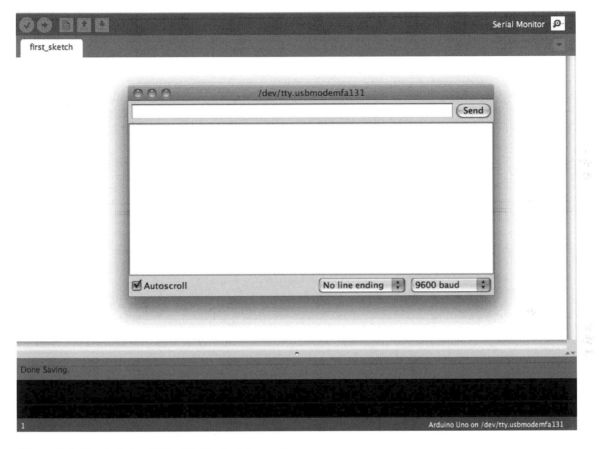

Figure 2-8. The Arduino IDE with the Serial monitor open

Any information sent from the Arduino board will appear in the big window. Above this window you will find an input window and a Send button. This is used if you want to send information from the computer to the Arduino board. At the bottom you will find two drop-down menus. The first one has options for line editing, which means the way the serial monitor rearranges the information received. The other drop down is where you set the speed of the communication, which has to be the same on both the computer and on your Arduino board.

Now that we have installed the IDE and have taken a quick tour, it's time to do something with it— which means writing some software for your Arduino board.

What Is Software?

Software is usually what we call a collection of programs and data that tells a computer what to do. Everything we install on our computer is normally some sort of software; and without any software, there wouldn't be much to do on our computers.

The Arduino is basically a small computer (which is also called a *microprocessor*) without any software on it from the start. It is like a clean sheet of paper, so we need software to be able to make the Arduino do stuff. But before we start writing software for the Arduino, we need to know how to give the Arduino instructions that it will understand. Computers and microprocessors like the Arduino are similar to humans when it comes to communicating. If you want me to get you a cup of coffee, you would have to ask me something like,

"Could you please get me a cup of coffee?"

Then, if I have the time and feel like it, I might go and get you a cup. But if you were to ask me,

"Pouvez-vous s'il vous plaît me faire une tasse de café?"

I would have no clue what you are talking about since I do not speak French.

It's same thing with computers and microprocessors. If you don't tell them to do stuff in a language they understand, they won't do anything. What computers and microprocessors understand is machine code, which is basically 0s and 1s.

To you, 00100101 might not have any meaning whatsoever, but to a processor this makes full sense. However, you should not feel intimidated by this in any way since most people with a good knowledge of programming don't know how to program at this low level. In fact, we probably would get nowhere if this were the only option.

Artificial languages, also known as programming languages, were created to make it easier to communicate instructions to computers. We use programming languages to construct programs that basically are a list of instructions for the computer to do. Learning how to program is not as hard as most people might think. For example, if you know how to explain how a cup of coffee is made, then you already understand the basic principles of writing a computer program. The good thing about computers is that they do not have feelings; so if you tell one to do something in a programming language that it understands, it will do it. You don't even have to say please. In contrast, if you ask me to get you a cup of coffee, I might not do it.

With the Arduino, we will be using a mix of two programming languages called C and C++. In a normal case, these programming languages might be a bit hard to use for a first-time programmer. But the Arduino way of programming was inspired by a piece of software called Wiring, which was made to make the use of electronics easier.

It only takes a few programming commands to get your Arduino to do stuff, which together make up the Arduino programming language. For this we need a piece of software: the Arduino IDE you just installed.

All human languages follow a set of rules and principles; if they did not, we would not be able to understand one another. If I were to say to you,

"Is the for today a going park to nice day."

It would not make any sense whatsoever. But if I rearrange the words to follow the standard rules of creating an English sentence, I would say:

"Today is a nice day for going to the park."

In this case, you probably would understand me better.

Computers work the same way, but in a stricter manner. When writing programs for computers, you have to follow certain rules on how you combine the commands—and they cannot be misspelled. The rules for writing programs are called *syntax*. The syntax refers to "how" we write the programs. "What" we write in programs are the *commands*. It is the syntax together with the commands that make a programming language. Again, like human languages, each programming language has different syntaxes and commands. Sometimes we also refer to this as *code* and code is what software is made of. So again, the Arduino IDE is the software we use to write programs for the Arduino board.

How We Write Code

Before we get started with writing programs for the Arduino, let's have a look what code actually consists of. The first thing you need to know about is variables.

Variables

Variables are like containers for something else. Variables allow us to store information within our programs; and the information can be known or unknown. It's like a cookie jar that we put stuff in. We can also assign a name to the variables so that we can use them independent of the information inside. This would be like putting a name tag on the cookie jar.

For example, if you only have one cookie jar and you put a key in it, it would not be that hard for you to remember that you have your key in that cookie jar. But if you have ten cookie jars with ten different things in them, it might be hard to remember where you put what. That's why it helps to put name tags on the cookie jar—and the same thing goes for variables. To help us remember what information is inside a variable, we need to give them a name. But variables are a bit pickier than cookie jars, so just giving them a name is not enough; we also have to tell them what kind of information we will be storing in the variable. The reason for this is that both numbers and letters can be stored as many types of variables. For example, the number 1 can both be stored as a number or a character, but not both at the same time. This is why you have to declare the type of a variable; so that the computer knows how you will use what's inside your program.

In programming for the Arduino in this book, we will mostly use two types of variables: integer variables and character variables. An *integer* is a number without any decimals. A number with decimals is called a *long*.

So for example, the number

12345

is an integer. If I add a period, making any number after the period a decimal, like this

1.2345

makes the number a long.

Characters are basically everything else you can think of that is available on a keyboard, like all letters

A B C D E

and so on, but even signs like

= ?   # " %

can be stored in a character variable. So before you create a variable, you need to know what kind of information you want store in it.

Creating a variable is also known as declaring a variable, and to make one we have to follow the syntax of the programming language. To declare a variable in a program, you would do the following (you can type this into the IDE window if you like):

```
int myVariablename;
```

In this case, `int` is short for integer, which declares what kind of information we will be storing in the variable (which is numbers without decimals). `myVariablename` is the actual name of the variable and this could be anything. Even though you can assign a variable any name you want, it's a good idea to give it a proper name. For example, if you want to store information from a sensor, you could name it `sensorValue`; or better yet, if it's a light sensor, name it `lightSensorValue`. The reason I use a capital letter on the second word in the variable name is because the name has to be a consistent string of characters. `sensor value` is not an acceptable name, but `sensorvalue` is; so just to make it simpler to read, I usually write the second word with a capital letter. It is also good to name your variables so that they make sense. If you start naming your variables `banana`, `apple`, or `lovePrada`, it will be hard to remember what kind information is actually stored in them.

The semicolon at the end tells the computer, or in our case the Arduino, where the line of code ends. WIthout the semicolon, the Arduino would just keep on reading that line of code thinking something will come after `myVariablename` and it will be stuck doing this forever. However, if you forget a semicolon in your code, the Arduino IDE tells you that something is wrong before you can send your program to the Arduino board.

So now you have declared an integer variable named `myVariablename`. In this case, the variable is empty; but if we know that we want to store something in it, we would have to write it like this

```
int myVariablename = 13;
```

This would not only create an integer variable called `myVariablename`, but also store the number 13 inside it. Then, any time we use `myVariablename` in our program, the Arduino reads it as the number 13. So the name is more for your sake since the Arduino never reads the name of the variable, it just opens it and picks out whatever is inside it. However, the Arduino does check what kind of variable it is, so you can't fool it by putting a character inside an `int` variable.

If you want to declare a character variable, you will have to write

```
char myCharacter;
```

And if you want to assign the variable a character from the start, you need to write it as

```
char myCharacter = 'H';
```

This differs from declaring `int` variables; you have to mark the character with ' ' or the Arduino will not recognize it as a character.

The Basic Structure of a Program

The structure of your code is important because it's rare that you will know from the start how your finished program will look. Usually, you start with writing the code for the basic parts or just one part of your wearable project. Then you test the code and if it works, you test it on your Arduino board; and if it works there, you continue with writing some more code. So it's always good to keep a good structure of your code so you can continue working with ease.

Another important part of structuring code is the syntax of the code. If it does not follow the syntax of how you should write Arduino code, your programs will not work. Later we'll see how we can verify the code to check for errors with the help of the IDE. Every time we do this, the Arduino will also try to compile your code. When the IDE tries to compile code, it's actually trying to translate your code into the actual language the Arduino board understands. If you have a syntax error at this point, the compiler can't translate your code. Basically this means that you have written code in the wrong way. It's usually only parts of your code and not the entire program that generates an error. Some IDEs help you with autocorrection features like filling in missing semicolons, but the Arduino IDE is very picky and you have to make sure on your own that everything is correct.

But let's have a look at how you actually write a program for the Arduino. Recall that programs for the Arduino are called sketches and this is something Arduino adopted from the Processing IDE. This is because the IDE works like a sketchpad where you quickly draw or write something down to test your idea. We will be using the IDE in the same sense: we write down some code, test it, and if it works, we write some more code.

When I start a new sketch, I always follow a three-step process.

1. I declare my variables.

2. I add what is called the setup.

3. I add the loop.

The setup and loop are part of the Arduino syntax and always have to be included in every sketch you write or the IDE will not even try to compile it.

To start your sketches with variables declarations, however, is optional. But you should make it a practice to always put your variables in the beginning of your sketches since this gives you a nice overview of them. For example, if I had a sensor and a button I wanted to connect to my Arduino, I would start with declaring two variables, like this:

```
int mySensor = 0;
int myButton = 2;
```

In these variables, the numbers actually relate to pins that are also numbers on your Arduino board where you connect your sensor. But for now, we will focus on the software; we will return to connecting stuff to the Arduino in the hardware chapter.

Adding the Setup

The next step is to add the setup. The *setup* is the name of a function that always needs to be included inside a sketch. A *function* is a portion within a program that performs a specific task. In an Arduino sketch, this is the first part of the program the Arduino board will look for and does whatever instructions it finds inside. It will only enter the setup once, and then it will continue to look for the loop. The following shows how you declare a setup inside an Arduino sketch (try it in your own IDE window):

```
void setup(){
  //enter commands here
}
```

void, in this case, means that this function ends when it reaches the end of the function. There are other functions that can return values, which we can then use in our sketches. The Arduino works like this: when it finds the setup function, it reads and does whatever command is put in setup, line by line.

This is why we use semicolons at the end of commands, so that the Arduino knows where every command ends and when it is time to move to a new line.

The curly brackets {} in the setup function are used to show where the function starts and where it ends. You always use a left (or an open) curly bracket { to show where something starts, and a right (or closed) curly bracket } to show where something ends. To write sketches, you will use a lot of curly brackets, and if you miss one of them, the sketch will not compile. A good tip is to always enter the left curly bracket and the right curly bracket at the same time so that you don't forget it later. The normal brackets () in the setup function are used for additional parameters. In the setup function, it does not take any additional parameters, so we just leave it empty every time.

Parameters allow you to send information to the function, so that the function can process that information. In some of the projects we'll work on, we will see how adding parameters to functions might come in handy.

In the setup function you may also find two slashes (//) with text that follows. The two slashes indicate that everything written afterward is not a part of the actual program. It has the effect of hiding the text from the Arduino so that you can add comments to your sketches. Adding comments is always good to do if you want to share your code with others, or use them as a helpful reminder for yourself, or to let the reader know what is going on at certain parts of the sketch. You'll see plenty of comments in the project code later in the book.

Adding the Loop

Next up we have the loop function. This is where the action happens. This is the part of the sketch where the Arduino spends most of its time while it's powered up.

To declare the loop, you write:

```
void loop(){
  //enter commands here
}
```

As the name suggests, this function enters a loop and it works like the setup reading line by line, but the difference is that once it reaches the end, it will not stop like the setup does. It jumps back to the start of the loop and does the same thing over and over again, as long as your Arduino has power. This does not mean that we have to do everything in the loop every time, but it is constructed this way because when we are working with the Arduino, we are usually waiting for something interesting to happen. If nothing happens, we loop the code one more time, and so on. When something does happen, we can choose to activate a separate part of code.

For example, I have a button and I want a light to turn on when someone pushes the button. In most cases, I don't know when someone is actually going to push my button. It might be in five seconds or it could be tomorrow. So that's why the loop runs over and over again; when someone pushes the button, the Arduino will be ready to detect that information and enter the part of the code that controls the light.

Basic Commands

So now that you know the basic syntax of an Arduino sketch, let's have a look at some of the basic commands available in the Arduino language. Commands are the actual instructions you give the Arduino board; they also follow a strict syntax for how you write them. If you don't write commands the correct way, the Arduino IDE will complain once you try to compile your code.

Setting pinMode

The pinMode function is used to set the mode of a digital pin on the Arduino board. The digital pins can be used both as an INPUT or an OUTPUT. This means that we can use these to both receive information coming into the Arduino board and we can use them to control something outside the Arduino board. But from the start, the Arduino board does not know how you will use the digital pins; so you need to tell it by using pinMode. Since we only need to tell the board once how we will use the digital pins, this command is always placed inside the void setup function, as follows:

```
int myPin = 13;

void setup(){
  pinMode(myPin,OUTPUT);
}
```

The pinMode command takes two parameters.

- The first is the pin on which you wish to set the mode. I have entered a variable called myPin.

- The second parameter is the actual mode you want the pin used as. I have declared it as an OUTPUT because I want to use it to control something outside the board. If I wanted to use the pin to read digital information coming into the board, I would use INPUT here instead.

Writing a Pin's State

Once you have declared a pin as an OUTPUT, you can set it to a state of either ON or OFF. To do this you would use the function digitalWrite, which takes two parameters:

```
void loop(){
  digitalWrite(myPin, HIGH);
}
```

As you can see, this command is placed in the loop because this is where most of our action takes place.

- The first parameter is still the myPin variable because we also have to name the pin that we want to set the state.

- HIGH, in this example, is the actual state and it means the same as ON. If I want to turn It OFF, I would just write LOW.

The digitalWrite command can be placed in the setup, but then it would only run once.

Adding a Delay

We could make a simple program with just the two commands from the previous example, adding a variable like so:

```
int myPin = 13;
```

```
void setup(){
  pinMode(myPin, OUTPUT);
}

void loop(){
  digitalWrite(myPin, HIGH);
  digitalWrite(myPin, LOW);
}
```

In this example, I have declared a variable called myPin and assigned it the value 13. I have declared it as an OUTPUT, and in the loop I am turning it on and off. However, if I were to connect something to myPin like a small lamp or a small motor, it would appear that nothing is happening apart from the lamp switching on. The thing is that even if the Arduino is a small computer, it is still a pretty fast one. The Arduino is able to turn on whatever is connected to myPin a couple of hundred thousand times per seconds. If we have a small lamp connected, it is very hard to see that the lamp is being turned ON and OFF. In fact, it is impossible for the human eye to detect this flickering, and it would just look like the lamp is on all the time.

So in this case we need to add the delay command, and as the name suggests, this command makes a pause in your sketch. The delay command counts in milliseconds, so to make a one-second delay, we would set the delay to 1000, like this:

```
int myPin = 13;

void setup(){
  pinMode(myPin, OUTPUT);
}

void loop(){
  digitalWrite(myPin, HIGH);
  delay(1000);
  digitalWrite(myPin, LOW);
  delay(1000);
}
```

I use two delay commands because, if I just use one delay between the digitalWrite commands, at the end of the loop it would just jump from OFF back to ON again, and we would not be able to tell that it actually went OFF. But in this case, we turn myPin to HIGH for a second and then we turn it LOW for a second. If we have a small lamp connected to pin 13, this would give us plenty of time to tell that the lamp goes ON and OFF.

We'll come back to this code in Chapter 3 when we check that our Arduino is working properly. For now, you can check that the code is valid by pressing the Verify button in your IDE window.

Summary

In this chapter, I have covered the very basics of getting started with writing code and how to install and use the IDE. Throughout all the projects in this book, I will gradually introduce more commands and uses as we go along; but if you need a complete overview of all the possibilities of the Arduino programming language IDE used, I suggest you have a look at the references on the Arduino web site at http://arduino.cc/en/Reference/HomePage.

CHAPTER 3

Hardware

Like most things in our daily life, we need stuff to do stuff. To be able to make new things, we need other things. Dealing with wearable projects is no exception, and you will need tools to be able to craft your projects. I like to believe that wearable prototyping with microcontrollers follows the same principle as any other craft. If you have a prior interest in sewing and fashion construction, you probably know that understanding the tools and materials is important, and the deeper your knowledge, the better your construction will be.

The same goes for working with electronics and microprocessors. There will always be more than one way to construct a circuit or program something, and the more you know about these things, the better your solution will be. Still, the most important thing is not that you know everything, but that you start learning; you will see that deeper knowledge comes from doing stuff with stuff.

In this chapter, you will cover the basic components of the Arduino Uno and LilyPad boards. I will also introduce you to the basics of electricity, as well as the different powering options for the Arduino boards.

The Arduino Hardware

Hardware refers to the equipment we use to construct things. We will be using Arduino boards and LilyPads as computation hardware in this book, but basically everything else that is physical is also referred to as hardware. All components, wires, tools and, even if it might sound counter intuitive, fabric count as hardware.

The Arduino board, however, needs some explaining. The Arduino board is also known as a *microcontroller*, which is the same thing as a small computer on a single, integrated circuit with a processor, memory, and controllable output and input pins. An integrated circuit is an electronic circuit that is manufactured using trace patterns. Today you can find integrated circuits in most electronic devices. If you ever opened a radio, or TV, or anything else electronic, you probably have seen an integrated circuit. It's the board all the electronic components are attached to. With the Arduino, the whole thing is an integrated circuit; what makes it an integrated circuit are the board and the combination of components.

A Closer Look

If you look closely at your Arduino board, you will see a lot of small lines going all over the place, as shown in Figure 3-1.

Figure 3-1. *Close-up of connection traces*

These are the trace patterns, which usually are thin lines of copper. These lines connect all the small components together. We are not going to go through every single component on the Arduino board because it would take way too long until we got to the fun stuff. Still, there are parts of the Arduino board we need to have a look at before you can start making your own wearable project. The first one is the ATmega chip, and Figure 3-2 shows where you can find it on the standard Arduino board.

Figure 3-2. *Close-up of the ATmega 328 chip on the Arduino board*

The ATmega chip is basically the brain of the Arduino board. You can find the same thing in your own computer, but in another form factor. The ATmega chip is also available in different form factors, and that's why you have to change the Arduino board type in your Arduino IDE—because different Arduino boards use different ATmega chips. For example, the LilyPad uses a smaller, surface-mounted ATmega chip. Surface-mounted means that it is soldered to the top of the board's surface.

In contrast, the Arduino Uno has a bigger DIP-mounted ATmega chip. DIP mount means that the chip is attached to the board either through holes that go through the board or, like the Arduino Uno, in a socket. The reason for putting the ATmega chip in a socket on the Uno board is that if you accidentally connect your Arduino board to something else in the wrong way, the chip might get burned. If this happens, you can pop out the chip and put in a new one. With the LilyPad, the problem is that it's very hard to replace a surface-mounted chip. This is why I prefer to do all my testing with a standard Arduino board like the Uno; if something happens, I can just buy a new ATmega chip rather than replace an entire board. But to be honest, I have never managed to destroy a single board—and I have used a lot of them.

The main reason I prefer to test things on a standard Arduino board is because doing so is fast. I love the design of the LilyPad, but it's made for wearable devices and therefore very small. This means it takes a bit longer to connect and test things with a LilyPad; so if your budget allows it, consider buying both the LilyPad and a standard Arduino board. Since both use an ATmega chip, the code you write is the same.

Microprocessors like the ATmega chip are amazing things that let us convert data into information. The way the Arduino is designed, it lets us read any information and control almost anything we can imagine.

On the Inside

Inside a microprocessor you find thousands of super-small transistors. Later on, we will be using bigger transistors, like the one shown in Figure 3-3.

Figure 3-3. IRFZ24 transistor

But the small ones found in microprocessors follow the same principle as the big ones. If I apply electricity to one of the legs of the transistor in Figure 3-3, the other two would connect to one another inside the transistor. A transistor works similar to a switch, where it is either on or off. This might sound like a simple electronic component, but in fact it is considered to be one of the most important technological inventions ever. Today it is the key active component of all modern technology.

The thing that makes the transistor so special is that it's also the component that made modern computers possible. With transistors it is possible to make what is called logical gates. A *logical gate* is a physical implementation of a Boolean function. This means that they can detect if something is true or false. While writing sketches for the Arduino, you can use Boolean variables, which are variables that can be only one of two things: true of false. A Boolean variable is declared the same as any other variable:

```
boolean myBoolean = true;
```

In our code, we would use the `boolean` to check if things are true; and if they are, we can choose to do something else. The transistor enables us to do the same thing in real life. Usually, big transistors like the one in Figure 3-3 are used to control high power with a lower-powered signal, as shown in Figure 3-4.

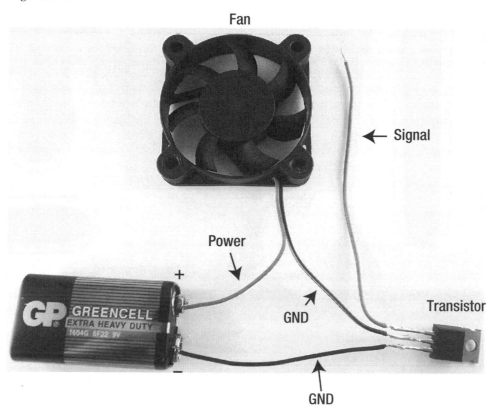

Figure 3-4. A fan connected to a battery with a transistor

In Figure 3-4, I have added a fan and a battery, and connected it to the transistor. The connection to the fan has two wires: a red one for power and a black one for ground. This is because electricity always has to go back to where it came from. I will get back to explaining electricity later on, but for now we just need to understand that if we don't have electricity going from the battery to the fan and back to the ground connection, nothing would happen.

I have cut the black wire and hooked each end to the legs of the transistor. Since these legs are not connected by default, the electricity cannot flow from the battery to the fan and back. However, if I were to give some electricity to the red "signal" wire connected to the transistor, it would connect the black wires, completing the connection between the battery and the fan. This would make the fan start spinning.

This might not seem an amazing thing, but if you think about it, a transistor allows us to make a logical question similar to the way humans communicate. In the case of the fan, we can ask the question if the fan is on or not. If we supply power to the signal pin, it would be true that the fan is on; and if there is no power on the signal pin, the statement would be false.

Still, the human communication is a bit more complicated than this and if you want to make a computer do more complicated things than turning a fan on and off, the processor needs to be a bit more complicated than just one transistor. But again, this is what is inside processors: thousands and thousands of very tiny transistors that enable us to ask the computer questions and set up rules for what to do and when to do it.

This is why it's a common misconception that you have to be good at math to be good at programming. This is actually not true at all. Computers are very good at logical operations like math equations, so we let computers do most of the math for us. To understand how a computer thinks, the thing you have to train yourself in is logical thinking so that you can ask it the right questions and give it the right instructions.

I told you that microprocessors like the Arduino don't actually understand programming languages either, so we have to use the Arduino IDE to compile our code to machine code. This is because all those zeroes and ones in the machine code actually set the pins of the transistors inside the microprocessor on and off. A zero is the same as off and one is the same as on. Programing languages are largely based on human languages. They are also partly based on computer syntax (not human language grammar), so the compiler knows how to translate into the zeros and ones that switch all the small transistors.

But enough about the inside of processors; let's have a look at the parts of the Arduino board that you will be using to create your projects.

Board Layout

Figures 3-5 and 3-6 show you a standard Arduino board (in this case, an Arduino Uno) and the LilyPad Simple board, showing the pin layout of these boards. No matter which standard board you use, the design layout always follows the same form factor. This is because a lot of people make add-on boards to the standard board—called "shields" or "piggyback boards"—that add extra functionality to the Arduino. This includes advanced sound generating, Internet connectivity, wireless communication, and more.

Depending on the project, we will be using different versions of Arduino boards. Some projects require a smaller board, for which we will use an Arduino Pro Mini. Some will be stitched in place, so we will use LilyPads. And for the projects that won't need a full number of pins, we will use the LilyPad Simple.

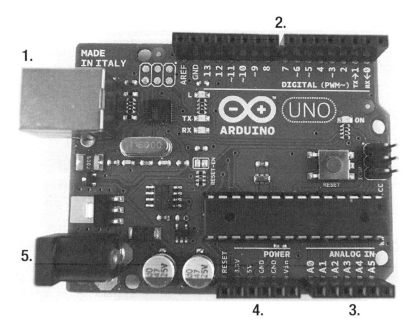

Figure 3-5. Overview of the Arduino Uno board

Figure 3-5 shows the following:

- USB connector
- Digital pins
- Analog pins
- Power pins

Figure 3-6. Overview of the LilyPad Simple board

Figure 3-6 shows the following:

- Analog pins A2, A3, A4, and A5
- Digital pins 5, 6, 9, 10, and 11
- Power pins and power connector
- Serial to USB connector

If this is the first time that you've use an Arduino board, there are a few part of the Arduino board that you need to keep track of; the first one is the USB connector.

USB Connector

A USB connector is shown in Figure 3-7. This is where you connect your Arduino board to your computer using a USB cable.

Figure 3-7. Close-up of the USB connector on a standard Arduino board

When the Arduino is connected to the computer, the computer powers the Arduino board through the USB cable. In order to tell that computer is powering the board, you should see a small green light on the board near the word ON, as shown in Figure 3-8.

Figure 3-8. A green light indicates that the Arduino board is powered

If you are using a LilyPad, you will need either a USB-to-serial cable or the Arduino simple USB converter. The standard Arduino boards, like the Uno, do not need an adapter for this since it has an onboard chip to handle the communication. Also, USB is a different communication protocol than what the Arduino uses and it is not supported by default, so it needs an extra chip to convert the signal to serial communication, which it does support. This is one of the things that have been removed from the LilyPad to make it smaller. The LilyPad also has a physical power switch that can be turned on and off.

■ **Note** When the LilyPad is connected over USB, it is always powered, even if the physical switch is set to OFF.

Digital Pins

On the Uno board we have 13 digital pins in total. On the same side you will also find one GND pin, which is short for "ground". All are shown in Figure 3-9. The digital pins are called digital pins because they only operate with zeros and ones, which, as you now know, is the same as on and off.

Figure 3-9. Digital pins from 0 to 13

Pins refer to the small holes in the board, and the digital pins have two states: on and off. If digital pins are on, there will be 5 volts in a hole; and if they are off, there will be 0 volts in a hole. The digital pins can be used as both inputs and outputs, which means that we can use them to either control electricity going out from the Arduino board or to tell if there is electricity going in to the Arduino board. The LilyPad also has digital pins, but a few less than the Uno. The LilyPad Simple has even fewer (see Figure 3-10); this is because when you reach the point where you are ready to finalize a wearable project, the project usually doesn't demand more.

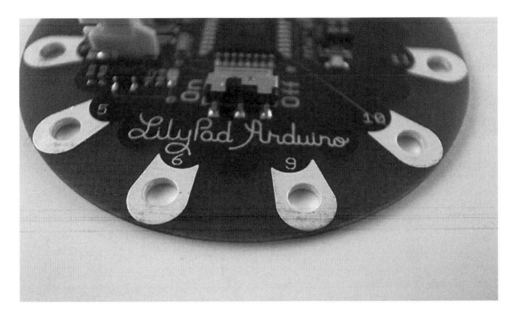

Figure 3-10. On the LilyPad Simple, the digital pins are numbered 5, 6, 9, 10, and 11

On the LilyPad Simple, it is much simpler to separate connections because there are fewer pins, which are placed farther apart. Having conductive thread connections too close is not good because they could accidentally come in contact with one another, which could cause errors or short circuits (more on conductive thread in Chapter 4).

Analog Pins

Opposite the digital pins are the analog pins, where we can connect sensors that measure things we sense in the real world. The problem with the real world is that most of the information is not digital. In other words, we are not like computers and our understanding of the world is not calculated in zeros and ones. As humans, we perceive things like light in a range of values. The problem with computers is that they can only understand two different states, on and off. So that's why the Arduino has analog pins, which are a bit different from digital pins.

Analog pins are the same as the digital ones in the sense that they are used as input pins, but what makes them different is that digital pins can only measure if something is on or off, or actually if there are 0 volts or 5 volts in the pin. The analog pins can measure a voltage range between 0 and 5 volts in 1024 steps. So if we connect an analog sensor to an analog pin, this sensor would give us a value between 0 and 1023, which means that if the value is 0, it is equal to 0 volts, and 1023 would be 5 volts. If the sensor gives you 511, it means that there are approximately 2.5 volts in the analog pin.

With analog pins, we can measure a lot of things in the real world, like temperature, distance, speed, and much more. If you can think of anything that you want to measure, there is a good chance there is a sensor for it. In fact, I have never found a situation where I couldn't find a suitable sensor to use. In most cases, there is the option to build the sensor yourself if need be. We will do exactly that in some of the projects in this book.

To the left of the analog pins, you will find the power pins, as seen in Figure 3-11.

Figure 3-11. The power and analog pins

Power Pins

The first pin, which says RESET, can be used to reset the Arduino board. If the board is powered, this makes the Arduino start the sketch from start. There is also a physical button that does the same thing; it is located next to the ATmega chip.

Next to the RESET is a pin that says 3.3V, which means there is always 3.3 volts in this pin. This pin is typically used when you make circuit connections outside the Arduino board and you need to power it. We also have the 5V pin, which is similar to the 3.3V, but there are always 5 volts in this pin when the Arduino board is powered. The reason the Arduino has a 3.3V and a 5V is that these are common voltages used by small electronic components.

Then you have two GND pins where you also connect anything you want to control or power from the Arduino board—because to complete a electronic circuit, power always has to go back to where it came from.

The last pin says VIN, which stands for "voltage in" and refers to external power sources. If you don't want to always power your board from a computer with a USB cable, you can attach an external power source. Depending on what you connect, this pin will provide the same amount of electricity provided by your power source (you can also connect a battery to VIN and GND to power your board, rather than use the external power source).

External Power

To connect an external power source, you use the DC jack, which is shown in Figure 3-12.

Figure 3-12. *The DC jack needs a minimum of 6 volts and a maximum of 17 volts.*

In the DC jack, you can connect any transformer that gives anything between 6 volts and 20 volts. Just make sure it is a DC transformer. You can find this information written on most transformers. The Arduino board needs at least 6 volts to run, and it can't handle more than 20 volts; but it's recommended to stay in between 9 volts and 12 volts. Six volts would power the Arduino board, but if you have anything else connected to the Arduino, this might not be enough.

A transformer is a normal power adapter that you use for laptop computers or electric razors and other low-powered electronics. They transform higher voltage electricity, like that in a wall socket, into a lower voltage. Figure 3-13 shows a transformer for an old Game Boy, and if you look at the sticker, you will find the information about the input and output voltage range.

Figure 3-13. Transformer supporting a 230V input and a 3V output

This particular transformer takes an input voltage up to 220 volts and transforms this into 3 volts. This transformer would not be enough for powering the Arduino Uno board, but it would power a LilyPad that takes an input of 2.7 volts to 5.5 volts. The Uno standard board has more components on the board than the LilyPad, so the standard board needs a bit more power. The standard board also has an onboard power regulator that can take a higher voltage input and lower it to the operational voltage of the ATmega chip. This is lacking on the LilyPad, so you have to make sure to stay within the operational voltage range, or you might end up burning the ATmega chip on the LilyPad.

On the LilyPad board you have two options for connecting external power, as shown in Figure 3-14. One is the plastic connector for a lithium battery pack that plugs in with a cable, and the other is the two pins next to the plastic connecter marked + and –.

Figure 3-14. *The two power connectors on the LilyPad*

Electricity

All the projects in this book are powered by electricity. Even though we use it on a daily basis, most of us have a hard time explaining what electricity actually is. In fact, the term electricity is very vague. The word was coined around the year 1600 AD and comes from the Latin word *Electricus*, meaning amber-like. It was the Greeks who figured out that when you rub two pieces of amber together, they generate an electrical effect. Luckily, the science of electricity didn't stop there, or you would have a lot of problems powering the projects in this book.

Until the late nineteenth century, there were few practical applications for electricity, and it's not until the last 100 years that we have come to rely on electricity as a source of power. We won't go through the entire history of electricity, but there are a few things you should know before you start playing around with electricity.

First, you should know that all the projects in this book are low voltage, and as long as you follow the instructions, they are completely safe. The worst thing that can happen is that you accidentally burn a small component. In fact, a sewing machine is probably the most dangerous tool you will use in any of the projects.

One of the misconceptions regarding electricity is that it is something constant. We count on the electricity in our wall sockets to always be at the same level, but this is not the case. Electricity moves a bit like water. You might have a constant flow of water, but sometimes the water moves a bit faster or slower—and it's the same with electricity.

Another misconception is that high voltage is dangerous, but in fact, it is high amperes that are dangerous. To better explain this misconception, you need to know a bit more about how electricity works.

Voltage, Current, and Resistance

I like to think of electricity as a round pipe filled with balls. The balls in the pipe are analogous to electrons and they move around by hitting one another. When one ball hits another, it moves forward until it hits another ball, and then that ball starts moving. It's like a row of billiard balls lined up. If you hit the one on the end hard enough, the balls will keep hitting one another, and they all move forward. This is how the electrons in electricity move. The electrons act the same as the billiard balls in the pipe; this is known as the *current*, which is measured in amperes.

■ **Note** Electricity always has to go back to where it came from so that the electrons can keep pushing each other around.

The force of the push between the billiard balls in the pipe is the same as the push between electrons, which is known as the *voltage*.

When we want to move electricity from one place to another, we usually use wires; and with the balls in the pipe, the pipe acts as the wire. The pipe adds what we call resistance; when the balls touch the pipe, it makes them slow down a bit.

In some cases resistance is a good thing. In many of the projects, we will be using a component called a *resistor* to slow down the flow of electrons. This is because we want to make sure that components on the receiving end can handle the electricity we are supplying them with. It's like squeezing the pipe a bit to make the balls pass even slower.

When electricity was discovered, scientists used an analogy with water, but I don't like this analogy since it is based on a mistake. At the time, scientists also tried to figure out the direction electricity flows, but they couldn't. However, they knew there were two types of electric charges, positive (+) and negative (–). So they decided, based on a guess, that electricity was a flow of positive charges flowing from positive to negative, and they used the analogy of the way water flows in a waterfall to explain it. It wasn't until 1897, when the electron was discovered, that scientists realized that electricity is a flow of negative charged electrons that flow from negative to positive. The problem with the waterfall analogy was that water would have to move up, not down. By the time this was realized, it was already standard practice to think of electricity as a flow from positive to negative; and it still is standard practice. The + is where the power comes from and the – is where it needs to go to for a circuit to be completed. If a circuit is not complete, nothing will happen.

Still, this is only true for DC electricity, and you should always make sure to use DC electricity with you Arduino board. AC/DC is not only a rock band from Australia, but also the abbreviation used for describing *alternating current* and *direct current*. All electronics are designed to handle either AC or DC electricity. If an electronic device is designed to handle DC power, AC power will short circuit the device and might destroy it.

When we are making electronics projects, we need to use DC electricity since it is what the Arduino is designed to handle. If you look at the transformer in Figure 3-13, near where it says 230V, there is a symbol that looks like the one shown in Figure 3-15.

Figure 3-15. The tilde is used to indicate alternating current

This symbol is used to indicate that the input power is AC. The symbol for DC looks like the one shown in Figure 3-16.

Figure 3-16. *This symbol indicates direct current*

The electricity you find in normal wall sockets is in most cases alternating current, so a transformer not only transforms higher voltages to lower, but also alternating current to direct current.

It is a common misconception that high voltage is dangerous because voltage only tells you the force of the push between electrons. If there is a low current (amperes) or, in other words, a low amount of electrons and high voltage, it is typically not dangerous. But high amperes are dangerous, even at low voltage. Again think of it as billiard balls in a round pipe. High voltage and low amperes would be like pushing one or two balls around the pipe very fast. But low voltage and high amperes would be like pushing a lot of balls through the pipe. So even at low speed, if there is too much resistance in the pipe, the balls could start colliding and get caught in the pipe. When this happens with electrons, it's bad news, since they start generating heat very fast.

The important thing to keep track of is the voltage in relation to amperes; because if you are dealing with high amperes, you want to make sure they have room to pass and that nothing gets in their way—like your body. I would say that anything that can supply more the 500 milliamperes should be handled with caution since this could severely hurt you.

Batteries

While you are building your project and testing stuff out, you probably will stick to powering your Arduino board with the USB cable; but once you are close to finishing your project, it will be time to switch to another power source to truly make your project wearable. This is when you will use batteries.

There are two types of batteries: primary and secondary. Primaries are the disposable kind that you throw away once they lose power. The secondary ones are the rechargeable kind that can be used over and over again.

■ **Note** Always make sure to throw your batteries in battery recycle bins since they contain harmful chemicals.

A battery is a collection of electrochemical cells, but in everyday use of the word, we usually refer to a single battery as one cell; in fact, most batteries are made of multiple cells. For example, a 1.5 volt AAA battery has one 1.5 volt cell, but a 3 volt battery has two 1.5 volt cells inside it.

A battery converts chemical energy to electronic energy. Depending on the type of battery you are using, the chemicals used in them are different. But the principle is the same: when you connect the negative end to the positive end, the chemicals on the inside react to each other and the outcome is electricity.

The two types of batteries are sub-divided by the kind of chemicals they use.

- *Zinc-carbon*: Used in most of the common, inexpensive AA, AAA, and dry-cell batteries.

- *Alkaline*: Commonly used in AA and dry batteries.

- *Lithium ion*: Often used in rechargeable batteries for high-performance devices like cell phones, digital cameras, and laptop computers. These are usually a bit more expensive.

- *Lead acid*: Used for products that need a longer shelf-life, like car batteries.

On the standard Arduino board, you can connect batteries to the DC jack with the appropriate connector for your type of battery. Personally, I like 9 volt batteries since they have a nice form factor and enough energy to power the Arduino for some time.

Battery Connectors

You have a nice selection of different battery connectors for the LilyPad since it is hard to connect batteries in a wearable project. A connector really helps. The first one is the LilyPad power supply (shown in Figure 3-17), which takes a standard AAA battery. Remember to never power the LilyPad boards with more than 5 volts.

Figure 3-17. The LilyPad power supply uses normal AAA batteries

It outputs 5 volts and has built-in short circuit protection, which is good when you are working with sensitive electronics. It also has an onboard On/Off switch. If you don't need as much power, there is also a coin cell connector, shown in Figure 3-18. It fits a 20mm 3V coin cell. Keep in mind that there is not a lot of power in these batteries, but in some cases you don't need a whole lot of power.

Figure 3-18. LilyPad coin cell battery holder

The LiPower connector (shown in Figure 3-19) allows for connecting lithium batteries and even includes a connector for a charger if needed. All battery connectors can be used with both the LilyPad and the LilyPad Simple.

Figure 3-19. The LilyPad LiPower uses 3.7V lithium batteries

Testing the Hardware

Now that you know the basics of the Arduino hardware, let's test to make certain that everything works as it should. For this, you will be using the Arduino IDE. On the Arduino board, there is a small LED mounted on the board next to pin 13. LED stands for *light emitting diode* and it's a small lamp on the Arduino board that can be used for testing and debugging. We are going to use it to make sure the Arduino IDE is installed correctly and that there is nothing wrong with the Arduino board. Let's start with the code, as follows:

```
int ledPin = 13;

void setup(){
pinMode(ledPin, OUTPUT);
}

void loop(){
digitalWrite(ledPin,HIGH);
delay(500);
digitalWrite(ledPin,LOW);
delay(500);
}
```

This is the same code we started in Chapter 2, but now we are going to test it on our Arduino board by taking the following steps:

1. Plug your Arduino into the computer using the USB cable. Start the Arduino IDE.

2. Check the Tools menu to ensure that the correct Arduino board is selected under Board and that you have selected the correct port under Serial Port.

3. Press the Verify/Compile button and wait for the "Done compiling" message. Check that you received a message in white text in the black window.

4. Press the Upload button and wait for the "Done uploading" message.

5. Check that the LED next to pin 13 is blinking (the LED is shown in Figure 3-20).

Figure 3-20. Pin 13 has an onboard LED connected to it.

If the LED is blinking with a half-second delay, then your IDE is installed correctly and your Arduino board is working. The LilyPad also has a small LED mount next to the ATmega chip. The code example works the same way on the LilyPad.

Summary

To do the entire field of electronics and microprocessors justice, I would need many more pages than I have for this book. But the good thing is that you don't need to know everything to get started doing stuff with electronics. It is still true that the more you know, the better your designs will become; but I always stress that it is more important get started making things because this is when the actual learning happens. Most of the things covered in this chapter will be revisited through projects later on, where we go through how the different parts work at a practical level.

There are a lot of options if you want to learn more about the basics of electronics and electronic components, but the ones worth mentioning are *Getting Started in Electronics* (Master Publishing, 2003) and *Engineer's Mini Notebook* (Radio Shack, 1985), both by Forrest Mims. These books are excellent introductions to electronics and are written and hand-drawn by Mims himself.

Charles Platt also wrote a very good introduction to electronics titled *Make: Electronics (Learning by Discovery)* (Make, 2009).

CHAPTER 4

Smart Materials and Tools

Smart materials have one or more properties that can change its state using external stimuli like stress, electricity, moisture, magnetic fields, and more. However, the term "smart materials" is also used to refer to materials combined with electronics. We will not bother with definition of the word, but instead focus on the most important aspect of smart materials, and that is how awesome they are. In this chapter, I will list a few of the smart materials that we'll use in the book, as well as some other ones that I have come across during my prototyping years. I will also introduce some tools that are good to have in your prototyping kit along with your standard sewing equipment.

Materials

In this section, we cover the materials and tools that you will use during the course of the book. Additional materials are introduced in some of the projects. The following are more of an honorary mention of tools and materials that are good and fun to have in general, and to experiment with beyond the projects in this book.

Thermochromic Ink

The name comes from the term *thermochromism*, which refers to the ability a substance has to change its own color depending on temperature. Thermochromic ink was made popular in the early 1990s by the Hypercolor clothing line from Generra Sportswear. Hypercolor clothing was a short-lived fad, but today thermochromic inks have made a small comeback. This has made it fairly easy to get your hands on thermochromic ink and opens a lot of potential for creative designs. There are two types of thermochromic inks: one that appears when heated and one that disappears when heated.

Figures 4-1 and 4-2 show fabric with thermochromic ink patterns before and after heat is applied.

Figure 4-1. *Thermochromic screen print on fabric*

A second, normal fabric color was applied under the thermochromic ink so it looks like the fabric changed color when the thermochromic ink was heated. You don't need an additional color if you don't want it. You can color any fabric with thermochromic ink and it will disappear when heated, revealing the fabric's original color. In most cases you do not need a lot of heat to make the ink disappear. But keep in mind that you are a bit limited in how you can control the spread of thermochromic ink since it reacts to body heat as well. With multiple fabric layers and Kanthal wire (described next) you can make some cool interactive patterns and shapes.

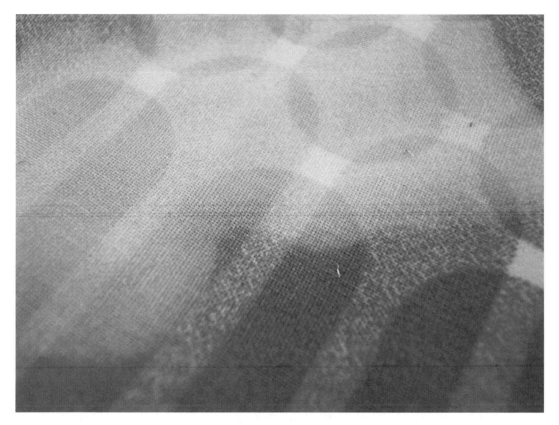

Figure 4-2. Thermochromic screen print after heat is applied

Kanthal Wire

Kanthal is a trademarked name for iron-chromium-aluminum alloys that are used for high-temperature applications. It is available in a range of resistances. When electricity is applied to Kanthal wire, it starts to generate heat. Standard Kanthal wire has a melting point of 1200°C (2200°F), which is pretty impressive, but probably nowhere near what you might need for a wearable project. You can use it, however, to generate "body-friendly" heat as well.

Conductive Foam

You probably have conductive foam somewhere in your house and you don't know it. Conductive foam is used to ground electronic appliances. For example, some stoves have conductive foam in places where metal is exposed to make sure that the electricity goes back to where it came from, and not through anybody that might come in contact with the metal area.

You can buy conductive foam in all shapes and sizes and with different resistances. An example is shown in Figure 4-3.

When you buy electronic components, some of them come packaged in conductive foam to protect the component from static electricity. Make sure to save that foam because you never know when it might come in handy. Conductive foams are used to make soft-pressure sensors and buttons. Or you can make your own stylus pen for your smartphone or tablet. To test whether a piece of foam is conductive or not, you can use a multimeter. (To learn more about using a multimeter, head over to Chapter 5.)

Touchscreens are usually resistive, which means that they can detect where your finger is because skin is conductive. This is why touchscreen devices don't work when you are wearing gloves. But a small piece of foam on the tip of a glove finger or a pen would work. Or if you want to make a pair of touchscreen gloves, you could use conductive thread (described in the next section).

Figure 4-3. Conductive foam with non-conductive center

Conductive Thread

We will use conductive thread as a substitute for wires in many projects in the book. When it comes to finalizing your project, you will find that in some cases it's not very practical to use wires for wearable projects. Conductive thread looks like normal gray thread (see Figure 4-4), but can conduct electricity. Most conductive threads are silver-plated and available in a range of resistances. In most cases you should not follow the resistance indicated by the supplier since it is hard to tell how much thread you will use before you start sewing. It's usually better to sew you connections and then measure the resistance to get a more exact resistance value. The more thread you add, the greater the resistance will be. You use a multimeter to measure resistance.

One thing to keep in mind when using conductive thread in wearables is that human skin also conducts electricity, and if the thread touches skin, it might interfere with the signal. But this also means that you can use conductive thread to make a sensor that detects when it's touched.

Figure 4-4. Roll of conductive thread

Conductive Textile

Conductive fabrics are textiles that have the ability to conduct electricity. Some textiles are made with metal strands woven into the fabric (see Figure 4-5) and others are made by impregnating normal fabrics with metal or carbon powders. The conductive areas can be coated onto fabric or embedded into fabric.

When it comes to making wearable projects, conductive textiles are great for making sensors or as a substitute for using cables. Conductive textiles offer more flexible design solutions. Examples of the way conductive textiles are normally used include the following:

- Static electricity shielding

- Signal and power transfer

- Heating elements

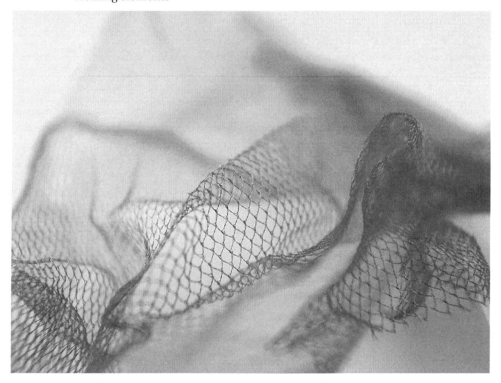

Figure 4-5. *Thin, conductive mesh fabric*

Conductive textiles are available with different material compounds that define the resistance in the material; this includes the following:

- *Electronylon:* The textile fibers have been coated with copper, which gives the material a very low resistance, if any.

- *Meshnet with copper-coated polyester fibers:* Available in different densities, some of which make the material see-through.

- *Electrolycra*: Looks and feels like normal Lycra, but it is conductive and can change its resistance when stretched.

- *Steel fabric*: Woven from very thin stainless steel fiber, but it feels like normal textile. Steel fabrics have a high resistance.

- *Zelt*: A low-budget alternative that uses a cooper-zinc coating. The down side to coated thread is that the conductive material might be accidentally stripped from the thread.

Most conductive fabrics come with resistance specifications, but you should never trust them since every piece of fabric has slight variation. In most cases you don't use the fabric as you bought it, instead you cut it into pieces; once this is done, it's better to measure the resistance yourself using a multimeter.

Some companies have developed more specialized conductive fabrics like the one in Figure 4-6 where the fabric is partly conductive. The conductive areas are separated by normal thread.

Figure 4-6. Conductive mesh fabric mixed with non-conductive thread

Conductive Velcro

Conductive Velcro (see Figure 4-7) looks like normal Velcro, but like other smart materials, it conducts electricity. You can use it for resealable flaps, tubes, or seams with other conductive fabrics or any material. It uses a silver coating and conducts along its length. In combination with the Arduino, it can be used as a switch or even a sensor that measures the amount of Velcro that is open by measuring the resistance in the Velcro.

Figure 4-7. Conductive Velcro

Conductive Paint

There are a variety of conductive paints. The compounds of the paints differ according to the application.

- Copper paints are highly conductive.

- Silver paint is typically used for repairing broken connections on PCB boards like the base board of the Arduino or LilyPad, onto which all the components are placed.

- Carbon-based paints aren't as conductive as metal-based paints, but they are good enough to make electronic connections. In Figure 4-8 you'll find a carbon- and water-based paint called Bare paint.

It's even possible to make your own conductive paint by mixing graphite carbon power with an insulator like liquid tape or paint. If you try to make your own conductive paint, you should expect some trial and error before you find a good formula that fits your project's needs.

Since carbon is conductive, you can even make simple sensors with a charcoal pen and paper. Keep in mind you need a lot of charcoal on the paper to make this work, and even if it does, a sensor made of paper has limited applications since it can easily break.

Figure 4-8. Conductive paint

Smart Wire

Smart wire (see Figure 4-9) looks like normal metal wire, but it is a bit smarter. The cool thing about this wire is that it remembers its original state, which is usually straight when you buy it. You can bend it into any shape you want, and if you heat it to 90°C (194°F), it will shift back to its original shape.

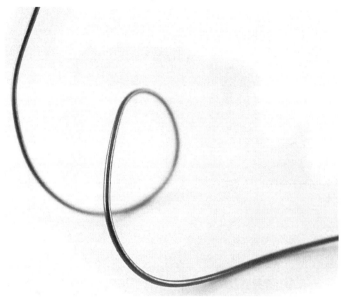

Figure 4-9. Smart wire that remembers shapes

The other great thing about smart wire is that you can train it to remember new shapes. To do this, you set it to a new position and heat it to 500°C (932°F) for 5 minutes. This can be done using a heating gun or even a candle flame. For example, bend the wire into an L shape and hold it over the open flame. At first, the wire will try to return to its original position, so you have to keep it steady until the tension releases. Then let the wire cool down. After it has cooled, you can bend it into a new shape. Put it in hot water and the wire will return to the L shape.

Smart wire is also often used in robotics and medicine, where thin smart wires are inserted into blood vessels to help them expand from normal body heat.

Nitinol Wire

Nitinol wire is also known as "shape memory alloy" or "muscle wire." It looks identical to any other metal wire. The difference is that nitinol wire shrinks approximately 5 percent in length if you heat it to 70°C (158°F). At 52°C (125°F) the wire resumes its original length. Nitinol wire is pretty strong and at a thickness of 0.5 millimeters (1/50th of an inch), muscle wire can lift up to 0.4 kilograms (almost a pound). The popular name "muscle wire" comes from its use in robotic arms, where the wire is used to simulate human muscles.

The tricky thing to using muscle wire in wearable projects is fastening the wire into fabrics, since it easily pulls itself loose. One of the best ways to prevent this is to use crimp beads and normal wires.

Tools

When it comes to selecting tools, it's subject to what you prefer and depends a lot on what you are building, but let's discuss some standard tools that are always good to have when dealing with any electronic and microprocessor prototyping.

Alligator Clips

Alligator clips are good for temporarily connecting stuff together (see Figure 4-10 and note the clips at the end of each wire). When it comes to normal electronic components, you use them with wires on a breadboard (see the next section). Alligator clips are especially handy when it comes to making wearables since you often use fabrics or other soft components, and it can be tricky to connect these things into a breadboard.

Figure 4-10. Alligator clips

Breadboard

Most electronic components are soldered together, but it might not be a good idea to solder before you learn how to actually connect a component the right way. Because if you solder something, and then find out you made a mistake, it's very tricky to desolder it. That's why you should always try stuff out on a breadboard first and if everything works fine, then you can solder, or in our case, sew things together. Figure 4-11 shows a typical breadboard.

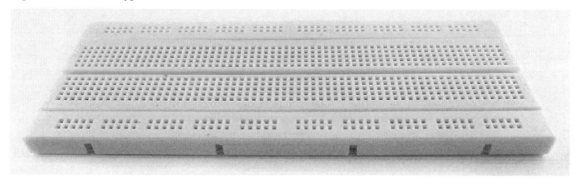

Figure 4-11. Breadboard

A breadboard is a piece of plastic; on the bottom of the inside there are metal strips that connect the small holes together in rows. The rows of holes are both connected in vertical and horizontal lines. It might be a bit confusing and hard to remember how the connections work if you never used a breadboard before. So when things don't work, you should also make it a standard practice to check your breadboard connections. Figure 4-12 shows how the rows are connected on this board.

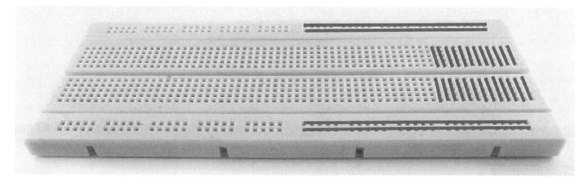

Figure 4-12. The connection of the breadboard

On the horizontal edges of the breadboard, the rows connect horizontally in two lines to the middle, and then there is a break in the connection. After the break, they continue the same way. In the middle of the board, the rows are connected vertically to the vertical middle, and then there is a break. On the other side of the break, they continue in a second vertical row.

Most of the projects in this book show figures of how circuits need to be sewn in place. But in most cases, it might be a good idea to try them out on a breadboard before you get started in order to help you understand the circuit and to try it out with an Arduino sketch. Sewing circuits takes a bit of time and testing them on a breadboard might save you a lot of time later on.

As an example, testing an LED connection by sewing the circuit might take about 10 minutes to sew in place on a LilyPad; but it can be connected within seconds with wires on a breadboard, as shown in

Figure 4-13. Connecting LED to the Arduino board

So again I recommend buying a standard Arduino board and a breadboard for testing. Once you feel confident about how to connect things, you can move on to using a LilyPad or an Arduino Mini and conductive thread.

Multimeter

A multimeter (see Figure 4-14) is an instrument used to measure amperes, volts, and resistance. It can also be used to check for electronic connections. A multimeter is always good to have close by while searching for errors. If a conductive thread breaks, we can use the multimeter to check the connections. If a connection is whole, the multimeter beeps; if there is no beep, the connection is broken.

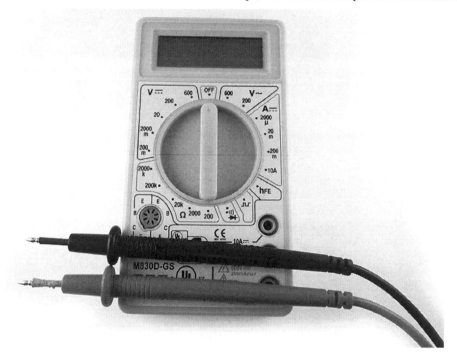

Figure 4-14. Multimeter

There are many different multimeters available, ranging from cheap to very expensive. If you are not super experienced with electronics, go for a cheaper one. Using a multimeter is covered in Chapter 5.

Camera

It might sound silly to have a camera in your prototyping kit, but to be honest, this was my most-used tool when I was first learning electronics and microprocessors—and it still is. While trying out new stuff, you are constantly connecting and reconnecting components; and then, when things work, you move on. The problem is that you might have to do something again, but you forgot what you did the last time you made it work. When this happens, it's priceless to have a picture bank of images to help you remember, or if you need help from someone more experienced, you can send a picture of what you are trying to do. It doesn't have to be a good camera as long as you can tell what is in the image.

Helping Hands

Helping hands, also called soldering clamps (see Figure 4-15), are a simple and very helpful tool used while soldering. When you start soldering, you'll soon realize that a third hand would help a lot—and this is when these guys come in handy. You can also attach magnifying glasses on the arms of a helping hand, which is also helpful when soldering really small components.

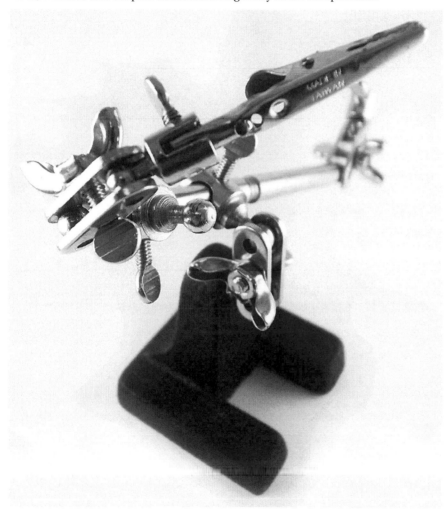

Figure 4-15. Helping hands

Needle-nose Pliers

A pair of pliers (see Figure 4-16) is always good to have around since some electronic components are small and hard, and in some cases needs to be bent, squeezed, or pulled. Needle-nose pliers are particularity nice when dealing with wearables because you are working with tiny components and sometimes in very narrow spaces.

Figure 4-16. Needle-nose pliers

Soldering Iron

A soldering iron (see Figure 4-17) is what you use when you solder. Soldering is like mini-welding, where you connect the metal parts of electronic components together by melting solder on to them, which makes an electronic connection. When it comes to soldering irons, I avoid the cheapest since they are not very good and usually have a short life span. I would not go for the most expensive one either since they can cost hundreds of dollars. A good idea is to go to your electronics store and ask which one is the best for you. I do suggest a soldering iron with regulatable heating so that you don't end up overheating your components.

Figure 4-17. Soldering iron

Wire Cutters

Wire cutters (see Figure 4-18) are a must-have when dealing with electronics because you will be dealing with a lot of wires.

Figure 4-18. Normal wire cutters

With a bit of finesse, you can also use them to strip wires; but if you don't want to master this art from the start, there are dedicated wire-stripping tools (see Figure 4-19) that are usually available at affordable prices.

Figure 4-19. Wire stripper with cable cutter

Summary

In addition to the material and tools mentioned in this chapter, you need a computer and a sewing machine, as well as your standard sewing equipment—like nice scissors, needles, and so on. It might take some time to get everything together, and it will cost a bit of money, so my suggestion is to not start with everything. Take baby steps, and get the stuff you need when you need it.

But you need to start somewhere, and the first investment I suggest you make is an Arduino board. There is a lot of learning that can be done with just the Arduino board, which gives it good value for your money. Each of the projects in this book introduces new materials and different tools and techniques. The projects start off fairly easy, with few components; and they gradually become more complex. So rather than using this chapter as a shopping guide, take a look at the individual projects because they may require additional components and materials.

CHAPTER 5

LED Bracelets

This chapter explains how to make two versions of an LED bracelet: a "soft" one and a "hard" one. Both bracelets are made using what is known as a parallel circuit, which is one of the most common electronic circuits. Both projects will also introduce you to two methods for making circuits.

- One uses soldering, which is more traditional in terms of electronics.
- The other one uses sewing and conductive thread.

At the end of this chapter, you will have new jewelry with extra "bling," as well as a fundamental understanding of how circuits work.

To start things nice and slow, this chapter introduces you to working with electronic components in relation to fabrics. The chapter also includes a tutorial of the basic use of a multimeter, a skill you'll need in many of the upcoming chapters. This chapter will not include the use of an Arduino board and it will not require any programming.

Materials and Tools Needed

The following are lists of the materials and tools you will need for making a soft bracelet and a hard bracelet.

Soft Bracelet

To create a soft bracelet, you will need the following:

- Conductive thread
- Needle-nose pliers
- Fabric
- LEDs
- Coin cell batteries
- LilyPad coin-cell battery clip
- Needles

- Sewing machine
- Metal snap-on buttons

Hard Bracelet

To create a hard bracelet, you will need the following:

- Solder
- Soldering iron
- Needle-nose pliers
- LEDs
- Metal rings
- Coin cell batteries
- Rare earth magnet

Using Multimeters

Using a multimeter is not much fun in itself, but it is a good skill to acquire; without one, you are left in the dark when it comes to electronics because you can't actually see the electricity running through your project. Multimeters can be complicated tools, so in this tutorial we will stick to the functions we use in this book.

You can use a multimeter for different things, like measuring voltage, resistance, and conductivity. Let's start with checking for conductivity, which means that a current flows through the connection being tested.

Conductivity

Start by setting the multimeter dial to the symbol shown in Figure 5-1. If you don't touch the probes, which are the red and black pens connected to the multimeter, the display should read O.L or 1, depending on the manufacturer. O.L means open loop, which in turn means that there is no connection between the probes.

If you connect the two probes together (see Figure 5-1), the multimeter should start to beep, which indicates that the multimeter has found conductivity between the probes.

Figure 5-1. *Finding conductivity with a multimeter*

This function is used for checking that things are conducting properly. To do a simple test, take some conductive thread (see Figure 5-2) and connect the probes to each end of the thread.

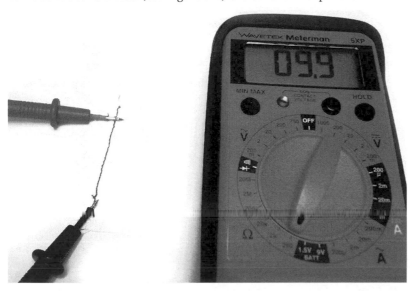

Figure 5-2. *Checking for conductivity in the conductive thread*

If the multimeter beeps, it means that the conductive thread conducts electricity between the probes.

Measuring Resistance

The second use for the multimeter is to check resistance, which we'll need to do quite a few times when using non-standard components, such as a zipper. To do this, turn the dial of the multimeter to the area with the Ω sign (see Figure 5-3). This area is subdivided into different ranges. Usually the range is from 200 to 2M. This sets the maximum range of your measurement. If the thing you are trying to measure is outside the range maximum, the display will show O.L.

At this point, you might wonder how you will know which range to use if you don't know the resistance of the thing you are trying to measure. Well, the easiest way is to start from the bottom (at 200) and work your way up.

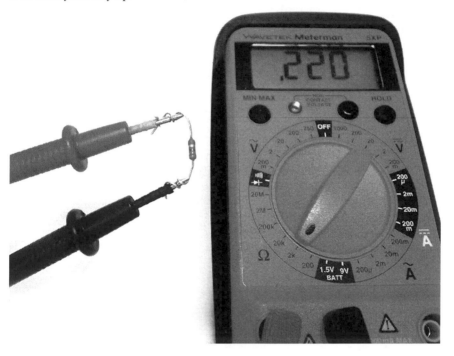

Figure 5-3. Measuring the resistance of a resistor

In Figure 5-3, the resistance of a resistor is measured. The dial is set to 2k, which means that the maximum value for this range is 2000 ohms. Note that the point is before the 220, which within the range of 0 to 2000 ohms means 220 ohms; this is also the resistance indicated on the package of the resistor in the figure.

■ **Note** The range is 0 to 2000 ohms because the dial is set at 2k. In other words, a reading of 2.000 on this setting is 2000 ohms, so .220 is 220 ohms.

In most cases, the resistance on the packaging of a component is an approximated value; it usually doesn't differ that much from the actual value. Resistors do not often have the exact same value. This is due to the manufacturing process, where the slightest change will affect the resistance. In fact, in most cases the resistance does not have to be 100 percent correct. A few ohms more or less will not affect your projects.

Measuring Voltage

To measure voltage, turn the dial to the symbol shown in Figure 5-4. On the opposite side you will find a similar symbol with a V, but with a tilde above it; the tilde indicates that that side is used to measure alternating current. The side used in Figure 5-4 is used to measure direct current, which we will use in all the projects in this book.

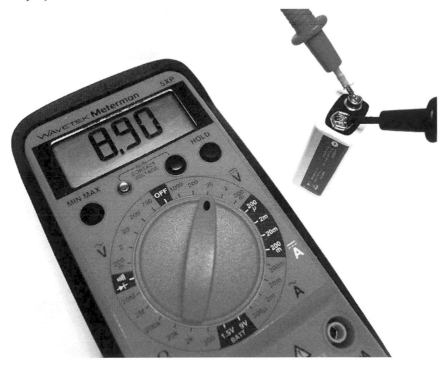

Figure 5-4. Measuring voltage

In Figure 5-4, the red probe is connected to the positive side of the battery and the black probe is connected to the negative. If I swapped them around, the multimeter would still tell me the voltage of the battery, but there would be a minus sign in front of the value. This shows you can also use a multimeter to check the direction of the voltage. You don't need to bother with this for resistance and conductivity since both are bidirectional, which means they go both ways.

Now that you are equipped to measure the important values in a circuit, it's time to work with some electronics.

Using LEDs

LED stands for *light emitting diode*. The diode part means that electricity can only travel through the component in one direction. When the electrons travel through the LED, they release energy in the form of photons. This effect is called *thermoluminescence* and the color of the LED depends on the distance of the energy gap inside the LED.

■ **Note** Without getting too technical, you could say that the energy gap has to do with the distance between the metal pieces inside the LED. If the gap is shorter, the color of the LED might be red; a bigger gap would make the color yellow.

LEDs are available in almost any shape or size you need. They can be as small as less than a millimeter. There are even LEDs that transmit ultraviolet and infrared light, which are not visible to human eyes. Infrared LEDs are used inside a TV remote to send signals to the TV, which has an infrared receiver. LEDs have very low power consumption and a long lifespan; this makes them an alternative to standard light bulbs, which have been banned in some countries because of their power ineffectiveness. Today you can find LEDs everywhere, such as bus signs, control panels, on laptop computers, and in traffic lights. You can also find them in newer car lights since LEDs consume less power than those found in older car lights.

There are a few easy ways that you can tell how to power an LED since they only take electricity in one direction. The first indication is the legs. If you look at an LED, you will find two legs; one leg is longer than the other. The longer leg indicates where to connect the power (+) and the shorter leg indicates where to connect the LED back to ground (–), as shown in Figure 5-5.

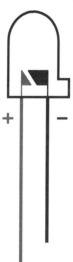

Figure 5-5. The longer leg of an LED indicates the positive side; the shorter leg indicates the negative side.

Suppose that you cut the legs of an LED or you just want to make sure that the long leg is the actual positive leg. Take a look at the small rim of the LED, which should have one flat side. This side indicates the negative leg. Another option is to hold up the LED to a light and look inside it. You should see two pieces of metal: one smaller, one bigger. The smaller one connects to the positive leg and the bigger one connects to the negative leg, as shown in Figure 5-6.

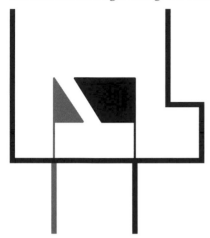

Figure 5-6. *Inside an LED, the smaller metal piece is connected to the positive leg and the bigger metal piece is connected to ground.*

LEDs are not only available in a large selection of colors, but also in a range of light intensities. The light intensity is called *lumen,* and the higher the voltage, the greater the intensity. More intensity sometimes requires more power. A 12V LED emits more light than a 3V LED. For this project, we will use 3V LEDs since they can be connected straight to a 3V coin cell battery.

While working with the Arduino, most times you end up using 3V LEDs since these can be controlled and powered from the digital pins without any extra components other than a resistor. The 3V LEDs are also the most common LEDs, which makes them the easiest to find and also the cheapest.

Serial vs. Parallel

To quickly test your LED, you can hook it up straight to your coin cell battery (see Figure 5-7) with the long LED on the positive side of the battery and the short LED on the negative side.

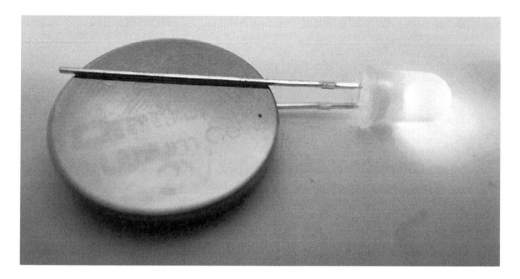

Figure 5-7. Single LED and coin cell battery

You can even add more LEDs using the same connections (see Figure 5-8).

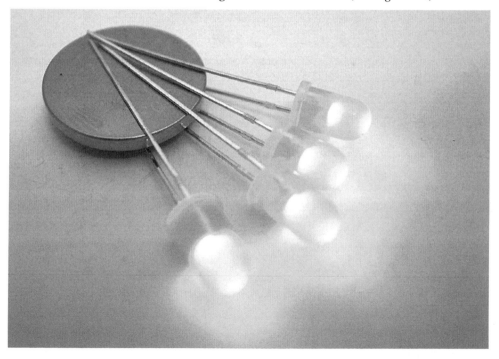

Figure 5-8. Multiple 3V LEDs can be connected straight to a 3V coin cell battery.

This type of connection is called a *parallel connection*. Electronic components can be connected in many different ways and serial and parallel connections are two of the most common connections. If you connect components, such as LEDs, in parallel, the same voltage will be applied to all the LEDs, as shown in Figure 5-9.

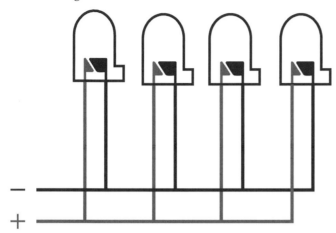

Figure 5-9. LEDs in a parallel connection

A *serial connection* means that you connect all the components from ground to the positive in a single path, and the positive and ground end at a power source. This makes the same current flow through all the components. Figure 5-10 shows how to make a serial connection with four LEDs.

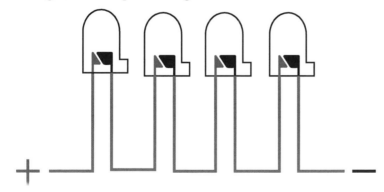

Figure 5-10. LEDs in a serial connection

If we hooked the four LEDs in series to the 3V battery, the voltage would drop since they are all sharing the same current flow. In other words, the LEDs need 3 volts each to light up, and if they are connected in series, it would be like dividing the 3 volts into four—and that would not leave enough power for each one to light up.

But when we connect them in parallel (see Figure 5-9), the same current is not passed through all of them; instead, each LED gets the current it needs and the right voltage, which makes it light up. This knowledge might come in handy, for example, if you have only a 6V battery to use with 3V LEDs. If you connect the LEDs in parallel, they will burn out; but if you connect two of them in series, the voltage drops between them, making it 3 volts, which would not burn the LEDs.

The same rule applies for batteries. If you have two 1.5V batteries and connect them in series, the voltage increases to 3 volts, but the amperes stay the same since the current has to flow through both batteries. But if you connect them in parallel, the voltage stays the same but the amperes multiply by the number of batteries, assuming they carry the same current.

Basic Schematic for Parallel LED Bracelet Circuit

Figure 5-11 shows an abstracted schematic of how the bracelets will work. Real electronic schematics look a bit different because they use symbols for components instead of illustrations of components.

In Figure 5-11, you will find that all the LEDs are connected in parallel to the battery's positive side. All the ground connections are also connected in parallel to one side of the button. The other side of the button is connected to the negative side of the battery. Note that there is a gap between the buttons; this is how you will turn the bracelet on and off. If the button is closed, the circuit is completed and the LEDs light up. If the button is open, there is no connection back to the negative side of the battery from the LEDs, and the LEDs remain off.

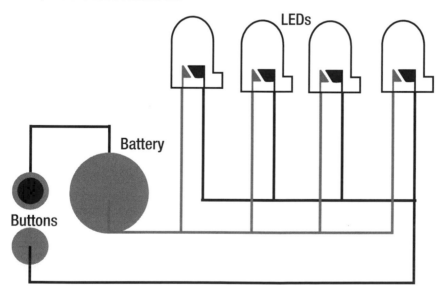

Figure 5-11. LEDs in a parallel connection to a battery and button

Soft Bracelet

Figure 5-7 shows the basic abstracted schematic you will use to construct your soft bracelet. Once you understand the schematic, feel free to make any artistic modifications you feel are necessary. The important thing to remember is that your conductive thread lines never cross each other. This might be tricky to remember if you are used to sewing, but new to sewing circuits. You should never sew a line over another using conductive thread if you don't want those lines connected to one another.

I chose a natural-colored hemp fabric for the bracelet because I want a low-tech/high-tech feel to it, but you can choose any fabric you want as long it's not conductive. The design is also an open circuit in order to give a better overview of the construction. If you want, you can use the same design and then cover it with fabric, only exposing the LEDs.

Step 1

Figure 5-12 shows a piece of hemp fabric that is 20 centimeters (8 inches) long and 6 centimeters (2.5 inches) wide. The first step is to make two 0.5 centimeter (1/5th of an inch) folds on both horizontal sides and sew them in place using conductive thread. To sew the lines, I used a sewing machine with conductive thread as the bobbin thread. Since conductive thread is usually a bit thick, it is not a good idea to use it as both spool and bobbin thread in a sewing machine; and it's really only needed on one side.

Figure 5-12. Seams sewn with conductive thread

Step 2

LEDs are not really made to be sewn into fabrics, but I'll describe a trick I picked up from one of my students that makes it a bit easier to both sew LEDs and tell which leg is which on the LED. Use your needle-nose pliers and roll the positive leg of the LED into a coil (see Figure 5-13).

Figure 5-13. Modifying the LED legs

I use a different shape for the negative leg in order to be able to tell which one is which. I use a rectangular shape, but you can use any shape you like as long as you remember what it means.

There are sewable LEDs available—like the LilyPad LEDs, which are placed on a small board with holes for sewing it in place. The board adds an extra cost, but sometimes this is worth it, depending on the project and the visual style you are looking for.

Step 3

The next step is to put all your components in place to check that everything fits nicely. In Figure 5-14 I marked my desired placement of all the components, as well as the connection that needs to be made. Make sure to use a pen that can easily be removed from the fabric.

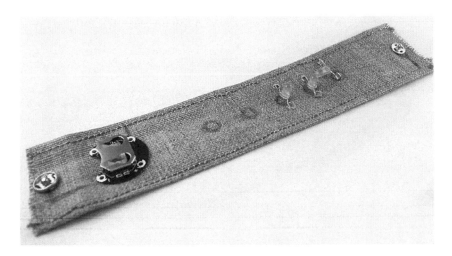

Figure 5-14. Marking the placement of components and needed connections

Step 4

Once the marks have been made, you can start making your connections using conductive thread. Since these are short connections and you need to stitch your components in place, I recommend doing this by hand. Using a sewing machine to sew components in place is never a good idea since the needle might hit the component and break.

Figure 5-15 shows that I have made a connection straight from the negative pin on the battery connector to one of the sides of the metal snap-on button. You need to make sure this is all done with the same piece of thread to ensure that the connection holds.

Figure 5-15. Ground connection from the battery holder to the button

You then attach the positive pin of the battery connector to the horizontal conductive thread line next to it, as shown in Figure 5-16. To make this connection secure, make a few loops in the hole of the battery connecter and pull the thread hard so it connects to the metal of the battery clip hole. To connect the thread to the machine-sewn line, stitch the thread in a few loops around the line and make a stitch straight through the line before making a knot in order to make sure that the thread does not slip away. This will act as the power line for your LEDs. Since we are going to connect them in parallel, all the positive legs of the LEDs need to go to the same power source.

Figure 5-16. Making the power connection

When sewing the LEDs in place, make sure that you connect the positive side of the LEDs to the end line that is the power line. In Figure 5-17 the circular legs are the positive leg of the LEDs and the negative square ones connect to the other line, which will act as the ground line. Make sure to sew the LEDs tightly in place to make a good connection with the conductive thread.

Figure 5-17. LED connected to each of the horizontal lines of conductive thread

At the end of the short side of the fabric, sew the other piece of your metal snap-on button in place with a connection to the ground line.

Step 5

Once everything is sewn in place, you should have something that looks similar to Figure 5-18. Now you can put a battery in the battery holder and snap the bracelet. The snap button holds your bracelet together, but also works as an on-and-off switch, completing the circuit.

Figure 5-18. The finished bracelet

Hard Bracelet

We will use two metal rings for the hard bracelet. I found metal rings in the jewelry section of a local clothing store at a cheap price; they came in a pack of twenty. Metal bracelets are a popular fashion accessory, so hopefully you won't have too much trouble finding them. Bring your multimeter to test that what you find is conductive.

This project will be built as an exposed circuit and follows the same principle shown in Figure 5-11. But in contrast to the soft bracelet, this bracelet will have a bit more solid construction and will require some soldering.

Making exposed circuits like this with low voltage is fine, but I would not recommend it with higher voltage and amperes than what is found in a coin cell battery. With these bracelets you are actually in contact with the electricity; but at a low ampere and voltage, it's pretty impossible to feel it. To avoid contact with the skin, an extra layer of fabric is usually enough. If you are dealing with higher voltage, a more secure material might be needed to insulate connections. Chapter 13's EL-wire dress project covers how to properly insulate higher-voltage connections.

Step 1

The first step is to put things in place. To help with this, use the magnet required for this project. I did not feel like incorporating any battery holder in the project because I wanted a clean look and I wanted the battery to be shown in the design; so to hold the battery in place at a later stage, you can use a magnet. The magnet I used is called a *rare earth magnet*; it is super strong for its size, which makes it perfect for holding the two metal rings together. Since the magnet is metal, it also helps connect both sides of the battery—which completes the circuit.

Figure 5-19 shows how you can hold the rings together with the help of the magnet; on the other side you can start attaching LEDs.

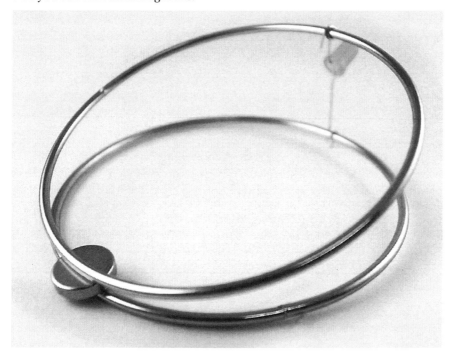

Figure 5-19. Magnet holding the rings together

The legs of the LEDs are used to separate the rings from one another (see Figure 5-20). Remember that the rings can't touch each other because the positive and negative leads of the LED need to stay separated or the bracelet will not light up (since electricity always takes the easiest path). If the rings touch, then the power will just flow from the positive to negative side of the battery, once we attach it—and not through the LEDs.

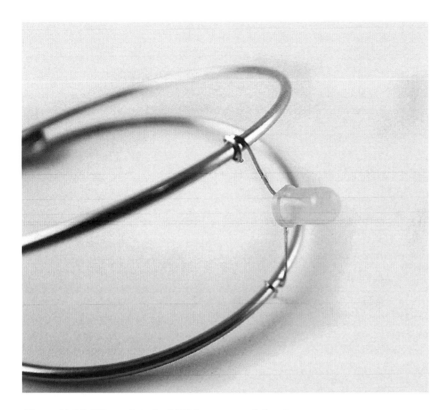

Figure 5-20. Wrapping the LED legs around the rings

To fasten the LEDs to the rings, you just wrap the legs around the rings with your desired spacing. The last part of the leg might be a bit hard to wrap, so it's a good idea to do this with your pliers. If your LEDs move around a lot at this stage, a helping hand or soldering clamps might come in handy (see Figure 5-21). Make sure that all the positive legs of the LEDs are connected to the same ring and that all the negative legs are connected to the other ring. The circuit will not work if you connect one in the opposite direction, so take your time making sure all the legs are connected in the correct direction.

Figure 5-21. Helping hands giving a hand

Step 2

Once you have wrapped your LEDs to the rings, you will notice that it's hard to make them stay in place; so to make a better connection, we will solder them in place.

Soldering is one of those things that is easy to learn, but hard to master. It is true that practice makes perfect. One good rule to learn is that you never heat the solder, but the area you want to solder. Figure 5-22 shows how the tip of the soldering iron is placed onto the leg of the LED and the metal ring. Keep the soldering iron steady for a few seconds, and then apply some solder close to the tip. When the ring and leg of the LED are heated enough, the solder will start to melt onto both.

■ **Caution** The problem with electronic components is that if you heat them for too long, they will melt or break. I usually heat my iron to around 350°C (650°F), so it's good to have a regulated soldering iron. It's also good practice to heat the target area for a bit and then see if the solder melts. If it doesn't melt, heat it a bit more but never for more than a few seconds at a time to avoid burning anything.

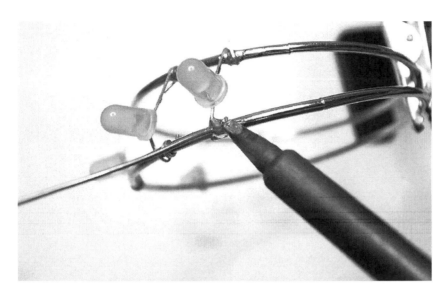

Figure 5-22. *Soldering the LEDs*

The tricky thing with soldering is that even if the solder melts, it sometimes melts it badly. This is called cold soldering, which means that the solder has melted onto the material but hasn't really attached. This makes for a bad electronic connection, and in some cases the solder will fall off. Figure 5-23 shows a typical, cold soldering joint. An indication of cold soldering is that the solder forms like a bubble onto the material like a water bubble on a leaf.

Figure 5-23. *A cold soldering joint*

A proper soldering joint should look something like that shown in Figure 5-24, where the solder has spread onto the material. It takes some training before you learn how to spot cold soldering as well as soldering, but another good rule is that more solder never helps. If you have enough solder on the material to cover your desired connection, just reheat the material until the solder reflows itself.

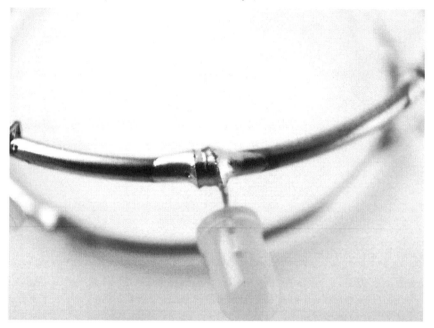

Figure 5-24. The solder should spread onto the material.

Another key to making good soldering is keeping your soldering iron clean at all times. If you leave solder on the tip of the soldering iron, it will burn on to the tip and slowly destroy the iron. If you don't have a soldering iron with a changeable tip, solder will eventually permanently destroy it. So every time you use your iron, make sure to clean it. Soldering sponges and tip cleaners are available for this purpose.

Step 3

The last step of the project is to attach the battery with the magnet. If you got your hands on a rare earth magnet, it should be strong enough to hold the battery, as well as the ring, in place. Make sure that the battery is connected the right way, with positive side of the battery to the ring that is connected to the positive legs of the LEDs. Place the magnet on top of the battery, and then place it between the rings—with one ring touching the battery and the other ring touching the magnet.

If you can't find a rare earth magnet, you could use two regular magnets for each side of the battery (as long as the magnets are small enough).

Finishing Up

The bracelets in this chapter show the core principle of making circuits, which is basically routing the flow of electricity. The thing to remember is that power flows from positive to negative, and for any electronic component to work, the power in it always needs to go back to where it came from. In other words, electricity needs to go from + to –.

Another thing to remember is that power always takes the easiest way back to where it came from. If it has more than one option, it will always take the option with less resistance. In the next chapter, we will use this principle to add interactivity to a project, which includes a more advanced circuit.

CHAPTER 6

Solar-Powered Glow-in-the-Dark Bag

This project demonstrates how to make a solar-powered glow-in-the-dark bag. As soon as night falls, the bag will automatically switch on, giving your bag extra "shine." The project introduces interactivity using advanced circuits. The project also introduces the use of solar power energy, which might come in handy as an alternative power source for future wearable projects. We will also look at how to make a battery charger as well as how to make your first sensor. This is the last chapter without the Arduino board. This chapter also acts as an example of why it is useful to use Arduino boards.

■ **Note** There are a lot of steps to this project, and since all the electronic components are fitted into the bag, I recommend you to read through the entire project guide before you get started so you can plan your work.

Materials and Tools Needed

The following are the materials and tools you will need for making the solar-powered glow-in-the-dark bag:

- 6V flexible solar panel
- EL panels
- 3V voltage inverter
- Wires
- IRFZ24 transistor
- Power diode
- Soldering iron
- Sewing machine
- 6V rechargeable battery pack
- Eyelets with washers

- Zipper

- Fabrics

- 10K resistor

- LDR

- Perfboard

Solar Panels

We will use batteries to power everything in this project. But once all the electronics are sewn into the bag, it might be tricky to charge the batteries when they run out of power. To keep them charged, we will add solar panels to the bag.

Solar panels are made of solar cells, also known as *photovoltaic cells*, and it's through the photovoltaic effect that these panels can generate electricity from sunlight. They can even generate electricity from artificial light like lightbulbs. Before we get carried away with thoughts of perpetual power, however, consider that a lightbulb uses more electricity than a solar panel can generate using the bulb as a light source.

There are different types of solar panels; for this project we will use a flexible solar panel. The most common solar panels are rigid, but the flexible ones are thinner and (of course) flexible, which makes them more suitable for wearable projects. If you can't find any flexible solar panels, normal ones still work but you might have to modify the design of the bag a bit. Just make certain that the panel doesn't output more voltage than what your battery pack can handle, which in this case is 6 volts. The voltage indication shown on solar panel packaging is usually the maximum output, which means that it needs to be a very clear and sunny day for your panel to output the maximum voltage.

Power Diode

If you looked at the first project in this book, you should be familiar with one type of diode, the light-emitting diode (LED). For this project, we will use a non-glowing diode simply called a diode or power diode. A diode is a two-terminal component with nonlinear resistance and conductance, which means electricity can only pass through the component in one direction.

We will use it for our battery charger to ensure that the electricity from the solar panel goes to the battery, but also prevents the solar panel from draining the battery when it is dark.

Resistors

Another new component used for this project is a resistor, which deserves a separate mention. A resistor is an electronic component designed to oppose an electric current by producing a voltage drop between its two ends in relation to the current. In other words, a resistor slows down the flow of current that will lower the voltage going into the resistor. Resistance is always measured in ohms and can also be presented as the Ω symbol. The two most common multipliers for resistance calculations are

- kilohm (kΩ), which equals 1000 Ω, and

- megohm (MΩ), which equals 1,000,000 Ω

All resistors are color-coded with four, five, or six color bands. These bands tell you the resistance. If you have a six color-banded resistor, then the first three bands are digits that follow the following color digit scheme:

- black 0
- brown 1
- red 2
- orange 3
- yellow 4
- green 5
- blue 6
- purple 7
- gray 8
- white 9

If the three bands are white, red, and green, it would translate to 925. The fourth band is the multiplier. You multiply the first three digits by this band to get the resistance of your resistor. The fourth band follows the following color scheme:

- silver 0.01
- gold 0.1
- black 1
- brown 10
- red 100
- orange 1k
- yellow 10k
- green 100k
- blue 1M
- purple 10M

The fifth band is the tolerance of the resistor and the sixth band is used for the temperature coefficient. The tolerance and temperature coefficient are usually a concern for circuits with high precision. Standard resistors are not made with 100 percent resistance accuracy, so the tolerance lets you know the permitted variations in resistance. Resistor resistance also changes a little bit in relation to temperature and this is indicated by the temperature coefficient. You don't need to worry about the tolerance and temperature coefficient for the projects in this book; you only need to keep track of the actual resistor value. I have never met anyone who knows all the colors by heart and I don't recommend that you spend a lot of time trying to memorize them. You can use the list in the book as reference; but if you find yourself without your copy of the book, you can use an online calculator. Googling "resistor calculator" finds tons of links to graphical calculators that allow you to punch in the color of a resistor to calculate its resistance.

Making a Battery Charger

To make the battery charger, we need the solar panel, power diode, and a 6V rechargeable battery. You can use either four 1.5 AAA batteries in series or you can use a battery pack, which are available in different form factors at most RC (radio control), robotics, or electronic stores.

Before we get started you should keep in mind the amount of milliamp hours (mAh) your batteries can hold. Most batteries have this information, as well as the voltage output, written on them.

■ **Note** Recall that amps are the measurement of current, so amp-hours are the amount of amps a battery can supply in an hour. We're using milliamp hours, so it is the amount of milliamps our batteries can supply in one hour. You can then extrapolate to calculate how long the battery will last: if your battery holds 10,000mAh and your circuit draws 100mAh, your battery will last for 100 hours. You can measure the current in a circuit with your multimeter on the A setting.

You also need to know the voltage and output of your solar panel. The flexible one I used output a maximum of 100mAh, which means that at optimal sunlight the panel will output 100 milliamperes per hour at 6 volts. If a battery holds 10,000mAh, it will take some time in the sun for it to charge (100 hours to be precise).

Now you might think "why not just use more solar panels or a bigger solar panel to charge the battery faster?" This is never a good idea because it might kill the batteries. In fact, most battery chargers regulate the amount of power going into the battery. We will not use a regulator for this charger, but we will follow the principle that you should not charge the battery with more than 10 percent of its capacity per hour. In this case we will use a battery pack with a capacity of 1100mAh—to be on the safe side. Since the solar panel outputs a 100mAh, it will take about 11 hours to fully charge the battery. But remember that this is 100mAh at a maximum, so it might take longer.

If you want to show off your shining bag for a longer period of time, I suggest a battery that carries more milliamp hours at the same voltage. The more milliamp hours a battery has, the longer it will last.

Figure 6-1 shows a schematic of the solar battery charger. The first step is to attach wires to the solar panel since most flexible solar panels come without cables. A common standard is to use red wires for power and black ones for ground, which I have done in the schematic as well. To do this, you will have to solder them on.

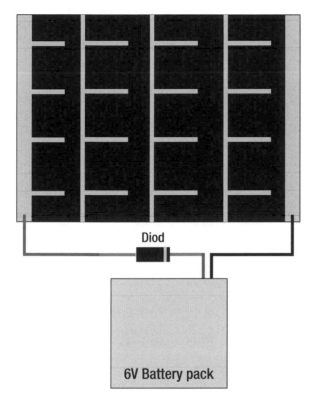

Figure 6-1. Solar battery charger schematic

The first step is to determine the positive and negative sides of the panel. At two of the edges you will find two silver strips, which are the power lines. If they are not marked, use a multimeter to determine which side is which. You can also check that the panel is working and giving some voltage output. If you don't remember how to do this, take a look at Chapter 5 for instruction on using a multimeter.

Like mine, your flexible panel is probably covered in a thin layer of shielding plastic. Your solder won't stick until you remove a small piece of the plastic at the ends to expose the metal strip. Figure 6-2 shows the cables attached to the solar panel.

Figure 6-2. *Cables soldered to the solar panel*

Once your cables are in place, you need to attach the power diode to the power cable before you can connect it to the battery (see Figure 6-3).

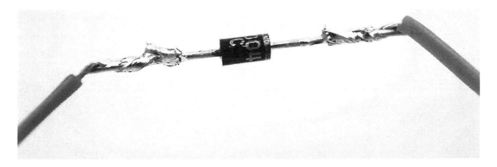

Figure 6-3. Diode connected between the solar panel and battery

Since electricity only flows through the diode in one direction, you have to make sure that you solder it in the right way. Diodes are marked with a line at one side to indicate which side is which. The line is the exit side of the diode, so this side should be connected to the battery and the other one to the solar panel. To get a better overview, take a look at Figure 6-1.

The last step is to connect the ground from the solar panel to the battery; and then the charging will begin. I would leave the ground cable for now, however, since there are a few mores steps to the construction before we are done; and to be on the safe side, we don't want power running through your project while you are working with it.

Be sure to cover the ends of the diode with sticky tape or electrical tape. I covered my ends with tape, bent the diode into a U shape, and then added some extra tape around it to prevent it from breaking inside the bag.

Making the Bag

Figure 6-4 shows the pattern I used for the bag in this project. It is a simple pattern, but keep in mind that making bags is a bit tricky—especially if you are adding electronics to the inside. If you choose to work with another pattern, I suggest using a simple one the first time.

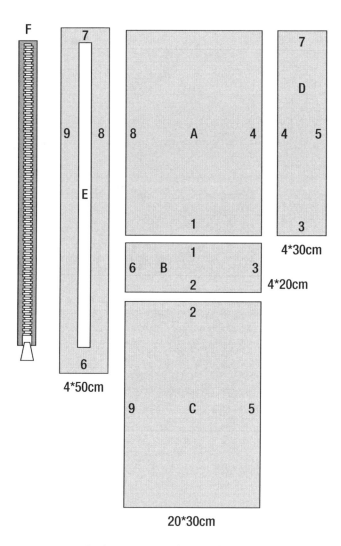

Figure 6-4. *The bag pattern. The numbers on the edges indicate how the sides connect to one another.*

Start by sewing pieces A, B, C, and D together at seams 1, 2, 3, 4, and 5, and you should end up with something like in Figure 6-5. The seam allowance used is approximately 0.5 centimeters (0.2 inches).

Figure 6-5. Pieces A, B, C, and D from the pattern sewn together

Once you have the four pieces sewn together, sew the zipper into piece E and attach it to the rest of the bag. The zipper should be long enough to cover the top of the bag and one of the short sides to make the design a bit more interesting. Seam 8 should start in the top corner on pieces A and B down to the bottom corner of pieces A and D. The same goes for seam 9, but on the opposite side from the top corner of pieces C and B down to the corner of C and D.

Once we have the shell of the bag done, it's time to start preparing the sensor that switches the bag on and off.

LDR Sensor Switch

A sensor is a device that detects some physical change and converts that into a signal. In this project we will be making a light sensor. For the sensor, we will use an LDR and a transistor. LDR stands for *light dependent resistor*. In contrast to a normal resistor with a fixed resistance, an LDR's resistance depends on light. If there is low light, the resistance will be higher; if there is bright light, the resistance will be lower in the LDR.

The transistor I recommend for this project is the IRFZ24, as shown in Figure 6-6. There are thousands of different transistors available, depending on the application. All of them have three legs, which are known as the gate, source, and drain (and also known as the collector, base, and emitter). Different combinations are used on different transistors. I found a transistor, the IRFZ24, and decided to stick with it until I actually need something else. The IRFZ24 can handle up to 60 volts and activates with a signal at a low 5 volts, which makes it good for most applications.

The IRFZ24 is a MOSFET transistor, which stands for *metal-oxide-semiconductor field-effect transistor*. It is used whenever you want to amplify a high electricity signal with a lower electricity signal. In this project we are going to use it to control the inverter, which powers the EL panel that will light up your bag (the EL panel is described in the "Adding the EL Panels" section).

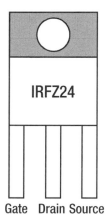

Gate Drain Source

Figure 6-6. Illustration of an IRFZ24 MOSFET transistor

Figure 6-6 shows the pin layout of the IRFZ24. The first leg is the gate, which needs to be activated with a power signal. The drain will connect to the source if the gate is activated. We want to control the ground connection between the inverter and the battery with the transistor. To do this you need to connect the transistor, as shown in Figure 6-7.

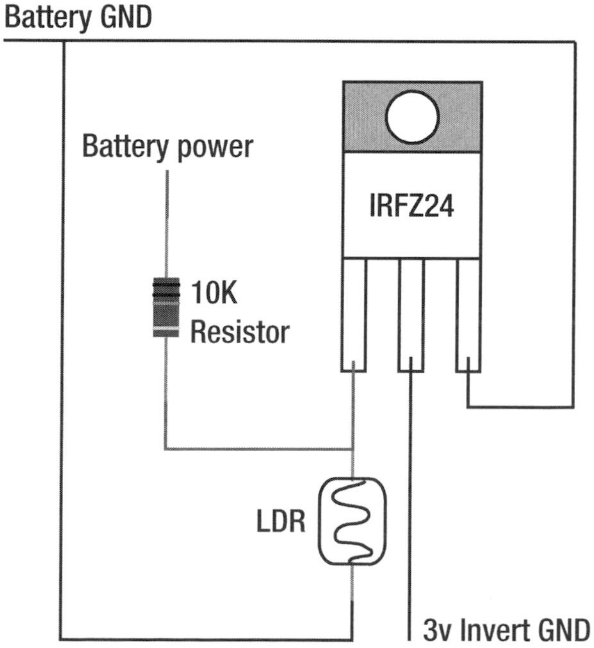

Battery GND

Battery power

IRFZ24

10K
Resistor

LDR

3v Invert GND

Figure 6-7. Light sensor switch

Figure 6-7 also shows a 10 kilohm resistor and the LDR on the signal to the gate. The signal is the electricity that controls the transistor. If it's low (0 volts), the transistor is off and if it's high (5 volts), the transistor switches on. The resistor is used as a pull up resistor, which ensures that signal settles at the expected level or, in other words, keeps the voltage value steady. On the same connection we have the LDR that will act as a pull down resistor. If there is light on the LDR, the resistance is low and it is much easier for the signal to go back to ground and not into the transistor: nothing happens. But if it's dark, the resistance is higher and it is much easier for the signal to pass through the gate, which closes the connection between the drain and source—and makes the EL panel light up.

To make the actual sensor circuit, I used a small piece of *perfboard*, which is a sheet with pre-drilled holes and copper pads on the holes for prototyping circuits. Perfboard is available in different sizes and form factors when it comes to hole connections. Some only have holes with separated copper pads and some have the holes connected in rows, as shown in Figure 6-8.

Figure 6-8. Components soldered onto a piece of perfboard

Figure 6-8 shows the components soldered onto a piece of perfboard and following the schematic in Figure 6-7. You usually put your components through the sheet without the copper pads, and then solder the legs on the other side.

The last stage is to add red and black cables for the power and ground. Always add cables a bit longer than you think you'll need because it is always better to be safe than sorry. If it turns out that the cables are too long, it's easier to cut them down than to add a new piece.

Adding the Solar Panel

The next step is to add the solar panel to the bag. As shown in Figure 6-9, you can start by cutting a hole in the bag for the solar panel about 2 centimeters (0.8 inches) smaller than the actual panel in either side A or C (see Figure 6-4). Then make a 1 centimeter diagonal cut in the four corners and fold the edges.

Figure 6-9. Hole cut for the solar panel with diagonal corner cuts

To actually fasten the solar panel to the bag is the hardest part. You can stitch it in place using nonconductive thread and a sewing machine (as shown in Figure 6-10) or sew it by hand. If you use a sewing machine, I recommend using a jeans needle in the machine so that it can puncture the panel.

■ **Caution** If the solar panel is the flexible kind, only try to sew the panel to the bag using a sewing machine.

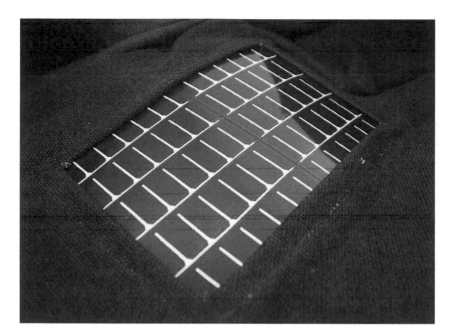

Figure 6-10. The solar panel sewn in place using a sewing machine

Adding the EL Panels

EL panels are plastic sheets containing phosphor that lights up when proper voltage is applied. EL stands for *electroluminescence*, which refers to the phenomenon of a material emitting light due to electronic current passing through it.

To make the EL panels light up we need to use AC power, not DC as with a battery. To transform DC to AC we will use a 3V inverter. The inverter takes a 3V DC input and outputs 110V AC. The inverter actually takes anything between 2.7 volts and 4.2 volts. Running two panels on one inverter is no problem. The panels are not at maximum brightness, but still give plenty of light in dark spaces. The only problem with using two panels is that the battery will not last as long.

For this project's bag, I decided I wanted a more fun shape than a square 10 × 10 centimeter panel form factor. I wrote my initials on the bag using eyelets on the side opposite the solar panels. First, I marked the size of the panels on the bag so that I knew how much space I had to work with. Then I drew my initials and started to punch holes into the bag using the hole puncher that came with my eyelets kit, as shown in Figure 6-11.

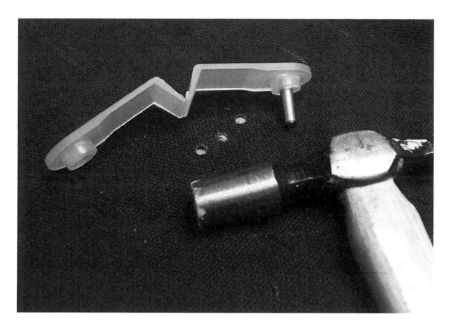

Figure 6-11. Punching holes for the eyelets

You can cut the EL panel (but not the wires) into any desired shape with normal scissors and stitch it in place with non-conductive thread. But I thought my design would look nicer with a backlit monogram.

You can start adding the eyelets once the hole pattern is made (see Figure 6-12), but be sure to watch your fingers if you are using a hammer to do this. There are dedicated tools for punching eyelets into fabrics if you prefer a safer option.

I used duct tape to attach the EL panels inside the bag since I did not want any stitching visible on the monogram side of the bag, and because duct tape sticks very well to fabric while remaining flexible. You could also add an additional layer of fabric over the panel like a pocket inside the bag.

Figure 6-12. *Eyelets punched in place*

Putting Everything Together

Take a good look at Figure 6-13 for a better idea on putting everything together; it shows the entire schematic of the inner workings of the solar-powered glow-in-the-dark bag.

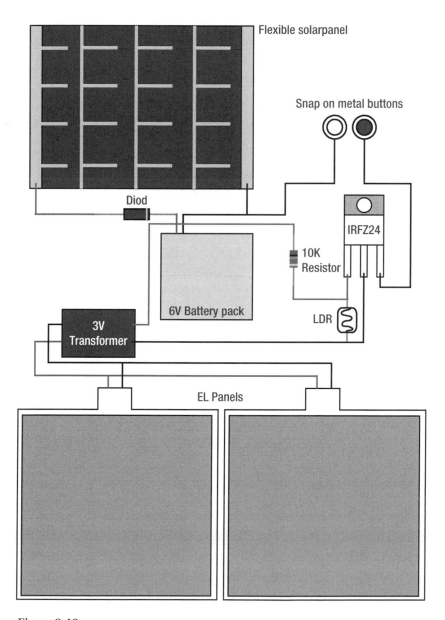

Figure 6-13.

At this point you might be wondering why I recommend using an inverter that takes a maximum input of 4.2 volts and power it with a 6V battery. The issue with this design is that the battery power is shared with the inverter and the signal to the transistor. If you use a battery pack of only 4 volts, there will not be enough power for both the signal and the panels.

I added the connection with the metal snap buttons so that the EL panel can be turned off manually to not drain the battery. Once in a while you will need to turn the bag off to allow the batteries to charge. You can put the metal snap buttons anywhere it's possible to snap them together. In my final design I put them in the hand straps, which was the last thing I sewed (along with the zipper).

To make a good connection between the button and wire, use conductive thread to stitch the buttons with the cables.

Before you stitch up the bag, you want to put the LDR in place. To do this, make a small hole in the bag on the same side as the solar panel and place an eyelet into the fabric big enough to fit the LDR through it. You want it on the same side as the solar panel because you don't want it to turn on the EL panel while you are charging it in the sun.

Once everything was in place in my bag, I stitched a lining fabric into the bag to hide all the electronics—but also for safety (see Figure 6-14). The reason for not using conductive thread in most of this project is that it would make the wiring very hard—and also because there are 110 volts going into the EL panels. With conductive thread you might end up with an open connection, and if you come in contact with the 110 volts, it might give you a nasty shock. The chances of this happening are slim, but again, it's better to be on the safe side. The thing to look out for is the connection between the EL panels and the inverter, which is the connection that carries 110 volts.

Figure 6-14. The lining was made using the same pattern as the outer bag fabric.

Once you have soldered the cables together, be sure to secure them with some electrical tape or a shrink tube. Shrink tube can be bought at any electronics store. It is a rubber tube to put over your cable connections once they are soldered. Once heated, the tube shrinks and isolates the connections.

Before you start soldering and stitching, however, I recommend setting up the entire schematic on a breadboard and studying it until you feel confident that you know what goes where. Doing this helps when you move from the security of a flat surface into the actual implementation inside the bag.

The Final Bag

Figure 16-15 shows the finished bag in daylight. As soon as you bring it into the dark or switch the light off in a room, the bag will light up, as shown in Figure 16-16. The light switches on very fast. You can also dim the light in a room by partially covering the LDR with your hand.

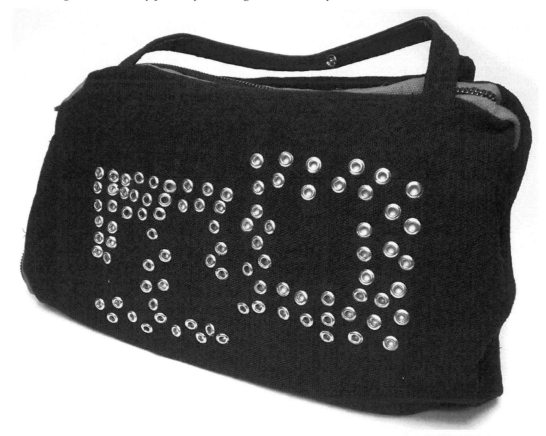

Figure 6-15. The finished bag in daylight

Figure 6-16. The finished bag in the dark

Wrapping Up

Even though this project does not require programming and an Arduino, it is still probably the hardest project in this book—construction-wise. But like most complex things, if you break it down into pieces, it becomes simpler. Still, this project is a good exercise in connecting electronics into wearable accessories, with minor risk of damaging any expensive parts.

When it comes to electronics, a lot of things can be done by just using electronics components without a microcontroller. Some think it might be easier to skip learning how to program and just rely on electronics, but this is not really true. It might be easier if you have a tutorial like this book, but once you reach the point where you want to do something else or quickly change something, knowing how to use an Arduino really comes in handy. For example, the glow-in-the-dark bag only has two functions: it's either on or off. If we wanted to add a new function, like sound, it would require an additional schematic even more complex than the one in this chapter. By using an Arduino board, it might not be harder than adding a few lines of code and one extra component.

From now on, the projects in this book will require an Arduino board and some programming. The next topic focuses on sound and music.

CHAPTER 7

Piano Tie

This project was inspired by an idea from my former students. They never finished the project, but later I found a blog post by Maureen Grants demonstrating her version of a soft-circuit musical tie (see the video at http://vimeo.com/15083685). The project takes the concept of a vintage piano tie and turns it into reality.

By making your own electrical piano tie, you will learn how to control inputs in the form of soft push buttons made from conductive fabric, and an output in the form of sound from your Arduino board. You will also learn the basics of computer-generated sound, as well as new commands and methods for writing sketches for your Arduino board.

Tools and Materials Needed

You will need the following tools and materials to create your piano tie:

- Conductive thread
- Conductive fabric
- Arduino/LilyPad
- Fabric
- LilyPad coin cell battery holder
- Sewing machine
- Piezo disc

Making Sounds with Piezos

A new component in this chapter is the piezo speaker. A speaker is something that generates sound when an electrical signal is applied to it. If you ever had a toy that beeps, you probably already know what a piezo speaker is. Piezo speakers are used in a large variety of devices and applications to generate sound. They are sometimes used as tweeters in less expensive speaker systems to generate higher audio frequencies.

Piezos consists of two metal plates and when electricity is applied through them, they move a bit. If this continues over time, they create small vibrations in the air—which is basically what sound is—and once these vibrations reach your ear, you hear the sound.

To generate sound in a piezo, you turn it on and off. This creates the vibrations; but it has to be done at a very high frequency. To turn a piezo on and off by hand to generate sound would not work; but with the help of the Arduino and some code, we will make this happen later on in this chapter. First you need to make the piano tie so you have something to activate the sounds with.

Cutting the Tie

To start, you will need two pieces of fabric cut following the pattern shown in Figure 7-1. One piece will be used for the outside of the tie and the other will be used as lining fabric, in which you will also make the circuit using conductive thread. This is a rough pattern that allows you to extend the length if needed. The easiest way to cut your fabric is to first draw half of the pattern. Next, fold the fabrics and place the pattern in the fold, and then cut the fabric. When you unfold the fabric, you get matching sides.

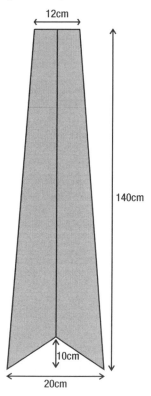

Figure 7-1. Pattern for the piano tie

Once you have your two pieces of fabric, it's time to sew the two diagonal ends together at the bottom of the tie. Most of the lining fabric will be hidden inside the tie, but we will use it to make our circuit connection with conductive thread and as a separation material for the soft push buttons.

Adding the Buttons

Most push buttons consist of two metal plates. When the button is pushed down, the two metal plates connect, thus completing a circuit. To make a soft push button we will follow the same principle, but using conductive fabric instead. To separate the conductive fabrics when the button is not pushed, we will use the actual tie fabric.

The first step is to mark the placement of the buttons that will act as the keys of the piano. Mark the keys on the front of the fabric and then punch a hole through both fabrics. Make them approximately 1 × 3 centimeters (0.3 × 1.2 inches). Be sure to make the holes a little smaller than the keys. I made seven keys since there are seven basic notes on a regular piano keyboard (see Figure 7-2).

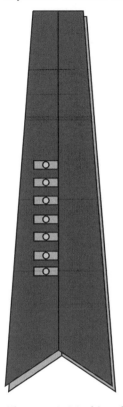

Figure 7-2. Marking the keys and making the holes

Once this is done, cut two pieces of conductive fabric for each key, the same size as your key markings. Then the goal is to attach your conductive pieces to the outside and inside of the tie so you have the two layers of fabric between the conductive pieces. Take your time with the outer keys since these will be visible, and make sure that the conductive pieces cover the holes and line up with the corresponding piece on the opposite side of the tie, as shown in Figure 7-3.

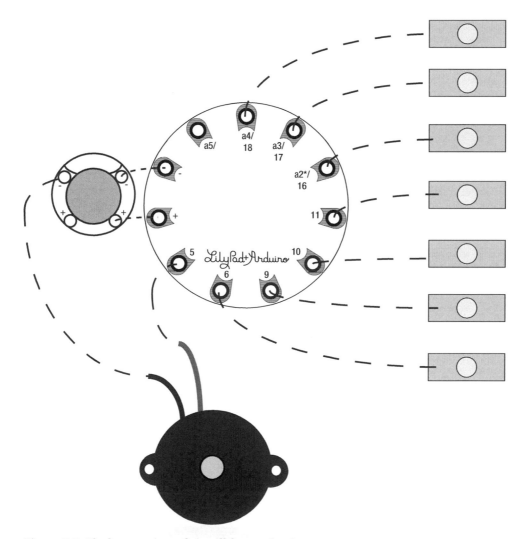

Figure 7-3. *The button pieces that will face each other*

The conductive pieces should only be attached to one side of each layer.

Once the conductive keys are in place, you should still be able to separate the two non-conductive layers, except at the bottom end of the tie where they are stitched together.

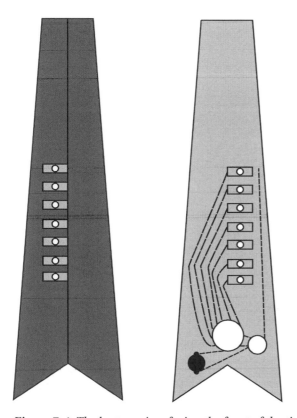

Figure 7-4. The button piece facing the front of the tie

Stitching the Schematic

Figure 7-5 is a simplified close-up of the connections that need to be made on the lining fabric, which will face the inside once the tie is sewn together. For this project, I recommend a regular Arduino LilyPad or a LilyPad Simple, which is shown in Figure 7-5.

All the reverse sides of the soft buttons are connected to a separate pin (either digital or analog). It does not matter where you connect the different keys as long as each key connects to a pin. At this stage, however, the thing you have to keep track of is the actual stitching so the different lines of conductive thread do not touch each other. You also have to make sure the thread is a single thread from the pin to the button. It is also a good idea to do a few extra loops at the pin of the LilyPad and the conductive fabric to secure it.

To power the tie, I also recommend a LilyPad coin cell holder since coin cell batteries are flat and easy to hide in small places.

The third component is the piezo disc. There are different kinds of piezos, but a common one, as shown in Figure 7-5, has a plastic casing with ears and holes on the side. This really helps when fastening the piezo to the fabric. Most piezos come with two wires. The red one needs to go to a digital pin and the black one to a ground connection. To make a connection, you need to strip the cables exposing the metal inside them, and then stitch a few laps of conductive thread around the exposed metal ends to secure it.

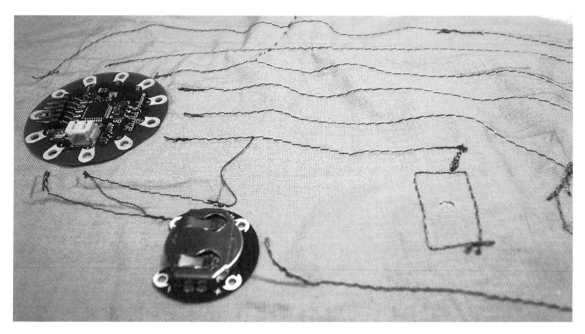

Figure 7-5. *Stitching the components together*

Checking the Layout

Before you get started stitching everything together, take a look at Figure 7-6 for the recommended placement of everything. The LilyPad is placed upside down at the bottom of the tie so that the USB adapter connector is facing down. This makes the connections to the keys a bit easier, and enables you to attach the USB to serial adapter for programming without the need to open the tie.

The battery holder is also placed at the bottom since once the tie is done, there will be an opening at this end in case you need to switch batteries.

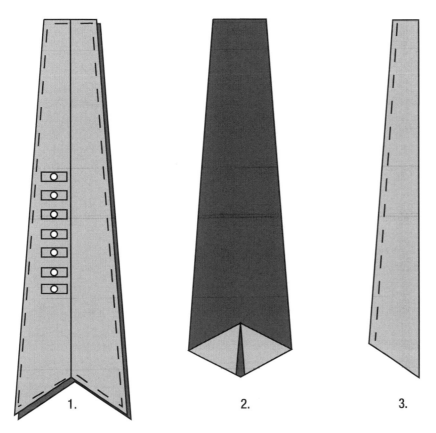

Figure 7-6. *Recommended placement of components inside the tie (left) and the conductive thread stitching pattern (right)*

The last step of this stage is to add a ground line from the negative connection on the battery to all the reverse sides of the soft push buttons. Then the goal is to add a connection from the front side of the key buttons to this line on the reverse side of the tie. Again, make sure the holes through the two pieces of non-conductive fabric line up so when the button key is pressed, the two pieces of conductive fabric touch each other.

When the soft push button key is pressed, power travels from the LilyPad back to the battery, and then the LilyPad can detect if the button is pushed or not. Figure 7-7 shows the connections made with conductive thread. Before the construction of the tie is done, two major things need to be checked. First, you need to check that all your connections conduct to where they are supposed to. This is done by using a multimeter; take your time to check that everything looks fine and that there are no short circuits. Instruction on how to use the multimeter to check your connections is covered in Chapter 5 if you need to refresh your memory.

You also need to test that the buttons actually work and the piezo plays sound. To do this we need to add a sketch to the LilyPad. So before you do the final stitching of the tie, let's take a look at some code.

121

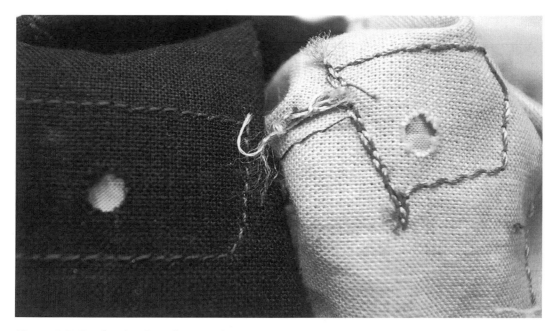

Figure 7-7. Conductive thread connections

Writing the Code

Before starting a new sketch, I always take some time to think about what it is I want to do. Because it's always hard to know how your entire sketch will look like once it's done, it's never a good idea to write the entire sketch in one try. When it comes to learning programming, an equally important part is to learn how to debug.

■ **Note** Debugging means looking for errors. Some claim that the word originated at Harvard University, where there was a problem with a Mark II computer in the 1940s. The problem turned out to be a moth caught in one of the computer's relays.

If you want to learn how to program, you will need to do a lot of debugging. This is why I like to take some time to think about what I want to do before I start to program—to see if I can break down the process into parts.

We need to know that the piezo speaker and seven buttons in this project work. Instead of testing everything at once, let's start to check that each key button works individually. To indicate that they work, use the onboard LED of the LilyPad, which is connected to pin 13.

Testing the Buttons

The following is the code that needs to be uploaded to your LilyPad:

```
//declares ledPin as pin 13
int ledPin=13;
//declares buttonPin as pin 6
int buttonPin=6;
//declares a variable which will be used to store the state of the buttonPin
int buttonState;

void setup(){
 //declare ledPin to be used as a output
 pinMode(ledPin, OUTPUT);
 //declare buttonPin to be used as a INPUT
 pinMode(buttonPin, INPUT);
 //Turn the buttons HIGH
 digitalWrite(buttonPin,HIGH);
}
void loop(){
  //checks the state of buttonPin and stores the information in buttonState
  buttonState=digitalRead(buttonPin);

  //checks is buttonState is the same as LOW
  if(buttonState==LOW){
  //if buttonsState is LOW turn the LED on
   digitalWrite(ledPin, HIGH);
  }else{
  //in all other cases turn it off
   digitalWrite(ledPin, LOW);
  }
}
```

This code keeps it simple, starting with checking one button at a time. The onboard LED needs to be declared as an OUTPUT since we will push power out from this pin to the LED to turn it on. On the button key side of things, we have declared pin 6 as an INPUT since this pin is connected to one side of the soft button on the tie and the other side is connected to the ground on the battery.

In the setup, we then power up the buttonPin. If you don't push the button, the pin will be powered. When you push the button, the power will go through the button and back to the ground of the battery. This is what you are checking for inside the loop with the digitalRead command. It checks over and over again and stores the information inside the buttonState variable. If there is no power in the pin, the digitalRead command will answer LOW, so the buttonState variable will contain the value LOW. If there is power in the pin, it will answer HIGH, so the buttonState variable will contain the value HIGH.

Inside the loop you also have the if statement. Between the brackets of the if statement, a logical question is declared: is buttonState equal to LOW? If it is, then do whatever is found between the following curly start and end bracket. The else part of the code connects to the if statement; it says, if the if statement is not true, then do whatever is inside the curly brackets after the else. If the if statement is true, then the digitalWrite command turns on power on the ledPin, else it will turn it off.

To clarify what happens, when you push the button, you redirect the power from the buttonPin to the ground of the battery, making it LOW. It might seem confusing that the buttonPin is HIGH and LOW at the same time, but when you push the button, you are actually stealing the power from the pin back to ground. So when the button is LOW (which means it's pushed), it's time to turn the LED HIGH. In all other cases, keep the LED LOW.

So if everything is connected properly, the LED on the LilyPad should turn on when you press the button connected to pin number 6. To check the rest of the buttons, change the number in the buttonPin variable declaration to a new number. At this point, you might notice that some of the key buttons are connected to analog pins a2, a3, and a4. If you look again, these pin are also assigned the numbers 14, 17, and 18 on the LilyPad Simple board. The analog pins can be used as digital pins if you declare them the same way as in the previous setup. The standard Arduino board works the same way. It has six analog pins. To use them as digital pins, their numbers follow the last digital pin on the opposite side of the board; this is 13, which would make the analog pins 14, 15, 16, 17, 18, and 19.

But since the analog pins are inputs, you could read the signal as an analog one as well, as follows:

```
int ledPin=13;
int buttonPin=A2;
int buttonState;

void setup(){
 pinMode(ledPin, OUTPUT);
 digitalWrite(A2,HIGH);
}

void loop(){
  buttonState=analogRead(buttonPin);

  if(buttonState<512){
   digitalWrite(ledPin, HIGH);
  }else{
   digitalWrite(ledPin, LOW);
  }
}
```

The difference is that you don't have to declare the analog pin as an INPUT in the setup since, if used as analog pins, they can only be used as inputs. Another difference is that the analogRead command, used instead of digitalRead, will answer with a value ranging from 0 to 1023 and not a HIGH or a LOW. Then the question in the if statement would be, is buttonState smaller than 512? Again we are using the trick of turning the analog pin HIGH, which means that we are powering up the pin and then stealing the power away from the pin. When the button is not pushed, the buttonState is above 512, and when you push it, the buttonState drops below 512, which turns the LED on.

In the case of buttons, it does not make much sense to read the buttons as analog since they only have two states, on or off, HIGH or LOW. But once you want to connect an input that has more than two states, you will need to use the analog pins.

Making Sound

Once you know that your buttons are working, you can move on to create a tone. Tones are what sounds are made of and notes are the names we assign to tones. You could also say that a note is a tone with duration over time. A tone can be played so fast that the human ear can't perceive it, so to be able to hear them we need to play them over and over for some time.

This might sound a bit strange, but when it comes to computer-generated tones, a speaker needs to be turned on and off at a super-high speed to generate tones. We are talking ons and offs with a delay in microseconds, and if this is not done with some duration, we will not be able to detect it. In the following code example, the code for turning on and off the speaker is put inside the loop, which will keep playing the tone forever—or at least as long as the LilyPad has power.

```
//declare piezo to pin number 5
int piezo=5;

void setup(){
  //declare piezo as a OUTPUT
  pinMode(piezo, OUTPUT);
}

void loop(){
  //turn the piezo on
  digitalWrite(piezo, HIGH);
  //wait for a bit
  delayMicroseconds(659);
  //turn the piezo off
  digitalWrite(piezo, LOW);
  //wait some more
  delayMicroseconds(659);
}
```

This is basically the same code for turning a LED on and off, but when connected to a piezo using a delay in microseconds it will make the piezo vibrate, which makes it sound. The difference in tone sounds is caused by the delay time between being on and off. In this case, it is the note E5, and to generate it, the speaker needs to be turned on and off at a frequency of 659.255 hertz (Hz). We are playing it at only a frequency of 659.0Hz, but I doubt that anyone will be able to tell the difference.

If your LilyPad plays the tone on the piezo using the previous code, it means that everything is connected as it should be. But before we move on, let's take a look at how you add additional tone. If you just added the same code inside the loop with a new delay time, it would just mash everything together, creating one tone that is wrong. To be able to play one tone after the other, we need to play each individual tone a couple of times before we move on to a new one, as shown next.

```
//declare piezo to pin number 5
int piezo=5;

void setup(){
  //declare piezo as a OUTPUT
  pinMode(piezo, OUTPUT);
}

void loop(){
  for(int i=0; i<100; i++){
    //turn the piezo on
    digitalWrite(piezo, HIGH);
    //wait for a bit
    delayMicroseconds(659);
    //turn the piezo off
    digitalWrite(piezo, LOW);
```

```
    //wait some more
    delayMicroseconds(659);
  }
  for(int j=0; j<100; j++){
    //turn the piezo on
    digitalWrite(piezo, HIGH);
    //wait for a bit
    delayMicroseconds(1760);
    //turn the piezo off
    digitalWrite(piezo, LOW);
    //wait some more
    delayMicroseconds(1760);
  }
}
```

This example code includes two for loops, in which I have put the code to generate each tone. for loops are used when you want to do something a certain number of times and you know how many times you want to do it. They are always declared using three parameters, which are

- The counter

- The end condition

- The increment of the counter

The counter is declared as any integer variable, and since this variable is seldom used outside the for loop, it is often named with a single character. You can start your counter at any number, but if you don't need the counter variable for anything else in your sketch, just start it at zero.

The end condition has to be a logical condition so that the for loop knows when to end. A for loop keeps looping any code inside it until this condition is met, when it jumps out the for loop and carries down your sketch. In both cases in the example code, the for loops keep looping as long as the counter is smaller than 100. In other words, they will loop 100 times before stopping.

The last parameter is the increment of the counter for each loop the for loop makes. To increase a variable by one, you can use the short command ++. So in our example, we add 1 to the counter for every loop.

It works the same with subtracting one with --. If you want to increase by five, you need to write the code as follows:

j=j+5

or

j+=5

Both mean the same thing: 5 is assigned to j, adding its current value.

The code example will first play the tone E5 100 times and then the tone A6 for an equal number of times. Bear in mind that even if the LilyPad is a small computer, it's still a fast one; so looping each tone 100 times will be very fast, but should still give you some time to distinguish each tone. If you want it to play the tones longer, you just change the end condition in the for loops.

Piecing the Code Together

The reason it is a good idea to divide your coding into parts is that it's easier to find a problem when you are only working with a small piece of code. There are two steps to get the code right:

1. The code has to compile, which means there can't be any syntax errors in it.

2. It has to work in real life with whatever you have connected to your LilyPad or Arduino Simple board.

But hopefully when you reach this point, both your buttons and sound work, and now the goal is to piece the two parts together. The goal is to have each soft button key play an individual tone when it is pressed. Table 7-1 contains a list of tones and their corresponding frequencies. A list of all notes and frequencies are found at the end of the chapter.

Table 7-1. *Tones and Frequencies*

Tone	Frequency
C5	523.25
C#5/Db5	554.37
D5	587.33
D#5/Eb5	622.25
E5	659.26
F5	698.46
F#5/Gb5	739.99
G5	783.99
G#5/Ab5	830.61
A5	880.00
A#5/Bb5	932.33
B5	987.77

Piano Code

I have not included every tone on a piano keyboard in Table 7-1 since on a typical modern piano there are 88 of them. The frequencies represent perfect tone, but adding decimals to code makes the code a bit messy; so the following example code rounds the numbers off. Do not worry, most pianos are not in perfect tune, and the nice thing with your piano tie is that once the code is done, this tie never needs to be retuned.

```
int keyC=18;
int keyD=17;
int keyE=16;
int keyF=11;
int keyG=10;
int keyB=9;
int keyA=6;
int piezo=5;

void setup(){
 pinMode(keyC,INPUT);
 digitalWrite(keyC,HIGH);
 pinMode(keyD,INPUT);
 digitalWrite(keyD,HIGH);
 pinMode(keyE,INPUT);
 digitalWrite(keyE,HIGH);
 pinMode(keyF,INPUT);
 digitalWrite(keyF,HIGH);
 pinMode(keyG,INPUT);
 digitalWrite(keyG,HIGH);
 pinMode(keyB,INPUT);
 digitalWrite(keyB,HIGH);
 pinMode(keyA,INPUT);
 digitalWrite(keyA,HIGH);
 digitalWrite(piezo,OUTPUT);
}

void loop(){

  if(digitalRead(keyC)==LOW){
   digitalWrite(piezo,HIGH);
   delayMicroseconds(523);
   digitalWrite(piezo,LOW);
   delayMicroseconds(523);
  }

  if(digitalRead(keyD)==LOW){
   digitalWrite(piezo,HIGH);
   delayMicroseconds(587);
   digitalWrite(piezo,LOW);
   delayMicroseconds(587);
  }
```

```
if(digitalRead(keyE)==LOW){
 digitalWrite(piezo,HIGH);
 delayMicroseconds(659);
 digitalWrite(piezo,LOW);
 delayMicroseconds(659);
}

if(digitalRead(keyF)==LOW){
 digitalWrite(piezo,HIGH);
 delayMicroseconds(698);
 digitalWrite(piezo,LOW);
 delayMicroseconds(698);
}

if(digitalRead(keyG)==LOW){
 digitalWrite(piezo,HIGH);
 delayMicroseconds(783);
 digitalWrite(piezo,LOW);
 delayMicroseconds(783);
}

if(digitalRead(keyA)==LOW){
 digitalWrite(piezo,HIGH);
 delayMicroseconds(880);
 digitalWrite(piezo,LOW);
 delayMicroseconds(880);
}

if(digitalRead(keyB)==LOW){
 digitalWrite(piezo,HIGH);
 delayMicroseconds(987);
 digitalWrite(piezo,LOW);
 delayMicroseconds(987);
}

}
```

All button keys are declared as inputs. Inside the code, each if statement checks that each individual key is pressed. If it is, it will generate the corresponding note. As you might notice, it only does this once; however, this is no problem for the Arduino Simple or LilyPad since they are very fast in performing whatever is inside the loop. It might just play the tone once, but once it hits the end of the loop, it starts over. If you are still pressing the key, it will play it again and so on until you release it. Even if you just press it for a half a second, the LilyPad will be able to loop this piece of code a couple of thousand times.

Synthesizing

I have called this project the "piano tie," but if you look at what it actually is, a more proper name would be "synth tie" or "synthesizer tie." A synthesizer is an electronic instrument capable of generating a large variety of sounds. The piano tie has this in common with most synthesizers in that it uses programmed algorithms to generate sound signals. In the last example, this part of the code would constitute as a very simple algorithm.

```
if(digitalRead(keyA)==LOW){
  digitalWrite(piezo,HIGH);
  delayMicroseconds(880);
  digitalWrite(piezo,LOW);
  delayMicroseconds(880);
}
```

If you take a look at the rest of the if statements in the example, they all follow the same pattern, and the only thing that changes is the delay time. Once you have started to learn programming, you soon realize that there is more than one way to write the code for something; and if you are new to programming, you often end up using more code than someone that has been programming for a while. There is nothing wrong with this and, in fact, this is how most people learn. But as you progress, you soon find steps to optimizing code, which is always good since it minimizes the area of debugging and it helps save memory space.

Arduino memory space is hardly a problem for most of the projects in this book; but once you are ready to move beyond it, you might run into a project where it might be an issue, so it's good to learn how to optimize your code as soon as possible.

In the previous example, the algorithm has the same functionality, and the only thing that changes is the delay time. So instead of writing the same four lines of commands seven times (once for each button), we can optimize by making it into a function. A function is a block of code that is reusable. Functions are given a name, and every time that name is called within your sketch, the program will jump to that block of code and execute any commands inside it. The following shows how we make the sound portion of the project a function:

```
void playTone(int delayTime){
  digitalWrite(piezo,HIGH);
  delayMicroseconds(delayTime);
  digitalWrite(piezo,LOW);
  delayMicroseconds(delayTime);
}
```

This is a declaration of a function with the name playTone. The void in front of the name is to indicate that this is a function that does not provide any information when called (recall that digitalRead provides information about whether a button is pressed or not). It will just do whatever is inside it. An integer variable is declared inside the braces, also known as a parameter, to indicate that every time this function is called you need to include a value or a variable with it. This value is then used as the delay time inside the function, where you also find the basic operation to generate a tone by turning the piezo on and off. So from now on, instead of writing the entire on and off code for each individual tone, you can just call this function with a delay time, such as

```
playTone(880);
```

The next step is to optimize the rest of the code a bit, as follows:

```
int keyC=18;
int keyD=17;
int keyE=16;
int keyF=11;
```

```
int keyG=10;
int keyB=9;
int keyA=6;
int piezo=5;

int toneC=523;
int toneD=587;
int toneE=659;
int toneF=698;
int toneG=783;
int toneB=880;
int toneA=987;

void setup(){
 pinMode(keyC,INPUT);
 digitalWrite(keyC,HIGH);
 pinMode(keyD,INPUT);
 digitalWrite(keyD,HIGH);
 pinMode(keyE,INPUT);
 digitalWrite(keyE,HIGH);
 pinMode(keyF,INPUT);
 digitalWrite(keyF,HIGH);
 pinMode(keyG,INPUT);
 digitalWrite(keyG,HIGH);
 pinMode(keyB,INPUT);
 digitalWrite(keyB,HIGH);
 pinMode(keyA,INPUT);
 digitalWrite(keyA,HIGH);
 digitalWrite(piezo,OUTPUT);
}

void loop(){

  if(digitalRead(keyC)==LOW){
    playTone(toneC);
  }

  if(digitalRead(keyD)==LOW){
    playTone(toneD);
  }

  if(digitalRead(keyE)==LOW){
    playTone(toneE);
  }

  if(digitalRead(keyF)==LOW){
    playTone(toneF);
  }

  if(digitalRead(keyG)==LOW){
    playTone(toneG);
  }
```

```
  if(digitalRead(keyA)==LOW){
    playTone(toneA);
  }

  if(digitalRead(keyB)==LOW){
    playTone(toneB);
  }

}

void playTone(int delayTime){
  digitalWrite(piezo,HIGH);
  delayMicroseconds(delayTime);
  digitalWrite(piezo,LOW);
  delayMicroseconds(delayTime);
}
```

When adding functions, make sure you put them outside the loop and setup curly brackets so that you can access them in the entire sketch.

■ **Note** This code has a few variables at the top of the file, where we can change them easily, rather having their values as "magic numbers" scattered throughout the code. Let's say, for example, we use tone C multiple times throughout the code; we just need to change its value in one place if we decide we want a slightly different tone. This makes the code much easier to maintain. Consider how tricky this could be if we'd simply used 523 throughout the code instead.

After trying the previous example, you might notice that the piano tie only plays a tone as long as you hold down the key button. If you think about normal pianos, they work a bit different—you hit a key and it keeps the tone for a bit. To make it easier to play melodies on your piano tie, we will modify the code once more so that your tie acts more like a normal piano.

```
void playTone(int delayTime){
  for(int i=0; i<50; i++){
    digitalWrite(piezo,HIGH);
    delayMicroseconds(delayTime);
    digitalWrite(piezo,LOW);
    delayMicroseconds(delayTime);
  }
}
```

The only thing you have to do is add a for loop to your function so that it keeps looping the tone for a while on its own. To modify the duration of the note, just change the end condition of your for loop.

Tone and noTone

To make working with sound even easier, there are functions included in the Arduino programming language called tone and noTone.

Using the tone Function

The tone function can be used with any digital pin and takes either two or three parameters. This function basically does the same thing as the function created earlier in this chapter. To call it, you need to include the pin you have connected your speaker to and the frequency you want to play, for example:

```
tone(pin, frequency);
```

With this function you can also set a tone duration as the last parameter, for example:

```
tone(pin, frequency, duration);
```

Using the noTone Function

The tone function will start to play a tone and will not stop until you call the noTone function. Since this function can be used on multiple pins, you also need to include the pin you on which you want to stop the playing, for example:

```
noTone(pin);
```

Piano Tie Code Using tone and noTone

The following example code uses tone and noTone, which, if you remember, are included in the Arduino language. In contrast to the earlier example, the code introduces while loops. In contrast to an if statement that only does everything inside it once (if the if condition is true), a while loop keeps looping as long as the condition is true. The noTone function is called outside all while loops at the beginning of the loop, so if none of the while loops are running, the speaker will be turned off.

```
int keyC=18;
int keyD=17;
int keyE=16;
int keyF=11;
int keyG=10;
int keyB=9;
int keyA=6;
int piezo=5;

int toneC=523;
int toneD=587;
int toneE=659;
int toneF=698;
int toneG=783;
int toneB=880;
int toneA=987;
```

133

```
void setup(){

 pinMode(keyC,INPUT);
 digitalWrite(keyC,HIGH);
 pinMode(keyD,INPUT);
 digitalWrite(keyD,HIGH);
 pinMode(keyE,INPUT);
 digitalWrite(keyE,HIGH);
 pinMode(keyF,INPUT);
 digitalWrite(keyF,HIGH);
 pinMode(keyG,INPUT);
 digitalWrite(keyG,HIGH);
 pinMode(keyB,INPUT);
 digitalWrite(keyB,HIGH);
 pinMode(keyA,INPUT);
 digitalWrite(keyA,HIGH);
 digitalWrite(piezo,OUTPUT);
}

void loop(){

 noTone(piezo);

 while(digitalRead(keyC)==LOW){
   tone(piezo, toneC);
 }

 while(digitalRead(keyD)==LOW){
   tone(piezo, toneD);
 }

 while(digitalRead(keyE)==LOW){
   tone(piezo, toneE);
 }

 while(digitalRead(keyF)==LOW){
   tone(piezo, toneF);
 }

 while(digitalRead(keyG)==LOW){
   tone(piezo, toneG);
 }

 while(digitalRead(keyA)==LOW){
   tone(piezo, toneA);
 }

 while (digitalRead(keyB)==LOW){
   tone(piezo, toneB);
 }

}
```

Finishing the Tie

To finish the tie, we must stitch it up. Figure 7-8 shows the three steps to finishing the tie.

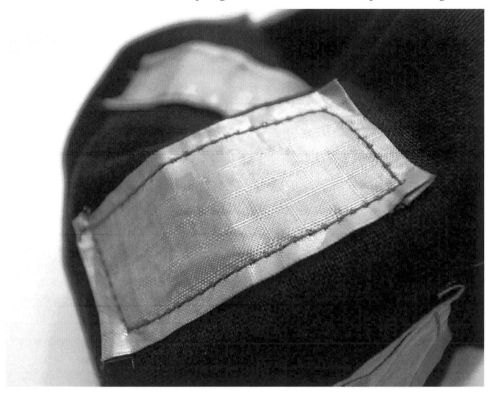

Figure 7-8. The last three steps to finish the tie

1. Start by stitching around the edges, but leave a hole at the very top since you need to turn the tie inside out in the next step.

2. Once you have the tie turned inside out, fold up the two flaps at the bottom, and stitch them in place.

3. Fold the tie in half and stitch the long sides together. Turn the tie inside out once more, completing your tie.

Wrapping Up

The piano tie project demonstrates the basics of computer-generated sound. Playing with computer-generated sound is a lot of fun, and once you understand the concepts taught in the chapter, there is a whole lot more that can be done.

This project introduced more complex interaction. The tie had multiple inputs in the form of the soft key buttons, and depending on which key was pushed, different things happened inside the program. With the tie, the output of all interactions were similar and the feedback was straightforward sound. But as I said before, other projects might not be as straightforward; therefore it is always good to break down your projects into parts. As soon as you have done something that can be tested, it is always good to take the time to actually test it. A quick verification of the code or a connection test on a conductive thread may take a minute or two, but it might also save hours later on. As your projects gradually become more complex with adding new functionality and construed parts, so will your debugging.

This project was based on a tie, but don't feel limited to this. A tie is a good start, but once you understand the basic construction of a soft push button, the project could be implemented into any garment you can think of. Who knows, a piano jacket might be the next big thing.

The next project focuses on implementing a security system into a bag, and continues with introducing more advanced methods for sound generating.

Notes and Frequencies

Table 7-2 is a list of notes and frequencies. It is also found inside the Arduino IDE in the example code toneKeyboard by Tom Igoe under file/examples/digital/toneKeyboard.

Table 7-2. Tones and Frequencies

Tone	Frequencies
B0	31
C1	33
CS1	35
D1	37
DS1	39
E1	41
F1	44
FS1	46
G1	49
GS1	52
A1	55
AS1	58
B1	62

Tone	Frequencies
C2	65
CS2	69
D2	73
DS2	78
E2	82
F2	87
FS2	93
G2	98
GS2	104
A2	110
AS2	117
B2	123
C3	131
CS3	139
D3	147
DS3	156
E3	165
F3	175
FS3	185
G3	196
GS3	208
A3	220

Tone	Frequencies
AS3	233
B3	247
C4	262
CS4	277
D4	294
DS4	311
E4	330
F4	349
FS4	370
G4	392
GS4	415
A4	440
AS4	466
B4	494
C5	523
CS5	554
D5	587
DS5	622
E5	659
F5	698
FS5	740
G5	784

Tone	Frequencies
GS5	831
A5	880
AS5	932
B5	988
C6	1047
CS6	1109
D6	1175
DS6	1245
E6	1319
F6	1397
FS6	1480
G6	1568
GS6	1661
A6	1760
AS6	1865
B6	1976
C7	2093
CS7	2217
D7	2349
DS7	2489
E7	2637
F7	2794

Tone	Frequencies
FS7	2960
G7	3136
GS7	3322
A7	3520
AS7	3729
B7	3951
C8	4186
CS8	4435
D8	4699
DS8	4978

CHAPTER 8

Bag Alarm

This project demonstrates how to add extra security to a bag. The project could be adapted to any bag. I chose a bag that holds one of my precious possessions, my laptop computer. To prevent any unauthorized persons from getting their hands on my laptop, the project implements a hidden security panel disguised as a normal zipper. Unless the bag is deactivated, it will sound an alarm to notify that someone is poking around my stuff.

This project introduces you to analog sensors and continues with more advanced sound generating with the Arduino. The project also introduces new commands in the Arduino programming language, as well as how to work with serial communication for sending data back to your computer.

Tool and Materials Needed

You will need the following tools and materials to make your bag alarm:

- Sewing machine
- Two pieces of normal fabric
- Normal button
- Conductive thread
- Arduino LilyPad
- Coin cell battery holder with 3V coin cell battery
- Piezo speaker
- One metal zipper
- 10 kilohm resistor

Cutting the Shape

The design for the laptop case is very simple and made from two pieces of fabric. I used two different fabrics for the inside and the outside of the bag, and, as in the piano tie project, the lining fabric will also act as the circuit board in which you will sew your connections using conductive thread.

Cut the two pieces of fabric into the shape found in Figure 8-1. Depending on the size of your laptop, you might need to change the measurements. The measurements found in Figure 8-1 fit a 13-inch laptop (10.25 × 32.25 inches).

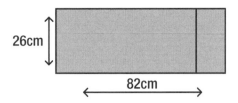

Figure 8-1. Pattern for laptop case

Once you have cut the fabric, it's time to cut a hole to fit your zipper in the outer fabric. This design folds the fabric up to the vertical mark. The placement of the zipper is optional, but I recommend it be placed somewhere in the middle of the bag because it will make for a nice pocket once the bag is stitched together.

But before we add the actual zipper, we need to modify it a bit to make it work as an analog sensor.

Analog Sensors

So far, the projects in this book have mostly dealt with digital actuators and sensors. Though it might seem a bit weird to think of buttons as sensors, they are; even though they only have two states, on and off. They also sense when they are being pushed.

A lot of things we find in the real world can't be reduced to only two states. Take light for example. We perceive it in a variety of ways and we have different words for different states of light. With sunlight, we call the morning light *dawn*, which is when the light is not so intense. Then we have daylight, dusk, and night. Earlier in the book, I explained that computers and microprocessors actually only understand two things: zeros and ones, and on and off. Explaining light to an Arduino in this way would mean that we could only tell it whether it's light or pitch dark. That is not much fun. If you want to measure things in the real world, data will come in a range of values, not just two states. There are also things like pressure, temperature, wind, and more that need to be measured in a range to make any sense.

So that's why there are analog pins on the Arduino board. These pins can measure the difference in resistance in a voltage range from 0 volts to 5 volts. This measurement is then divided into 1024 steps. So when the command analogRead() is called from inside a sketch, the Arduino will check what is going on in the analog pin and answer with an integer ranging from 0 to 1023. It will never actually say 1024 since the Arduino starts counting from 0. If it answers 0, it means that there are 0 volts in the pin, and if it answers 1023, it means that there are 5 volts going into the pin. To use the analogRead() command, you always have to name the pin you want to read from as well, as follows:

```
analogRead(pin);
```

But before we get to the coding, we need to modify the zipper so that we can use it as an analog sensor.

■ **Note** Remember that an analog pin will always answer with a value, even if there is no sensor connected to the pin.

Making an Analog Zipper Sensor

I won't lie to you, making a good analog zipper sensor takes some time and you want to take your time making it since it might not work properly if you don't. The zipper will be used for a side pocket; to actually open the bag you will use a button. We will use the zipper to enter a security code; if someone opens the bag using the button without entering the code, the bag sounds an alarm.

You will need a metal zipper, a 10 kilohm resistor, and conductive thread. Make sure that the zipper is metal by using a multimeter to make a conductive test, as explained in Chapter 5. A non-metal zipper could be made into an analog sensor, but using a metal one makes it much easier to conduct properly.

The mission is to make small loops between every tooth of the zipper using a single thread of conductive thread, as shown in Figure 8-2, almost all the way up the zipper. This has to be done on both sides of the zipper teeth using separate threads for the two sides. This is the crucial part: be sure to make your stitching snug because if it is not tight enough, the thread might get tangled while opening and closing the zipper. Each tooth needs to be able to connect to the teeth on the opposite side in order to make the zipper work. Later on I will explain the theory behind making the zipper into a sensor.

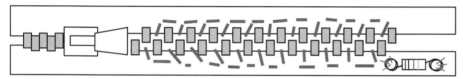

Figure 8-2. Modifying the zipper

You need to add the resistor at the end of one side of the zipper, as shown in Figure 8-2. To stitch it in place, it helps to make loops on the legs so that you can stitch around them to place the resistor into the zipper. It doesn't matter which side of the resistor you put things, but make sure that the side closest to the zipper actually connects with the thread all along that side of the zipper. Make sure that the legs of the resistors are well-connected to the conductive thread. You can just stitch the other side of the resistor in place for now.

The resistor is used because it is very hard to calculate the exact resistance of the thread. A 10K resistor works for the setup I used, with one side highly conductive; on the other side I used conductive thread with some resistance. Depending on the kind of thread resistance and the amount that you use, you might need to switch to a higher or lower resistor.

The final stitching is shown in Figure 8-3.

Figure 8-3. *The actual stitching*

Once you have sewn all the way around your zipper, make it conduct even better by also stitching your thread on the back side of the zipper (see Figure 8-4).

Figure 8-4. *Making an extra run of thread under your stitching on the back side helps.*

Theory Behind the Zipper

The first time I saw a zipper used with electronics was in a video of a Joo Youn Paek "Zipper Orchestra" installation. Real-life zippers were used as a physical controller of videos of people opening and closing zippers on their clothing.

I have seen different construction methods to make a zipper into a sensor, but they all follow the same principles. In fact, you probably often use a similar sensor component without thinking about it. The sensor I have in mind is either a potentiometer, which you can find in most volume knobs, or a slider, which is found on sound mixer boards. If it rotates around its own axis, it's a potentiometer (see Figure 8-5); if it moves in a linear motion, it's a slider.

But they do the same thing: change the resistance of current going through them. Both have three points, one voltage input, one ground connection, and one pin that gives the resistance signal. When you turn the dial on a potentiometer, it moves a small piece of metal inside that makes it easier or harder for the power to move to ground. The leftovers are what we can measure using the Arduino. In other words, the easier it is for the electricity to flow from positive to ground, the lower the resistance signal will be.

Figure 8-5. A standard potentiometer

Later, we will add the following three connections from the zipper to the LilyPad:

- One to the side of the resistor not connected to the zipper.

- One between the resistor and the zipper.

- One at the end of the opposite side of the zipper, as shown in Figure 8-6.

You will read the resistance at the point between the resistor and the zipper. On the other side of the resistor, you will add power; then, at the end of the other side of the zipper, you will add a ground connection. Now, when you open or close the zipper, you will let more or less power through to the ground connection; you will be able to read this information on an analog pin.

Testing the Zipper

Once you are done stitching the zipper, it is time to test it. The zipper might be the most crucial component in the entire book to test because once it is put in place on the bag, it is very hard to change it. But for testing, we will just add some temporary cables to connect it to the Arduino. I recommend using a normal Arduino board for this since it's much quicker to test with. Figure 8-6 shows how to connect your zipper to the Arduino board.

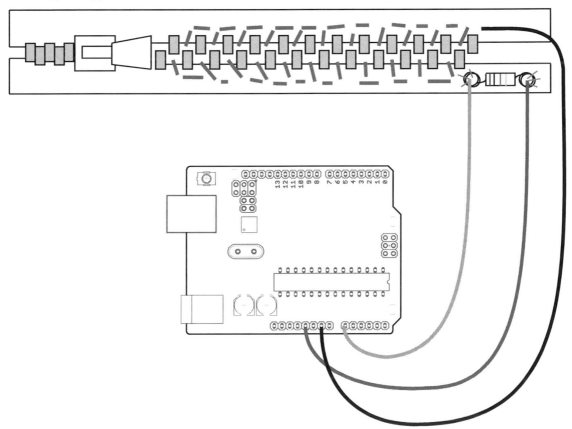

Figure 8-6. Hooking up the zipper to the Arduino 5V, GND, and analog pin 0

The red wire goes from the resistor to 5V on the Arduino. The other side of the resistor connects to analog pin 0, and the black cable connects the other side of the zipper to ground.

To be able to read information on your computer from the Arduino board, you will need to set up serial communication. When making your own sensor, like the zipper, or when you try out a new sensor for the first time, it's hard to tell what kind of values it will generate by looking at it from the outside. So you will need to have a look from the inside.

Serial Communication

Serial communication is the process of sending data between machines one byte at a time. In contrast to parallel communication, like your internet connection, several bits are sent as a whole package.

The Arduino board is not set by default to include serial communication since this takes extra memory space on your Arduino board; and if you don't use communication in your project, this is a waste of space. So every time you need to communicate between the Arduino and something else, you need to initiate the communication. This is not as hard as it might sound. The command for starting communication is `Serial.begin()`, and you always put this command in the setup section of the code since you only need to start communication once. When you initiate serial communication, you also have to declare a speed for which you want to communicate. This speed is always set in baud, which means symbols or pulses per second. These speeds are fixed so you can't choose any speed you want. The following are the available speeds on the Arduino:

- 300
- 1200
- 2400
- 4800
- 9600
- 14,400
- 19,200
- 28,800
- 38,400
- 57,600
- 115,200

You would write the following in your setup to initiate a speed:

```
Serial.begin(Baud);
```

The serial speed has to be the same on the two devices talking to each other. So if you set up the Arduino to send data at 9600 baud, your computer needs to be set to the same speed to be able to read the information. To read data from the Arduino, the Arduino IDE has a built-in serial monitor that opens with the last button on the right on the IDE. This brings up a new window with a drop-down menu where you can set the speed of the computer (see Figure 8-7). There is also an input window for sending information from the computer to the Arduino.

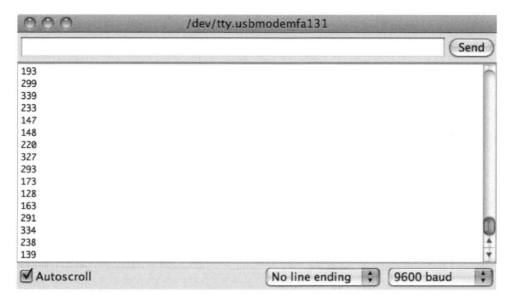

Figure 8-7. Serial monitor printing data

To print information from the Arduino, you can use either the Serial.println() or the Serial.print() command.

- The Serial.println() command is mostly used so we humans can read the data in the serial monitor. If you use the Serial.println(), the data will appear in the serial monitor like in Figure 8-7, where new data appears on a new line.

- If you use Serial.print(), each new message appears after the last message on the same line. After a few messages, it is impossible to tell which message is which. Computers know which message is which, but it is hard for us humans to distinguish the information.

We will use serial communication to test that the zipper works; this will also measure the minimum and maximum values of your zipper so that you can determine the range of values you have to work with. The analog pins can handle a range of data from 0 to 1023, but this doesn't mean that all sensors will output this range.

Test Code

Use the following code to test that the zipper works. It reads the data from the zipper and displays it on your serial monitor.

```
//Declares a variable to store zipper data
int zipperValue=0;
//Declares a variable for the zipper pin connected to the zipper
int zipperPin=0;
```

```
void setup(){
  //Initiates serial communication with the speed of 9600 Baud
  Serial.begin(9600);
}

void loop(){
  //Store the information for the zipper into zipperValue
  zipperValue=analogRead(zipperPin);
  //Sends the information from the Arduino adding it to a new line
  Serial.println(zipperValue);
  //wait for some time
  delay(300);
}
```

If you followed the construction of the zipper shown in Figure 8-2, you should have a space at the top of the zipper without conductive thread. This means that when the zipper is fully opened, the two sides of the zipper do not connect. If you are running your code and have your monitor open, you should get a value of 1023 because when the two sides do not connect, there is no ground connection and all the power goes back to the analog pin. The value should drop as you start closing the zipper. With my zipper, once the two sides of conductive thread touch, the value drops from 1023 to around 300. There is a steady drop to around 10 when the zipper is fully closed. When the zipper is fully open, it will return to 1023 since the two sides are not touching, and all the power in the zipper transfers back into the analog pin. As soon as they touch, the value drops to 300, and the value continues to drop the more you close the zipper. The value becomes lower since it will become easier for the electricity to travel to ground than back into the analog pin.

Since it is hard to make an exact replica of the zipper I made, your values might be in a different range; but if you have a range of 100 values, this is more than enough because it can be made into a bigger, more logical range with code.

There is a command called map() in the Arduino language that takes a value from one range and re-maps it into a different range, keeping it in the same relative position it had in the old range. The command is used as follows:

```
map(sensorValue, min, max, newMin, newMax);
```

This command takes five parameters:

- The first one is the actual sensor value.

- The second and third represent the current range of values for that particular sensor. You need to check this yourself, like you did previously with the zipper test code.

- The fourth and fifth parameters represent the new desired range.

So let's say that my zipper gives me values that range from 1023 to 0. I want it to give me values in the range of 0 to 2000 so that I can use the following code:

```
//Declares a variable to store zipper data
int zipperValue=0;
//Declares a varible for the zipper pin conncted to the zipper
int zipperPin=0;
```

```
void setup(){
  //Initiates serial communication with the speed of 9600 Baud
  Serial.begin(9600);
}

void loop(){
  //Store the information for the zipper into zipperValue
  zipperValue=analogRead(zipperPin);
  //checks that the values is below 1000
  if(zipperValue<1000){
    //re-maps the zipperValue to a new range
    int newZipperValue=map(zipperValue, 0, 1023, 0, 2000);
    //Sends the information from the Arduino adding it to a new line
    Serial.println(newZipperValue);
    //wait for some time
    delay(300);
  }
}
```

Since I know that when the zipper is fully open it will give me a value above 1000, I can use this information to detect when someone starts to close the zipper. If the zipper is fully opened, it will not print these values. But once the zipper is moved, the two sides connect and the printing starts. Yet before it prints, the value from the zipper is re-mapped to a range from 0 to 2000 and stored into a new zipper value, which is then printed. The reason for adding the actual value read from the zipper into the function is because the function needs to know the current value within its actual range to be able to calculate what the equivalent is in the desired range. For example, if the zipper gives a value of 150 in the 0 to 300 range, this would be re-mapped to 1000 since this would be the equivalent value in the 0 to 2000 range.

The map command will come in handy later because we will use the values from the zipper to test how you can use sensors to generate sound.

Making the Circuit

Figure 8-8 shows all the necessary connections that need to be made to complete the circuit.

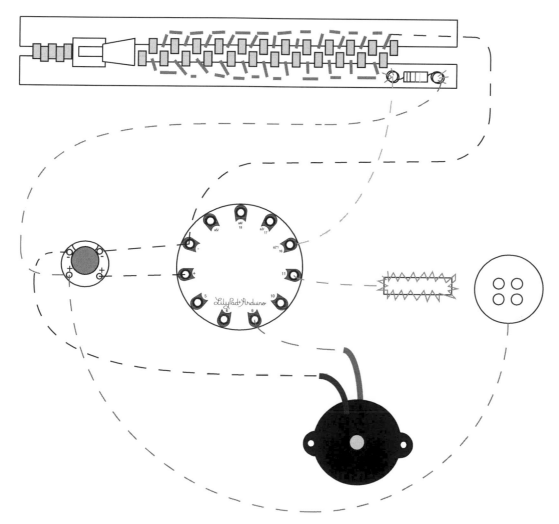

Figure 8-8. The battery holder, piezo, LilyPad, and zipper

If you are using the pattern for the laptop bag, the best placement for the components would be close to the zipper and inside the lining fabric. That way, all the components can be accessed through the zipper hole.

You will need to add a piezo speaker for sounding the alarm. Make sure to connect the speaker to a digital pin and a ground connection. You can use either the ground on the battery holder or the ground connection of the LilyPad. Since all components need to be connected to ground, the ground connection is the same for all. The zipper might be the trickiest part to connect since this is placed on the fabric facing the outside. It is powered straight from the battery holder (together with the LilyPad) and then connected to one of the analog pins of the LilyPad. If you use an analog pin other than the one in the picture, make sure to switch the pin in the code. The last connection from the zipper is the ground connection.

Stitching the Bag

The last part of the construction is a button and a buttonhole. To put this in place, the bag needs to be stitched up. You can still mark the placement of the button and hole, and make the conductive thread stitching before you stitch the bag together.

To stitch the bag, start with stitching the cover and lining fabric together along the sides, like shown in Figure 8-9, and then turn it inside out through the zipper hole. Make sure that the right side of the zipper is facing the lining fabric since the whole thing will be turned inside out.

Then fold the fabric up to the vertical mark and stitch up the side, turn it inside out once again, and you have a nearly finished laptop cover.

When stitching together the bag and all components, make sure none of the conductive threads come in contact with one another. If two connections need to cross each other, use the lining fabric as a separator where you stitch the connections under and above one another.

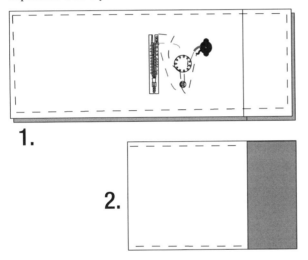

Figure 8-9. *Stitching the laptop cover*

Making the Button Hole

The button will be a part of the bag alarm system. The plan is to use the zipper to enter the security code and the button to detect if someone is opening the bag. If the zipper is not set in the right position, the alarm will go off. But again, to be able to detect if a standard button is opened or closed we need to modify it with some conductive thread.

This button will follow the same principle as the soft button keys in the piano tie project. You need two conductive areas that can connect and detach, which will open or close a circuit. This button has a different construction method compared to the soft button keys. Rather than modify the button, you will use conductive thread to make the buttonhole and to stitch the button in place. The idea is that the neck of the button will touch the buttonhole and conduct.

Start marking your buttonhole on the laptop flap, which covers the opening of the bag when closed.

I recommend using a sewing machine with a buttonhole mode since making buttonholes takes a lot of time to do by hand. Remember, if you are using a thick conductive thread in the machine, be sure to go slowly since thick thread can easily get stuck in your machine. Once the hole is stitched, carefully cut the hole, as shown in Figure 8-10.

Figure 8-10. Use a sewing machine to make the buttonhole

Next, line up your button, and using conductive thread, sew it into place like a normal button, as shown in Figure 8-11. Don't be shy with the thread at this point because you want the thread between the button and the fabric to make contact with the thread in the buttonhole. Once this is done, connect the buttonhole to a digital pin and the button to the power connection of your battery. Once you have your LilyPad running, you will have power going in; if the button is closed, the power will go back to the digital pin and you will be able to read this from your sketch.

Figure 8-11. The button is stitched like a regular button using conductive thread.

Sounding the Alarm

Once the construction of the bag is done, it is time to code. But before we get down to the main sketch, it might be a good idea to check that each part works by using the code examples from the piano tie to play a tone for the piezo. You should also check that you can turn the LilyPad onboard LED on and off with the button.

To test the zipper, once again we can continue with the code example presented earlier in this chapter; but instead of printing the data back to the serial monitor, we can use it to generate sound with the piezo.

```
//Declares a variable to store zipper data
int zipperValue=0;
//Declares a variable for the zipper pin connected to the zipper
int zipperPin=0;
int piezo=9;

void setup(){
  //Initiates serial communication with the speed of 9600 Baud
  Serial.begin(9600);
  //Declare piezo as a output
  pinMode(piezo,OUTPUT);
}

void loop(){
  //Store the information for the zipper into zipperValue
  zipperValue=analogRead(zipperPin);
  //checks that the values is below 1000
  if(zipperValue<1000){
    //re-maps the zipperValue to a new range
    int newZipperValue=map(zipperValue, 0, 300, 500, 2000);
    //play some tones with the help of the zipper value
    digitalWrite(piezo,HIGH);
    delayMicroseconds(newZipperValue);
    digitalWrite(piezo,LOW);
    delayMicroseconds(newZipperValue);
  }
}
```

We have added code to generate a tone, but instead of using fixed values for the delay, we use the re-mapped values from the zipper. If you want a different range of tones, refer to the tone list at the end of Chapter 7 and replace the desired range in the map function.

The resistance in the zipper will be higher or lower as you open or close it. This will be re-mapped into a higher or lower value in the new range, which in turn will be used as the delay time for generating the tone. This zipper is acting as an *oscillator*, an electronic component that generates a repetitive signal.

Bag Alarm Code

Before we get started with the coding, let's pause to think how the interaction will work with the bag so we know how to construct the sketch. The plan is to use the zipper as a code input device where you must enter the correct key before opening the button on the bag, or the alarm will go off.

The first step is to detect that the zipper is placed in the right position. The next step is to detect whether the button is open so that we know if the alarm needs to sound or not.

You need to choose the physical position on your zipper to act as the key. Let's start with an easy key, where you choose one position. To check the position, use the code example for printing the zipper data. Set the zipper to your desired position. My zipper gave a range from 0 to 300, and when I set it to a position in the middle, it gave a value around 130. When you do this with your zipper (while printing the values in the serial monitor), you will probably see that the values jump around a bit and do not stay at a constant value. This is always to be expected when making your own sensors. It very hard to make a precise sensor by hand, but the good thing is that you can calibrate this with code.

If I know that the position I want will give me a value around 130, I can increase the range a bit to look for a value in between 120 and 140. It's hard to find the exact same position twice on a zipper, so having some margin for error helps. You will probably need a different range with your zipper since it might have a different range of values; your key position might also differ from mine.

Once you know this, you can start with the overall code, as follows:

```
//Declares a variable to store zipper data
int zipperValue=0;
//Declares a variable for the zipper pin connected to the zipper
int zipperPin=0;
//Declare a variable for piezo
int piezo=9;
//Declare a variable for the button
int buttonPin=11;
////Declare a variable to store the state of the button
int buttonState=0;

void setup(){
  noTone(9);
  //Initiates serial communication with the speed of 9600 Baud
  Serial.begin(9600);
  //Declare piezo as a output
  pinMode(piezo,OUTPUT);
  //Declare piezo as a output
  pinMode(buttonPin,INPUT);
}

void loop(){
  //reads the buttons and stores the state
  buttonState=digitalRead(buttonPin);
  //checks if the button is opened
  if(buttonState==LOW){
    //stores the information from the zipper
    int zipperValue=analogRead(zipperPin);
    //re-maps the zipperValue to a new range
    int newZipperValue=map(zipperValue, 0, 300, 0, 2000);
    //Check if the zipper is set to the right position and
    //if it is turn the sound off
    if(newZipperValue > 120 && newZipperValue < 140){
      noTone(9);
    }else{
      //If the zipper is set wrong activate the alarm function
```

```
    soundAlarm(500,1000);
    }
  }
}

void soundAlarm(int delay1, int delay2){
  //As long as the button is open keep the alarm on
  while(buttonState==LOW){
    //play the alarm sound
    for(int i=0; i<500; i++){
      tone(9,delay1,100);
    }
    for(int i=0; i<500; i++){
      tone(9,delay2,100);
    }
    // Checks if the button is closed
    buttonState=digitalRead(buttonPin);
  }
}
```

When you open the button, this activates most of the sketch. First, the code will store and re-map the value of the zipper and check if it's in the range of the key code (see the next section for a detailed explanation of the &&). If it's not, it will sound the alarm. The code for the alarm is moved into a function that takes two variables for the two alarm tones. Then inside the function, the sketch will keep looping the sound portion of the code over and over again until the button is closed again. The button also acts as the reset of the alarm system and as long it is closed, the alarm will be off.

You might forget the code position on your zipper or you might want interaction that is more fun. So once you try the previous code example and make it work, you can move on to the next sketch, which implements a longer key code.

Using &&

In the last code example, the if statement checked the position of the zipper using &&, which are used in programming as a logical AND. If you want to check two thing at the same time—as with the if statement where you want to know if the zipper value is bigger than 120 but smaller than 140—you use && to separate what are actually two questions.

```
if( value1 < 10 && value2 < 10)
```

This logical question asks, is value1 smaller than 10 *and* is value2 smaller than 10? It would also work the same if you want to know if two or more things are the same as something else:

```
if ( value1 = = value2 && value3 = = valu4 && value5 = = value6)
```

Breaking into the Bag

The idea for the interaction in this project comes from old heist movies that often include a scene where someone cracks a safe by turning and listening to the safe dial. When the right digit is entered into a safe in the movies, the safe always makes a clicking sound, and the safe expert uses this sound to figure out the combination of the lock. The idea is to do the same thing with the zipper, where the piezo clicks when you enter the correct position. For this, we need a new sketch.

```
//Declares a variable to store zipper data
int zipperValue=0;
//Declares a variable for the zipper pin connected to the zipper
int zipperPin=0;
//Declare a variable for piezo
int piezo=9;
//Declare a variable for the button
int buttonPin=11;
//Declare a variable to store the state of the button
int buttonState=0;
//Variable for counting the lock picking
int keyCode=0;

void setup(){
  //Declare piezo as a output
  pinMode(piezo, OUTPUT);
  //Declare buttonPin as a input
  pinMode(buttonPin, INPUT);
  //Turn button pin HIGH
  digitalWrite(buttonPin,HIGH);
}

void loop(){
  //Make sure that no sound is play
  noTone(9);
  //Store the values for the zipper
  zipperValue=analogRead(zipperPin);
  //If the zipper is in the right position and if it is time to enter
  if(zipperValue >= 10 && zipperValue <= 50 && keyCode==0){
    //Beep once
    beep();
    //increase keyCode to 1
    keyCode++;
  }
  //If the zipper is in the right position and if it is time to enter
  if(zipperValue >= 50 && zipperValue <= 100 && keyCode==1){
    //Beep once
    beep();
    //increase keyCode to 2
    keyCode++;
  }
  //If the zipper is in the right position and if it is time to enter
  if(zipperValue >= 100 && zipperValue <= 150 && keyCode==2){
    //Beep once
    beep();
    //increase keyCode to 3
    keyCode++;
  }
  if(zipperValue >= 150 && zipperValue <= 200 && keyCode==3){
```

CHAPTER 8 ■ BAG ALARM

```
      //Beep once
      beep();
      //increase keyCode to 4
      keyCode++;
    }
    if(zipperValue >= 200 && zipperValue <= 250 && keyCode==4){
      //Beep once
      beep();
      //increase keyCode to 5
      keyCode++;
    }
    //checks if the button is open
    if(digitalRead(buttonPin)==HIGH){
      //if the button is open and keyCode is not 5
      if(keyCode != 5){
        //activate the alarm
        soundAlarm(500,1000);
      }
      //as long as the button is open do nothing
      while(digitalRead(buttonPin)==HIGH){};

      //reset the keyCode
      keyCode=0;
    }
    //delay for fine tuning
    delay(300);
}


void soundAlarm(int delay1, int delay2){
  //As long as the button is open keep the alarm on
  while(digitalRead(buttonPin)==HIGH){
    //play the alarm sound
    for(int i=0; i<500; i++){
      tone(9,delay1,100);
    }
    for(int i=0; i<500; i++){
      tone(9,delay2,100);
    }
  }
}

void beep(){
  //make a beep sound
  for(int i=0; i<50; i++){
    tone(9,800,100);
  }
}
```

Note that this sketch does not use a re-mapped value, but uses the actual value range from the zipper. The trick to entering the key code is the following part of the code, which is repeated inside the loop:

```
if(zipperValue > 150 && zipperValue < 200 && keyCode==3){
  beep();
  keyCode++;
}
```

It first checks that the zipper is set to a position between the value range of 150 and 200, but it also checks if the keyCode variable is 3. You need to count them to be able to enter a key combination since you might need to move the zipper over a position that is a key position. In the example code, the keyCode is set so you can just drag the zipper across and you will have entered the right code. I wrote the example this way to help you understand it, but once you do, you can move around the number that is compared with keyCode so that you have to find the correct combination by moving the zipper forward and backward. If you hit the right spot, it activates the beep() function, which causes a small beep noise.

If someone opens the button, the following code will be activated:

```
if(digitalRead(buttonPin)==LOW){
  if(keyCode != 5){
    soundAlarm(500,1000);
  }
  while(digitalRead(buttonPin)==LOW){};
  keyCode=0;
}
```

First it checks that all five key codes have been hit with the zipper; if not, the alarm is activated. The while loop is added to wait until the button is closed again before resetting the key code to 0, which will make the entire system start over again.

There is a delay added at the bottom of the loop. This can be changed to modify how sensitive the code hacker has to be with his hands. The longer the delay, the greater the sensitivity needed to find the right spot.

Once every key position has been hit, it is safe to open the bag without sounding the alarm.

Bag of Fun

It's obvious that this alarm system will not prevent anyone from simply stealing the entire bag. Still, it might catch a nosey friend or two. It is a bit sad, however, to leave the project assuming the worst in people. The magic with programming is that we can switch the entire concept of the project if we want to—and why not? Instead of making a bag based on paranoia, let's use it to add extra joy in pulling your computer from your bag. The same technology can be used to play a nice melody every time you open the bag.

Melodies are sequences of notes and pauses; if you've had a look at the piano tie chapter, you should already be familiar with how notes are made. But since there is nothing to play notes on in this bag, we have to make the LilyPad play for us—which is no problem.

To store a melody on the LilyPad, we first have to store notes, and by now you know that a note is the frequency; so you will need to store delay times for different frequencies. When you have a collection of data that needs to be stored in a sketch, you can use an array.

Using Arrays

An *array* is a collection of variables that can be accessed by an index number. Every new piece of data that is stored in an array is given an index number, which refers to the datum's position in the array. The first datum that is stored is given the index number 0 since this is the first position, the second will be indexed 1, and so on. To declare an array would do the following:

```
int myArray[] = { 11, 22, 33, 44, 55};
```

This will store the numbers 11, 22, 33, 44, and 55 in the positions 0, 1, 2, 3, and 4 since computers start counting from 0. To grab data from an array, you call the array with the index number for the data you want to retrieve:

```
myArray[2]
```

You always have to declare the type of data you want to store in the array. If you want to store characters instead of numbers, you need to declare it as follows:

```
char myArray[] = {A,B, C, D, E};
```

If at first you don't know what you want to store in it, you can just declare an array indicating the number of positions you need, but leave it empty until you fill a position with a value.

```
int myArray[20];
```

To add a value to a position in an array, you indicate the position number and add the value. This data will be erased by the new data if something is already stored in the position.

```
myArray [2] = 255;
```

Storing the Notes and Making Melodies

The following example shows how the notes are stored in one array. A second array is used to store the names of the notes on the same position so that melodies can be composed more easily than using the actual delay time.

```
int delayTimes[] ={1047, 1175, 1319, 1397, 1568, 1760, 1976};

char toneNames[] = { 'C', 'D', 'E', 'F', 'G', 'B', 'A',};

char melody[] = { 'E', 'F', 'E', 'G', 'D', 'A', 'B', 'A', 'E', 'E', 'A', 'B', 'A', 'A',};

int piezo=9;

void setup(){
  pinMode(piezo, OUTPUT);
}
```

```
void loop(){
  playMelody();
}


void playMelody(){
  for(int i=0; i<sizeof(melody); i++){
    for(int j=0; j<sizeof(toneNames); j++){
      if(melody[i]==toneNames[j]){
        for(int k=0; k<50; k++){
          digitalWrite(piezo, HIGH);
          delayMicroseconds(delayTimes[j]);
          digitalWrite(piezo, LOW);
          delayMicroseconds(delayTimes[j]);
        }
      }
    }
  }
}
```

What might seem to be the most complicated part in this sketch is the play melody function, which has three different for loops. The number of times the first one loops depends on the length of the melody array. You can use the sizeof() command to make the Arduino count the number of positions in an array:

```
sizeof(myArray)
```

This command returns the number of positions in the array. The second for loop loops depending on the number of positions it finds in the toneNames array. This is how the melody is generated inside the third for loop. The first note is selected from the melody array, then the code checks where this note can be found in the noteNames array. When it finds the position, it uses the delay time that is stored in the same position as the noteName, and then plays the note. The third for loop is used to give the note duration.

Once you have the example done, you can start implementing the bag alarm code. The plan is that you will use the zipper to set the speed of the melody, and when the button on the bag is opened, the bag will play the song until you close the button again or fully open the zipper.

```
//The delay time of the notes
int delayTimes[] ={1911 , 1500 , 1400 , 1300 , 1211 , 1054, 1};
//The name of the notes
char toneNames[] = { 'C', 'D', 'E', 'F', 'G', 'R', 'A', 'R'};
//The melody
char melody[] = { 'D', 'P', 'B', 'D', 'A', 'D', 'P', 'G', 'A', 'D', 'P', 'A', 'D', 'P'};
//The different duration for the notes
int duration[] = {8,8,1,8,8,4,8,8,4,4,8};
//Declare piezo to pin 9
int piezo=9;
//Declare zipperPin to analog 0
int zipperPin=0;
//Variable for storing the zipper value
int zipperValue=0;
```

```
//Variable for storing the bpm value
int bpm = 0;
//Declare pin number 11 as button pin
int buttonPin=11;
//Variable for storing the state of the pin
int buttonState=0;

void setup(){
  //Declare piezo as a output
  pinMode(piezo, OUTPUT);
  //Declare buttonPin as a input
  pinMode(buttonPin, INPUT);
  //Turn button pin HIGH
  digitalWrite(buttonPin,HIGH);
}

void loop(){
  //Read and store the state of the button
  buttonState = digitalRead(buttonPin);
  //If the button is pushed enter the if sentence
  if(buttonState == LOW){
    //play melody
    playMelody();
  }
}

void playMelody(){
  //Storing the data from zipper
  zipperValue=analogRead(zipperPin);
  //loop the size of the melody array
  for(int i=0; i<sizeof(melody); i++){
    //loop the size of the tones array
    for(int j=0; j<sizeof(toneNames); j++){
      //if the melody not and the tone name is the same
      if(melody[i]==toneNames[j]){
        //loop the duration depending on where the zipper is placed
        for(int k=0; k<map(analogRead(zipperPin), 0 , 1023, 0 , 2000)/duration[j]; k++){
          //plays the tone
          digitalWrite(piezo, HIGH);
          delayMicroseconds(delayTimes[j]);
          digitalWrite(piezo, LOW);
          delayMicroseconds(delayTimes[j]);
        }
        //adds a small pause in between tones
        delay(duration[j]*1.40);
      }
    }
  }
}
```

The only problem with this code example is that I am not a very good composer; so once you get the sketch working, you might want to compose your own melody. To do this, you just switch out the notes in the melody array; but if you add a melody that is longer than the one in the example, don't forget to add duration for these notes in the duration array.

Wrapping Up

We further explored adding sound to your project; you can use the components as an alarm system or as extra flare when opening a normal bag. In this project, the bag was a laptop case, which was fairly easy to sew (the finished bag is shown in Figure 8-12), but once you understand the inner workings and circuits, you can implement it in any bag you want.

Working with computer-generated sound is a lot of fun and can be as complex as you want. This is a case where understanding the basics of sound really helps if you want to develop a more complex project. I also recommend reading other books on the subject. Unfortunately, there are too few pages in this book to cover everything that can be said about sound and computers, and I doubt that I would be the right person for the job anyway. However, we will not leave the subject of sound yet. The next project continues working with sound, but also adds the possibility of using sound as an input.

Figure 8-12. The finished laptop bag

CHAPTER 9

Beatbox Hoodie

This project finds its inspiration from hip-hop music and clothing. Many rappers and MCs have made the hoodie an icon within street fashion, and I think it's time to physically incorporate music into this garment by making the actual garment a beatbox sequencer. A *sequencer* is a device or software used to record, edit, or play music. The beatbox hoodie's sounds will be programmed, but what separates the sequencer in this project from a normal one is that this sequencer will be voice activated. Rapping and beatboxing at the same time is hard, but with this hoodie you can at least bring the beat at any time.

This project builds on the construction methods from previous chapters and introduces the use of skin resistance as a possible input for your Arduino Mini Pro or LilyPad. It also introduces you to some more advanced programming methods for generating sound.

Tools and Materials Needed

The following tools and materials are needed to make your beatbox hoodie:

- Fabric
- Sewing machine
- Normal thread
- Conductive thread
- LilyPad
- Two, small 8 ohm speakers
- Rib knit fabric
- Two types of normal fabric
- 1 megohm resistor
- Battery pack
- Long zipper or buttons
- ADMP microphone

Making a Hoodie

Start by cutting out all the pieces needed for the hoodie. Figure 9-1 shows the suggested shapes for a zip/button hoodie. I have not included any measurements for this pattern since it's hard to assume a design that will fit all people.

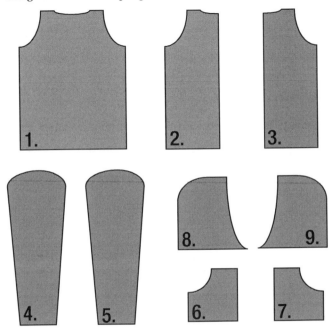

Figure 9-1. Zip hoodie pattern

The hoodie's individual pattern pieces, shown in Figure 9-1, are as follows:

1. Back
2. Front, right side
3. Front, left side
4. Left arm
5. Right arm
6. Right pocket
7. Left pocket
8. Hood, left side
9. Hood, right side

A popular trick to make your pattern fit your personal body shape is to use one of your own T-shirts for measurement. To cut each of the pattern pieces, do as follows:

- *The back of the hoodie (piece 1 in Figure 9-1).* Start by placing your T-shirt on the fabric of your choice with the arms of the T-shirt folded in, as shown in Figure 9-2. Then cut around the edges, adding about 2 centimeters around the shape.

Figure 9-2. Using a T-shirt for measurement

- *The front of the hoodie (pieces 2 and 3).* Fold the back piece in half and add about 4 centimeters to the straight edge. Cut out the shape. Repeat this for the other piece (we need two pieces to make a zipper front).

- *The arms (pieces 4 and 5).* Use the T-shirt's arm to get the shape where the arm is stitched to the hoodie. Extend the shape for the arm to fit the length of your arm and then cut the shape on folded fabric, adding about 2 centimeters to the bottom of the arm. Make the fold of the fabric at the top of the arms (top being the edge that joins the shoulders, as shown in Figure 9-3). Now you should have one piece of fabric. When you later stitch the horizontal bottom edges together, you will have a tube that is the arm. Once you are done with the first arm, repeat the process for the opposite arm.

Figure 9-3. Cutting the arm pieces

- *The pockets (pieces 6 and 7).* Now you cut the pockets. Remember that the shape in Figure 9-1 is just a suggestion that you can modify according to how deep and big you want your pockets. Cover the rounded edge with some rib knit fabric.

- *The hood (pieces 8 and 9).* You can modify the shape of the hood as long as you make certain that your head can fit in it. Repeat cutting the shape for the opposite side of the hood.

To help isolate the circuit that you will sew into your hoodie, you need to repeat all these steps for the lining fabric, which will be placed on the inside of the hoodie.

Stitching Things

The following instructions are for stitching both the hoodie's lining and the outer hoodie. But you should wait before stitching the lining together because some of its pieces need to be modified with conductive thread, as explained later. At this point, however, you can make the outer hoodie so you know what to expect when the time comes to piece the lining pieces together.

1. Start by stitching together the back and front right side (pieces 1 and 2) at the short vertical line and at the shoulder; but remember to leave holes for your arms. Then do the same for the front left side (piece 3).

2. The next step is to sew the arms (pieces 4 and 5) together along the underside. You should end up with something that looks like Figure 9-4 (don't complete this step on the lining until you've stitched the conductive thread, as discussed in the Button Arm and Hoodie Lining section).

Figure 9-4. *The stitched up arm*

3. This third step might be a bit confusing, so take your time and make sure you have it right before you start stitching. It's time to sew the arms to the rest of the body piece. You do this by turning the arms inside out and add them from the inside of the body piece, as shown in Figure 9-5. Then line up each arm with the hole for the arm in the body piece and pin it in place. Next, stitch around the end of the arm. The outside of the body and arm fabric should be facing each other before you start stitching.

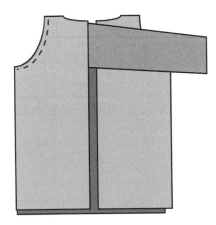

Figure 9-5. Turn the arm inside out and stitch it together with the body piece

4. The last step is to add the hood. Start stitching the hood (pieces 8 and 9) together from the neck along the rounded edge, up to where your forehead will be. Next, line up the hood with the body piece. To make certain you get it straight, you can fold the neck line of the body piece in half and use that mark to line it with the middle of the back of the hood.

After following these steps, hopefully you will have something that looks like a hoodie once you turn everything the right side out. Don't worry about the rough edges for now; those will be fixed once you add the outer fabric at the end.

Skin Buttons

In this project, we will use yet another button construction method. The problem I found with soft push buttons constructed like in the piano tie project is that they need pressure from both sides or need a solid surface behind it to work properly. It worked fine with the tie, but it's hard to press the buttons against your arm, especially if the fabric moves around.

Instead, we will let the skin on your fingers help. High ampere electricity is dangerous because the human body is a very good conductor. But this fact comes in handy in this project because it enables us to make touch-sensitive points on your hoodie using only a 1 megohm resistor and some conductive thread. Figure 9-6 shows how you can test your own body resistance with a multimeter.

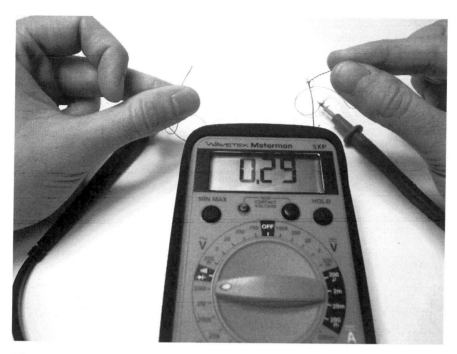

Figure 9-6. Testing skin resistance

Figure 9-6 shows that there is a very high resistance between my fingertips, but electricity is still able to pass from one hand to the other. This resistance needs to be counted to make a reference value when you build in your buttons so that you can read these values with your Arduino board.

If you use too much voltage to power a sensor and the sensor has a very large resistance, you would not be able to tell that the sensor actually affects the current going back to the analog pin (the difference would be relatively tiny). With the circuit set up in Figure 9-6, the way you act as a sensor is that when you grab the wires, you "steal" a bit of the electricity from the analog pin and pass it through your body back to ground. Since your body has a very high resistance (which means that it can only "steal" very little electricity), you need to lower the input voltage to a noticeable level in the analog pin. This is the reason we add a 1 megohm resistor; the multimeter tells me that my body, from hand to hand, has a resistance of about 2.9 megohms.

Before you get start with the hoodie, it might be a good idea to try this at a smaller scale. To do this, closely stitch two lines of conductive thread with very low resistance on a piece of fabric, like shown in Figure 9-7.

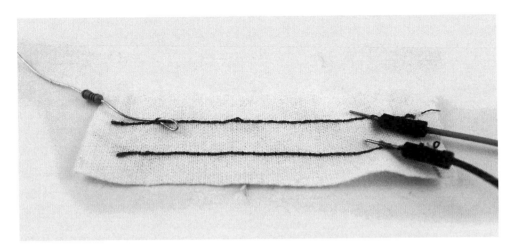

Figure 9-7. Making a test sensor

The reason for using conductive thread with low resistance is to make a good power connection. In this case, we are going to use a 1 megohm resistor to make the reference value lower, but it could also be done by using conductive thread with a very high resistance. As I said before, however, it is difficult to know the amount of thread you will use to make a connection, which makes it very hard to calculate your final resistance. Also, if you stretch conductive thread, the resistance will change. In some cases this is a good thing— for example, if you want to make a stretch sensor using conductive thread or fabric— but we need a steady value.

You can hook two wires to the two lines of thread. The wire connected to the same thread as the resistor is connected to an analog pin and the other wire is connected to GND. The other side of the resistor is then connected to 5V.

Use the following code to print the values from the analog pin to the serial monitor:

```
int analogInPin = 0;

int sensorValue = 0;


void setup() {
  Serial.begin(9600);
}

void loop() {
  sensorValue = analogRead(analogInPin);
  Serial.print("Value is: ");
  Serial.println(sensorValue);
  delay(500);
}
```

If you don't touch the two threads, this sketch will print the values to your monitor as:

```
Value is: 1023
```

It is a good idea to add text explaining the data when you print values from more than one sensor. To print text with the `Serial.print()` command, you have to enclose the text with quotation marks inside the brackets of the command. The trick to making the text and data appear on the same line is to do a `Serial.print()` on the text and then a `Serial.prinln()` on the data, which adds a new line after the data is sent.

My test sensor's value stuck around 1000 and above when left alone. Placing my finger over both lines of thread caused the value to drop below 1000. For this project we will just use this technique to make on-and-off switches, but the same sensor could be used as a proper analog sensor reading a full range of values on your entire body. If you place one finger from each hand on each thread, you will see that you get an entirely different value reading. This is because there is much more resistance in the skin between your hands than the skin on your fingertips.

■ **Note** An important part of making this analog button is that the lines of thread don't connect to each other.

Once you have tested the sensor on a smaller scale, it's time to move on to modifying the lining fabric for one of the hoodie arms using the same technique.

The final hoodie has eight buttons, but both the standard Arduino board and the LilyPad only have six analog pins, and the LilyPad Simple has only four. Don't worry, because since we're still only using these buttons as on-and-off switches, you can read them on the digital pins. When the digital pins go LOW, this doesn't mean that there is 0 volts. Depending on which microcontroller you are using, anything around approximately 2.5 volts and below will register as LOW.

■ **Note** To poke you finger into a 5V connection with low amperes is not dangerous at all, and I am prepared to bet that you couldn't even feel anything. That said, I would never recommend making sensors using a higher voltage and current than that available in the Arduino pins.

Button Arm and Hoodie Lining

The steps in this section are for the hoodie lining only. First, you need to choose which arm on your hoodie will act as the button arm. If you are right-handed, I suggest the left arm as the button arm, and vice versa. Then mark where you want your buttons placed on the arm, as shown in Figure 9-8. You can be a bit creative with the placement of the buttons as long as you remember that you will have ten lines of thread running up the arm that cannot cross each other.

The bottom line in Figure 9-8 is the GND thread, which has eight parallel lines going to the buttons; and there are eight separate lines running up the arm for each button. To stitch the lines, I recommend using a sewing machine with regular spool thread and conductive thread for the bobbin thread since this will stitch the conductive thread to one side of the fabric, leaving the other side non-conductive. I also recommend that you stitch the conductive thread connections on the arm as shown in Figure 9-7 before you close the arm since it is very difficult to once the arm is closed into a tube shape. This is important because you want the non-conductive side facing your body. If the conductive thread comes in contact with your body, the circuit will not work. As the stitches will be made onto the lining fabric, you want the conductive thread to end up on the inside of the hoodie, between the lining and the outer fabric.

173

Next, stitch the front hoodie piece to the back piece of the lining fabric, and then stitch the arms in place. As before, make sure that the arm is the right way around so that once you are finished, the conductive stitching will be on top of the arm.

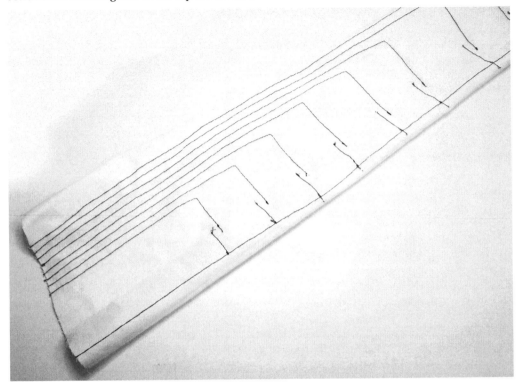

Figure 9-8. Conductive thread circuit for the buttons

The last step is to put the lining hood in place. If everything goes well, you should have a hoodie in the lining fabric that looks turned inside out since it will be covered with the outer fabric later on.

Completing the Circuit

Figure 9-9 is a schematic of all components and connections that need to be made. I recommend using a normal LilyPad or an Arduino Pro Mini in this project because you will need the extra pins offered on these boards to be able to connect all the buttons, the two speakers, and the microphone. I used a LilyPad, which you see in the schematic.

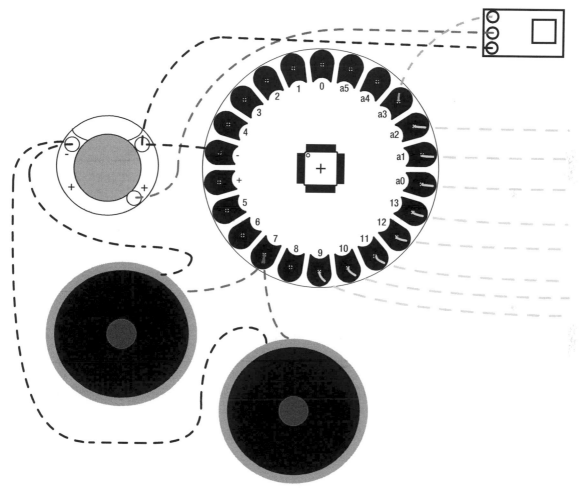

Figure 9-9. Schematic of a beatbox hoodie

■ **Caution** It is important that none of the thread connections come in contact with one another.

All the yellow (lightest) lines are the signal connections for your buttons that run along the arm of the lining fabric. The blue line (the top connector from the microphone) is for the analog output for the microphone, which we read on an analog pin. The red lines from the speaker are connected to the same digital pin. The black lines are ground connections.

The red line from the battery is power going into the Arduino, where you will also connect the 1 megohm resistor for each of the yellow lines running across the button arm. The rest of the arm connections are found in Figure 9-10.

To make the connections, start by placing all the components on the hoodie lining. The speakers go on each side of the hood. The microphone also goes on the hood close to where your mouth will be located and I found the best place to put the Arduino Pro Mini or LilyPad was on the shoulder close to the arm connection. The battery pack is placed on the front of the hoodie where the pocket will be placed so that you can make an opening into the inside of the hoodie to access the battery.

Next, mark all the connections back to the Arduino/LilyPad and start stitching. You have to make sure the conductive thread ends up on the side of the lining fabric that faces the inside of the outer fabric.

You can use a sewing machine for this to speed up the process.

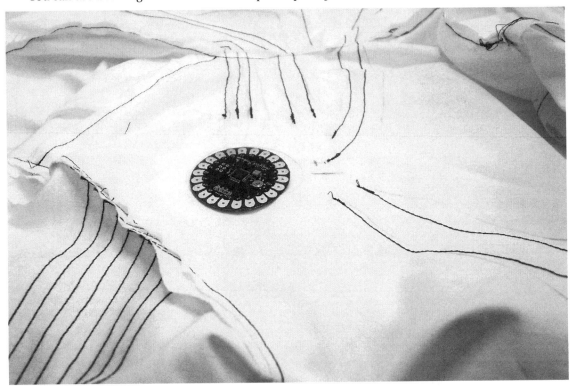

Figure 9-10. Connect all components back to the Arduino LilyPad

Connecting the Speakers

To generate the sound in this project, I recommend using 8 ohm loud speakers instead of piezos. Piezos will work, but normal loud speakers generate a nicer sound than the sharp tones in piezos. I found some cheap and very flat speakers at SparkFun Electronics, which fit this project perfectly.

The difference between the piezo and loud speakers is that speakers have two magnets inside them, one is permanent and one is electrical. A loud speaker or "speaker" is an electroacoustic transducer that produces sound as a response to an electrical signal like the piezo. But instead of being constructed of two metal pieces like a piezo disk, it usually consists of a paper coil that supports a voice coil electromagnet, which is basically a coil of copper wire. When electricity is applied to a roll of copper wire, a magnetic field is created around the wire. The permanent magnet will attract the voice coil, making it move slightly. If this is done at high speed, it will make the speaker vibrate and generate tones.

You can temporarily put some sticky tape over the speakers to hold them in place on the hood while you stitch the cables into the thread. The speakers come with normal cables that you have to strip and stitch with conductive thread to the corresponding connection. I found the best way to do this is to stitch loops around the exposed cable along the conductive thread connection line and then stitch a couple of loops straight through it, tangling the stripped speaker cable as much as possible with conductive thread to keep it in place.

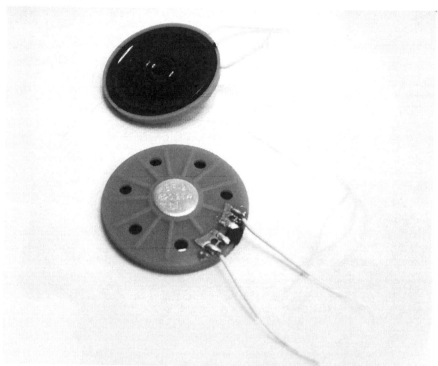

Figure 9-11. Small, loud speakers

Once the lining fabric is placed inside the hoodie, stitch a circle around the speaker through both fabrics to keep it in place; but for now, you can just leave it in place with the sticky tape.

The Microphone

It's possible to build your own microphone circuits, but I doubt that you can make one as tiny as the ADMP401 from SparkFun Electronics. Make sure you get the one with the breakout board since the ADMP401 is also available without it. Microphone kits with an amplifier are a common beginner's kit for soldering, and if you can't get your hands on the ADMP401, try to find one that is powered with 5 volts or lower. Other microphones are probably a bit bigger, however, so try to find one as small as possible.

If you do switch to another microphone circuit, you might need to modify the construction method a bit. Microphones are also electroacoustic transducers, which means that they are basically the same thing as a speaker but they work in the opposite direction. Instead of generating sound when electricity is applied to them, they generate a little bit of electricity.

You can use peizos as sensors by hooking them up to an analog pin. If you try this, you will soon realize that you need very loud sound to tell any value difference. This is why most microphones also have a small amplifier in their circuit, which amplifies the low electric signal generated from sound into a bigger electronics signal. You will also need to connect the ADMP401 to ground and power.

Figure 9-12. The ADMP401 with breakout board

Before you connect the microphone module to the lining fabric of the hoodie, you can try hooking it up through a breadboard and an Arduino, and test it with the following code example:

```
const int analogPin = 0;

int micValue = 0;
```

```
void setup() {

  Serial.begin(9600);
}

void loop() {
  micValue = analogRead(analogPin);
  Serial.print(micValue);
  delay(200);
}
```

This simple sketch will print the data from the microphone to your serial monitor at high speed because you don't want too long a delay since it will be hard to tell the changes sound makes to the analog value. The microphone gave me a steady value around 344 when there was no sound. When there was sound, the value jumped above 350 and under 340. This does not mean that high sound gives high values and vice versa. It's true that sound vibrations go up and down, but to be able to actually detect frequency in a sound recording, you need more processing power than the Arduino because sound oscillations are extremely fast.

This is not a problem in this project because you will use the sound as a beat trigger in the sequencer; and then you only need to detect when there is sound close to the microphone. Later on we will calibrate the microphone inside the sketch a bit so the sequencer can't be triggered by all sound but only sound close to it.

The ADMP401 breakout board is sold without pins attached to the pin holes, which makes it easy to stitch in place. Stitch it into the hoodie close to where you mouth will be located, but make certain that the three threads do not come in contact with one another.

Battery Pack

I choose the AAA LilyPad power supply for powering the hoodie since AAA batteries can hold more amperes than a coin cell battery, which makes them last a bit longer. You can use any battery pack you want as long as the output power is between 3 volts and 5 volts. The AAA battery pack is a bit big, so put it in the front of the hoodie where the pocket will be added to cover the battery pack. To make changing the battery easier, create a hidden opening inside the pocket. Another nice thing about the AAA battery pack is that it has a small, onboard power switch so that the beatbox hoodie can be switched on and off from there.

Arm Buttons

I won't lie, this part is a bit tricky. In order to make the arm buttons you need to put the lining fabric into the outer hoodie fabric. Once you have put fabrics in place, you need to make stitches from the top fabric into the lining fabric to make small pads made from conductive thread that will act as your button (mimicking the gap between the threads that exists in the lining). You need two for each button, where one connects to the thread that goes to a pin and the other one connects to the power line. Figure 9-13 shows an illustration of this. You also need to attach a 1 megohm resistor on every pin connection and connect the other side to power.

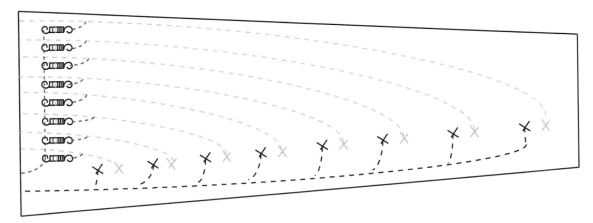

Figure 9-13. Arm button connections

The pads' stitching needs to be close enough so that you can touch both with one finger, but still separated far enough so that they won't come in contact by accident.

Coding the Sequencer

The goal is to create a so-called step sequencer with the beatbox hoodie. A step sequencer records sound without any exact time. Instead, the timing of each step is separated by the column of buttons on your arm. The idea is that when you press a button on the arm, the recording will start on that position. In this project, the hoodie will act as an eight-step sequencer. But there is a slight difference from normal sequencers: the hoodie will not record any sound; rather you will use your voice as the input for the beat count on every step of the sequence. For example, if you hold one button down and make two beats with your mouth, you have specified that there are two beats in that step in the sequence. This means the sound will play twice.

This all means that the sequencer will act as a button and the sound will be created by the Arduino when it is told the number of beats in a step. The sequencer has eight steps, which it loops through. If you hold down one touch button, it starts recording on that step. If you then say "boom, boom" it will record two beats on that step in the sequence. And if you let go, the remaining steps will be quiet; but when you reach the step you just recorded, it will play the sound of that step two times and so on.

When it comes to the sounds to play, you probably want to be able to change the sound for each step or else it won't be much fun. For this you will need an additional input. To keep things simple, we will use the buttons so that you don't need to add any additional components. To keep the interaction simple, use the time it takes to record as an input for changing the sound plays. So the longer you take to record the beat count, the deeper the tone will get. If you hold the button for a very short time, making three quick sounds with your mouth, the sequencers will play three quick beeps in this step.

The Code

This sketch has the following three major parts:

- The playBeat function

- The voiceActive function

- The loop, which acts as the step sequencer

The playBeat plays the actual sound. The voiceActive keeps track on all the buttons. Sound input and everything comes together in the loop, where each step is played over and over again.

One thing you might notice in the following code is that 14, 15, and 16 are used as digital pins. Pins 14, 15, and 16 are actually the analog pins 0, 1, and 2. The analog pins act as analog pins by default, but can be declared and used as digital pins.

```
//Declare pin 7 as speaker
int speaker = 7;
//Add pins 9 through 16 to button array
int button[]={9,10,11,12,13,14,15,16};
//Declare array for keeping track on button presses
int buttonPress[] = {0,0,0,0,0,0,0,0};
//Declare array for store tone pitches
int tonePitch[] = {0,0,0,0,0,0,0,0};
//Declare a variable for microphone
int mic=A3;
//Declare variable for storing time
long timer=0;
//Variable for microphone threshold
int micMin=340;
//Variable for microphone threshold
int micMax=350;

void setup(){
  //Loop all the button pins
  for(int i=0; i<8; i++){
    //Declare all buttons as inputs
    pinMode(button[i], INPUT);
    //Set them HIGH to make sure everything is off from the start
    digitalWrite(button[i],HIGH);
  }
  //Declare speaker as a output
  pinMode(speaker,OUTPUT);
}

void loop(){
/*Runs the playBeat function 8 times for every loop. Every time the function is called it will
play it a different amount of times depending on the voice input. The function will also be
different depending on how long each button is pushed. In this case all functions will be
played with the same duration*/
  playBeat(buttonPress[0], tonePitch[0],20);
  playBeat(buttonPress[1], tonePitch[1],20);
  playBeat(buttonPress[2], tonePitch[2],20);
  playBeat(buttonPress[3], tonePitch[3],20);
  playBeat(buttonPress[4], tonePitch[4],20);
  playBeat(buttonPress[5], tonePitch[5],20);
  playBeat(buttonPress[6], tonePitch[6],20);
  playBeat(buttonPress[7], tonePitch[7],20);
}
```

```
//Declares the playBeat function with three parameters for how many times
//it will play, delayTime for the pitch and duration of the tone
void playBeat(int times, int delayTime, int duration){
  //Store how long time has passed since the Arduino was turned on
  timer=millis();
  //Run the voiceActive function to check if a buttons is pushed before
  //entering the for loops
  voiceActive();
  //Makes an amount of loops depending on the voice input
  for(int j=0; j<times; j++){
    //Makes amount of loops depending on the duration added in the main loop
    for(int k=0; k<duration; k++){
      //Turns the speaker high
      digitalWrite(speaker,HIGH);
      //Makes a pause depending on how long a buttons was pushed
      delayMicroseconds(delayTime);
      //Turns the speaker off
      digitalWrite(speaker,LOW);
      //Makes a pause depending on how long a buttons was pushed
      delayMicroseconds(delayTime);
      //Runs the voiceActive function in every loop to check if a buttons is pushed
      voiceActive();
    }
    //Delay to add a pause in between notes
    delay(200);
  }
  //If there is no voice beat recorded make a delay to fulfil the step of
  //the sequencer
  if(times==0){
    delay(200);
  }
}

//Declare voiceActive function which checks if any of the buttons are
//pushed and records the sound input
void voiceActive(){
  //Loops the amount of buttons
  for(int k=0; k<8; k++){
    //Checks if any of the buttons are pushed
    if(digitalRead(button[k])==LOW){
      //Reset the buttons press counter
      buttonPress[k]=0;;
      //As long as a button goes low wait
      while(digitalRead(button[k])==LOW){
        //If the microphone is activted while the button is low
        if(analogRead(mic)>micMax ||analogRead(mic)<micMin ){
          //Add a to button presses every time the microphone picks up a sound
          buttonPress[k]++;
          //Wait until there is no sound
          while(analogRead(mic)> micMax ||analogRead(mic)< micMin ){}
        }
      // Sets a new timer minus the last timer to calculate how long the buttons
```

```
      // was held down
      long newTime=millis()-timer;
      //Uses the time it took to hold down the button to generate a pitch to play
      //multiplying it by two and a half
      tonePitch[k]=newTime*2.5;
    }
  }
 }
}
```

Time Is the Key

Time is very important in this project because you are combining interaction with sound. If something interferes with the part of code that generates the sound, the sound can come out the wrong way. Without interfering with the sound, you need to be able to register when you push a button to record a new sound at a step at the same time you want to play every step.

This is why the voiceActive() function is called inside the playBeat() function before the looped tones and inside the for loops; else there would be a delay before the new recording started and the entire sound would play out before anything happens. But when you press buttons, you expect them to do something straightaway; this is why the button status is checked at multiple parts of the code.

Another time issue with this project is that you want to know how long a button was pushed to calculate the new pitch. For this you will use the millis() command.

millis()

The millis() command returns the amount of milliseconds that have passed since the Arduino was turned on. As you can imagine, the number becomes very big in time so it's always good to store this value in a variable declared as a long. Long variables can also handle numbers with decimals and can store more numbers compared to what integer variables can store.

Two timers are used in the sketch for this project. One at the start of the loop that checks the amount of time that has passed since the Arduino started, and one inside the voiceActive() function. The second timer is declared as the current time passed minus the first timer, which tells you the amount of time that has passed since one of the buttons was pushed. This is then multiplied by 2.5 to calculate the pitch. The time it takes to push a button works by itself as a sound pitch, but multiplying it speeds up the process at bit so you don't have to push the button as long to reach deeper tones.

Keep in mind that the millis() command starts counting from power up and not reset. If you manually reset your sketch by pushing the reset buttons on your Arduino board, this will just reset the sketch. You have to power the board on and off to reset the time.

Stereo vs. Mono

You might have noticed that the speakers are connected to the same digital pin, which makes them play the same tones on both speakers. There are two reasons for this. The first one has to do with time. Generating two different tones at the same time is what constitutes stereo playback. To be able to generate two different tones at the same time, the microprocessors need to be able to handle multiple threads—which the Arduino can't do by default. The Arduino can only do three things at a time: do whatever is inside the loop, keep track on the analog pins, and handle serial communication. To generate two sounds at the same time, two different bits of code need to run at the same time; the Arduino is not equipped to handle this.

Nothing is impossible, however, and with creative coding and good knowledge about the microprocessor, I have seen this made possible by David Cuartielles, one of the Arduino founders. But that is beyond the scope of this book and probably requires a book in itself to be properly explained.

So for this project we will stick to playing mono sound on both speakers. Yet, another reason for connecting both speakers to the same pin is simply to lower the volume a bit. Even if they are small speakers, they are still pretty loud—especially so close to the ear. If they share the sound signal, it will lower the volume a bit.

Final Stitching

Hopefully, you now have a working beatbox hoodie. It's time to do the final stitching. Start by stitching the edges around the front and hood. Leave a small gap near where your battery is placed and add some Velcro for the opening so that the batteries can be accessed when they need changing. Make sure you do this inside out and leave an opening so you can turn it right side out once you have stitched the opening. If you plan to use a zipper to open and close the hoodie, you need to add it at this stage. Once this is done, you can stitch the hole and arm opening from the outside.

To keep the speakers in place inside the hoodie, you can stitch around them through both fabrics. You can do this with a sewing machine if you are skillful enough, but keep in mind that making a perfect circle is a bit tricky. An option for a more seamless design is to cover the speakers inside the hoodie (only in the lining fabric) with a small fabric patch stitched around them.

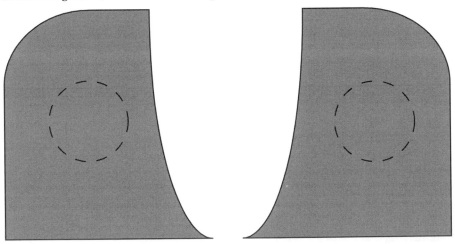

Figure 9-14. Stitching around the speakers to keep them in place

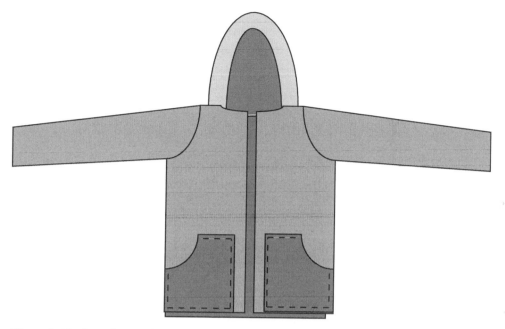

Figure 9-15. Completing the hoodie

The next step is to add the pocket to you hoodie. Make a 0.5 centimeter hold along the edges and stitch it in place. If you use buttons instead of a zipper, now is the time to add them.

And then you have finished the beatbox hoodie.

Figure 9-16. Playing the finished beatbox hoodie

Wrapping Up

Wearable projects take a very long time to construct, so making a first attempt at a beatbox hoodie by using a store-bought hoodie is not at all considered cheating. Implementing a sequencer into the garment is tricky enough. Even if the circuit seems straightforward, it always becomes complex when it comes to wearable devices since you can't always connect things in a straight path; so planning your construction is always important.

But even with the most careful planning mistakes can still happen. I urge you not to be disappointed by mistakes. Making mistakes is a huge part of learning about prototyping and electronics, and it is usually when you make mistakes that you learn how to make improvements. And you should always try to make improvements.

Once you understand how the sketch in this project works, you should try to start modifying it a bit so that the project really becomes your own. You could make tweaks to the pitches or, if you are up to the challenge, add buttons to both arms.

By completing this project you should have gained a good understanding of constructing circuits using conductive thread. You should have also gained some knowledge about using time in your sketches and the importance of timing when it comes to generating sound.

For the next project we will try to add some sunshine to rainy days.

CHAPTER 10

Sunshine Umbrella

Mixing electronics and rain might not sound like a good idea, but people usually think this for the wrong reason. Water alone is not what damages electronic components. It is even possible to wash the LilyPad if you want to; the important thing is to make sure that the LilyPad is dry once you turn it back on. Short circuits are what can destroy an electronic component. The problem with water is that it is a very good conductor, thus making it great for creating short circuits. But applied in the right way, water can be used as an input to your Arduino.

With this project, we will add some light to rainy days by adding LEDs into an ordinary umbrella—where more rain will add more light. So you can look forward to bad weather from now on! Through this project you will learn the importance of proper insulating. You will also learn how multiplexing works and how it can be used to add controlling points to your Arduino.

Materials and Tools Needed

You will need the following materials and tools for your sunshine umbrella:

- Umbrella

- LEDs

- Conductive thread

- Wire

- Soldering iron

- Sewing needle

- 5V battery pack

- Arduino Pro Mini

- 10 kilohm resistors

- 220 ohm resistors

- Electrical tape

Getting Started

Before we get started with the construction portion of this project, you need to know the basic theory behind both the sensor and the light output. Prior project constructions have been a bit flexible when it came to where you put what. The LEDs in this project, however, have to be placed in a very precise order or the project will not work. This special connecting of the LEDs is also known as a *matrix*, and to control them you need to know a bit about multiplexing.

Multiplexing

Multiplexing, also known as muxing, is a method where you take multiple analog messages or digital data streams and transfer them over a shared medium. There are also different types of methods for multiplexing. Even though what we attempt in this chapter is not as complicated as the most complex data transfer systems for multiplexing, it might still be a bit tricky to grasp the concept at first glance, so take your time and read this chapter a couple of times if you need to.

So far in this book, you have connected the positive, long leg side of a LED to the power source and the negative, short leg of the LED to the ground connection (see Figure 10-1) when you powered LEDs. If you want to control multiple LEDs from an Arduino, you hook each long LED leg to a digital pin and share the ground with all the negative legs.

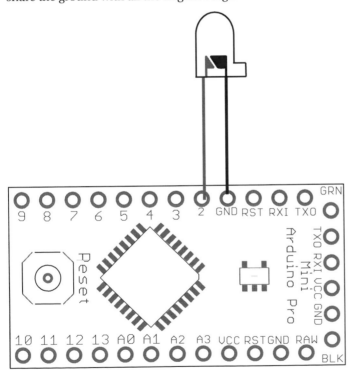

Figure 10-1. Controlling a single LED

This limits the amount of LEDs that can be controlled from your Arduino to the number of digital pins and analog pins you have. To add more control, you can add components like a bit shift register or maybe a TLC4950, which is an LED driver. These chips have additional pins that can be controlled from the Arduino using fewer pins. The nice thing about chips like the TLC is that they can also be connected, adding more controllable outputs without the use of more pins on your Arduino. When chips are connected like this, the connection is also referred to as "daisy chaining."

But if you don't feel like spending the extra money to buy TLCs, knowing how to multiplex might come in handy. Multiplexing is also a technique used in many displays where the speed of computers is used to trick the human eye. Since the multiplexed control signal is shared with more than one component, only one component can be on at a time. In this project, only one LED will be on at a time. But since computers are very fast at doing this, we can turn the LEDs on and off, and switch between them so quickly that the eye won't detect it, making it appear as if more than one LED is on at a time. Figure 10-2 shows a simple circuit where four LEDs have been set up with a multiplexed signal. This connection is also known as a matrix (and no, I am not talking about the movie).

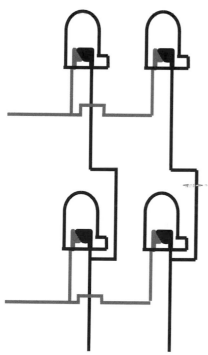

Figure 10-2. A four LED matrix

A matrix connection uses the fact that LEDs can only pass current in one direction with a multiplexed signal, so you can control multiple LED with fewer wires. If you power one of the power connections in Figure 10-2 and open up a ground connection, electricity will try to travel through your circuit. The only open connection will be through the LED between power and ground, which will make one LED light up (see Figure 10-3).

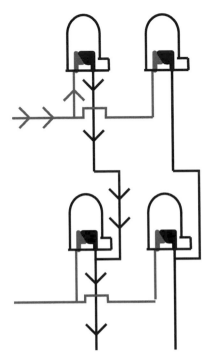

Figure 10-3. Controlling a single LED in the matrix

If you activate power line 1 and ground 1, LED 1 will light up, as we see in Figure 10-3 (note that you can think of this as a coordinate in the matrix, with the origin at the top left; the LED we light up here is at position 1,1). So, only one LED can be on at a time because you have more LEDs sharing the same connection. However, if you leave the previous connections open and try to light up LED 4 by opening power line 2 and ground line 2, this will light up all four LEDs and not only 1 and 4.

In a matrix, one LED can be controlled at a time because LEDs are also diodes, which only pass electricity one way; but if more than one power and ground connection is open, it is possible for the electricity to pass through more than one LED. So this brings us back to the trick.

The trick is to use what is known as the *persistence of vision* to your advantage. Persistence of vision is a human eye phenomenon in which an image persists one twenty-fifth of a second on the retina. In other words, we can still see images a twenty-fifth of a second after they are gone.

This is when the speed of computers really comes in handy since we can turn LEDs on and off quickly and switch between them at such a high speed that it is impossible to tell that there is only one on at a time. In fact, this is how most LED-based displays work. For example, if you take a picture of a bus sign with a high shutter speed, the photo will show that the display is only partly lit.

You can quickly test this by hooking up a matrix of LEDs on a breadboard and to your Arduino, as shown in Figure 10-4.

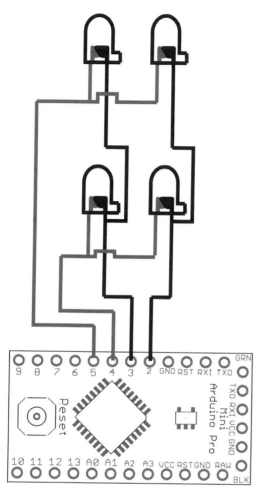

Figure 10-4. *Controlling a four LED matrix with the Arduino Pro Mini*

You can then try to control the LEDs with the following code:

```
//declare pin 2 as ground line
int gndLine1 = 2;
//declare pin 3 as ground line
int gndLine2 = 3;
//declare pin 4 as power line
int powerLine1 = 4;
//declare pin 5 as power line
int powerLine2 = 5;


void setup(){
```

```
   //declare all pins as outputs
   pinMode(powerLine1,OUTPUT);
   pinMode(powerLine2,OUTPUT);
   pinMode(gndLine1,OUTPUT);
   pinMode(gndLine2,OUTPUT);
   //Set the move of the ground lines high to block ground connection
   digitalWrite(gndLine1,HIGH);
   digitalWrite(gndLine1,HIGH);
}

void loop(){
   //Turn on led 1
   activateLine(gndLine1,powerLine1);
   //wait for a bit
   delay(500);

   //Turn on led 2
   activateLine(gndLine1,powerLine2);
   //wait for a bit
   delay(500);

   //Turn on led 3
   activateLine(gndLine2,powerLine1);
   //Wait for a bit
   delay(500);

   //Turn on led 4
   activateLine(gndLine2,powerLine2);
   //Wait for a bit
   delay(500);
}

void activateLine(int gnd, int power){
   //Turn everything off
   digitalWrite(gndLine1,HIGH);
   digitalWrite(gndLine2,HIGH);
   digitalWrite(powerLine1,LOW);
   digitalWrite(powerLine2,LOW);
   //Activate lines
   digitalWrite(gnd, LOW);
   digitalWrite(power, HIGH);
}
```

This code example implements an Arduino trick of using digital pins as ground connections. The problem is if you connect the ground line in Figure 10-4 straight to normal ground, the matrix will not work because we need to be able to turn the ground on and off. If a digital pin goes low, this opens a connection to ground in the pin; and if it is turned high, they will push out 5 volts, which blocks the ground connection. If you push power to both legs on an LED, nothing will happen since they only light up if current is passed through them from + to – in the right direction.

The LEDs in the loop are cycled one after the other, turning them on and off using the activateLines function. The function first blocks the gnd and sets the power to low to turn everything off, and then activates the desired lines, which it takes as two parameters. With a delay of 500 milliseconds, you should be able to see them go on and off one by one. If you try to upload the code again, changing the delay to 5 milliseconds, all the LEDs should appear to be on all the time—but in fact they are actually on one at a time.

Multiplexing a matrix like this makes for a messy and long sketch, so later on we will turn this code into a more practical function. This is only to give you a better overview of how multiplexing LEDs works in principle.

You might have noticed that in Figure 10-4 we are still using four digital pins to control four LEDs, which is the same amount you would use if you connected the LEDs straight to digital pins and ground. But the beauty of a matrix reveals itself once you add additional power and ground cables to the mix, as shown in Figure 10-5.

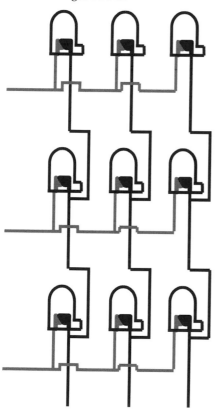

Figure 10 5. Adding two wires to the matrix adds four more LEDs

With two additional wires (making it six in total), you can control nine LEDs, which otherwise would have required nine digital pins plus ground connections. If you add just two connections more, you can control 16 LEDs and so on. So with one Arduino board using the analog pins as digital outputs, you can control up to 180 LEDs if they are connected in a matrix.

But to keep the wiring and programming in this project at a reasonable size, we will not go so far as to add 180 LEDs into the umbrella; but once you understand the basics of multiplexing and the circuitry of a matrix, it really is easy to add more wires.

Most displays are made this way because it makes them more power efficient and easier to control. The previous code example might not be the most efficient way to multiplex; later on we will look at how it can be done by implementing a function to turn the LEDs on and off.

Sensing Water

As I said, water is a very good conductor of electricity. This is why it's bad to pour water or liquids into electronics that are powered on—it causes a short circuit, which makes components burn. If you drop an electronic device into water while it is powered off, however, there is a good chance you can save it if you just let it dry properly before you turn it back on. Matters are worse with liquids that have sugar in them since once the liquid evaporates, it leaves sugar crystals behind. Sugar also conducts electricity and if you have sugar connecting connections that should not be connected, they might burn.

But enough about destroying electronics; let's focus on how to safely make a sensor that can be used to sense water. The sensor you will implement works similar to a button. A button is basically two metal plates that join two connections together, so doing the same with water is perfectly safe as long as you keep your Arduino board away from the water.

As usual, it's always good to try things out on a smaller scale before you start the construction of the entire project; so grab an Arduino board, two wires, and a 10 kilohm resistor. You should connect them as shown in Figure 10-6.

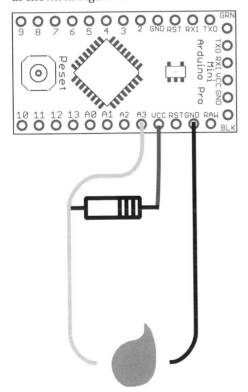

Figure 10-6. Water sensor

The resistor connects to the VCC or 5V, depending on which Arduino board you are using. The other side of the resistor connects to an analog pin and the connection is extended with a cable that you need to strip. Then the black cable is a straight ground cable. If the two ends connect by being placed in water, all the electricity should go back to ground and you will get a low reading on your analog pin. The following is example code for you to try out with your water sensor:

```
//Variable for the sensor
int waterSensor = A3;
//Declare pin 13 as led to show the connection
int led = 13;
//Variable to store the value from the sensor
int waterValue = 0;

void setup() {
  //Start serial communication
  Serial.begin(9600);
  //Declare led as a output
  pinMode(led,OUTPUT);
}

void loop() {
  //Store the value from the sensor
  waterValue = analogRead(waterSensor);
  //Print the value from the sensor to the serial monitor
  Serial.println(waterValue);
  //If the value is Lower than 500
  if(waterValue < 500){
    //Turn on the on board led
    digitalWrite(led, HIGH);
    //In all other cases then lower then 10
  }else{
    //Leave the led off
    digitalWrite(led,LOW);
  }
}
```

With this code you can use either the serial monitor or look at the onboard LED to check if the proper connection is made in the water. This code assumes that you are placing the wires fairly close in the water. You might need to modify the threshold value in your if statement if you are not getting the connection.

Remember that it is safe to put the wires into water, but be sure to keep your Arduino board at a safe distance from the water.

Constructing the Umbrella

You really need patience for the construction portion of the project and you should take your time constructing it since all the LEDs need to be connected the right way or the multiplexing will not work. Also, this project is meant to be used outside, so making sure everything is properly insulated is important.

195

Stitching the Water Sensor

You will use conductive thread stitched into the umbrella for the water sensing (see Figure 10-7). You will need two lines stitched in parallel along the top and down your umbrella. The lines should be close, but not so close that they touch. The lines do not need to be straight; instead, you can be a bit creative and make a nice pattern using the conductive thread.

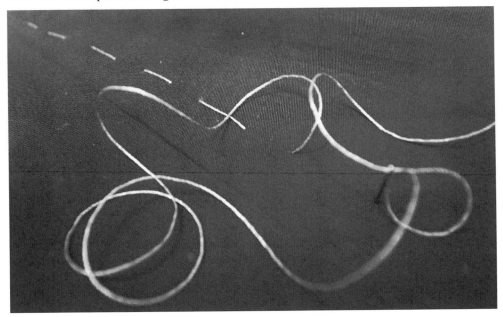

Figure 10-7. Stitching the water sensor into the umbrella

To be sure that you catch as much rain as possible, I suggest having two sensors on opposite sides of the umbrella to make the interaction a bit nicer. Once you have stitched all the conductive thread lines on the top of the umbrella, it's time to add the cables for the power and ground to the inside of the umbrella, as shown in Figure 10-8.

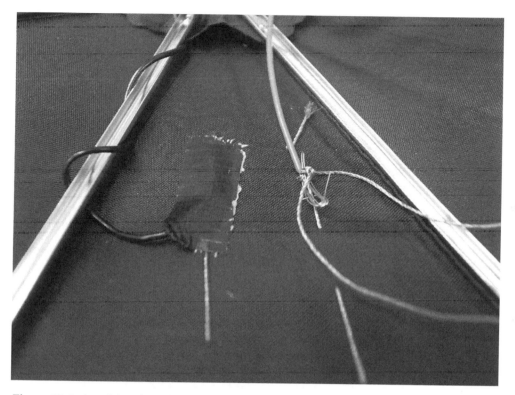

Figure 10-8. Attaching the cables to the conductive thread

The reason for adding normal wires to the conductive thread on the inside of the umbrella is that umbrellas are usually constructed of metal, and we don't want any short circuits since the conductive thread is basically an open wire. There would certainly be a danger of that if we trailed bare thread around the inside of the umbrella. To attach the wires to the thread, I made a loop of the stripped part of the wire and made knots through it and around it using conductive thread. Then I used duct tape to cover up and hold the connections in place.

Really make sure that the knots are tight so that you have a good connection between your conductive thread and wires. The length of the wires depends on where you will place the Arduino later on, but I suggest measuring the pole of the umbrella and adding a bit more to be generous. It's better to have a wire that is too long, which you can cut, than one that is too short and needs to be extended.

Soldering the Matrix

Take a deep breath and relax for a bit before you get started with this part; it might be a bit tricky, even if you are experienced in soldering. To keep the project at a reasonable level, I suggest adding no more than 20 LEDs the first time, since putting them in place is a bit time-consuming.

The LED matrix can't be pre-soldered, so you will need to solder parts of it inside the umbrella. And I have to say, soldering inside an umbrella is the hardest soldering I have ever done—but still far from impossible. Remember to be patient and careful since most umbrellas are made of a thin material that is easy to burn holes into.

A bit of preparation with the LEDs can ease the process. You can solder all the ground connections together. Since you have 20 LEDs, you will be making a 4×5 matrix, which means that you will connect five LEDs together in four ground lines. The controlling power cable will be added later on across the circular lines, like in Figure 10-9.

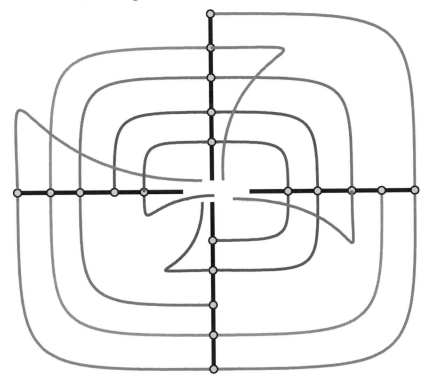

Figure 10-9. Umbrella matrix

Start by soldering together the ground connections of five LEDs for each of the four straight lines. The method I've found the easiest is to take one LED at a time and solder a wire to the bottom of the leg, and then solder the other wire to the top of the leg, as shown in Figure 10-10. The length of the wire between the LEDs depends on the amount of space you want between them. You need to measure your umbrella to be certain.

Figure 10-10. Soldering the ground line to the LED

Once you have soldered the ground wire to one LED, cover the leg with electrical tape. Once you have five LEDs connected to the same ground wire, it's time to add it to the umbrella. The umbrella I used had a convenient groove in the metal arms where the LED leg fit perfectly. Just make sure that the leg is insulated so it does not come in contact with the metal. To be on the safe side, add electrical tape to the metal rod. To hold the wire in place, cover it with more electrical tape around the arm. Figure 10-11 shows an LED in the groove of the umbrella's arm.

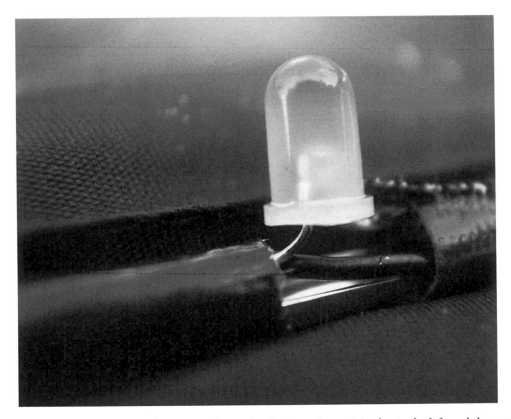

Figure 10-11. Attaching the LEDs to the umbrella (note the positive leg to the left and the ground wire continuing up the umbrella, ready to go into the groove)

Once you have added all four lines of LEDs into the umbrella, it is time to add the controlling power connections as described in Figure 10-9. To do this, you need to solder a joining cable from one LED to another around the umbrella, as shown in Figure 10-12. It is easier to start with the last LED in a series so you don't forget to add extra wire up to your Arduino board at the other end before you cut the wire.

Make sure to also insulate the power cables since the positive leg will be bent in the opposite direction of the LED's negative leg; and if you have an umbrella with a metal construction, you don't want any of the legs to come in contact with the metal.

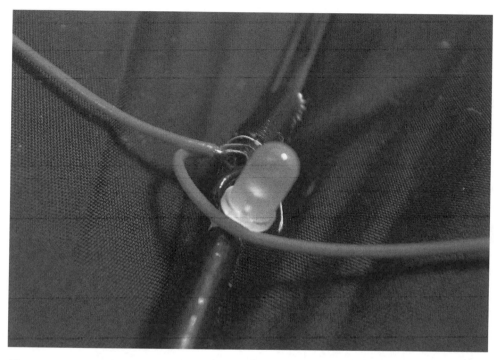

Figure 10-12. Adding the power wires around the umbrella

When you are done, you should have something that looks like Figure 10-13, where you have 12 wire ends going into the pole of your umbrella, waiting to be connected to your Arduino board. Nine of the wires are for the LEDs and the others are for each sensor and one shared ground cable.

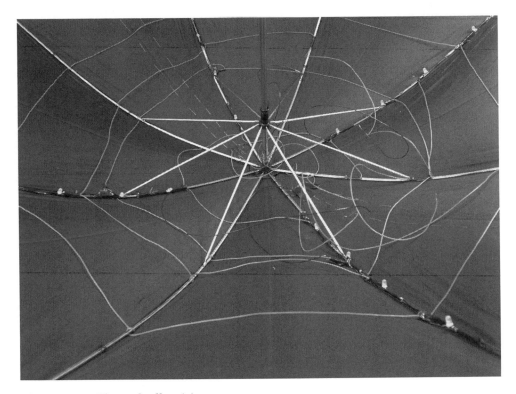

Figure 10-13. *The umbrella wiring*

Hooking Everything Up

Once you have pulled all your wires to the center of your umbrella, it's time to hook them up to your Arduino board. Take a look at Figure 10-14 to see what goes where.

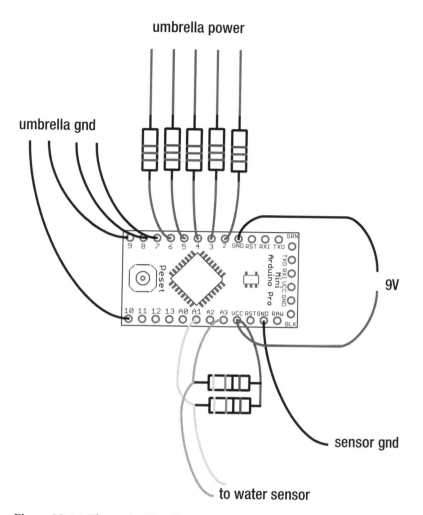

Figure 10-14. The umbrella schematic

You will need to add 220 ohm resistors to the power wires, as well as two 10 kilohm resistors for the water sensor. I found it easier to add the resistors on the cables before you attach them to the Arduino board. Also add wires for your battery connection. You can use whatever battery pack you feel fits the project, but if you want to leave your project intact once it's done, I recommend a 9V battery and a 9V battery clip. If you are using a LilyPad, make sure to use a battery with lower voltage since the LilyPad can only handle up to 5 volts. The 9V battery will last much longer than the smaller LilyPad batteries. Since there is no good place to sew a battery pack, you don't really need one—so a battery clip will do just fine. You can hold the battery in place against the umbrella pole using cable ties.

Once you have everything hooked up and ready to go, it's time to write a sketch that sheds some light inside the umbrella.

Writing the Code

Once all your LEDs are connected in the matrix, it might be a good idea to test that they are all connected the right way.

LED Test Code

The following code example loops each individual LED, switching each LED on one by one along the ground line:

```
//Declare pins as power pins
int power[]={2,3,4,5,6};
//Declare pins as ground pins
int gnd[]={7,8,9,10};

void setup(){
//Set up power pins as outputs
 for(int i=0; i<5; i++){
  pinMode(power[i],OUTPUT);
 }
//Set up ground pins as output and turn them high to block the connection
  for(int i=0; i<4; i++){
   pinMode(gnd[i],OUTPUT);
   digitalWrite(gnd[i],HIGH);
  }
}

void loop(){
 //Start looping all ground lines
 for(int i=0; i<4;i++){
   //For every ground line loop all the power lines
   for(int j=0; j<5;j++){
    //Turn each led on
    digitalWrite(gnd[i],LOW);
    digitalWrite(power[j],HIGH);
    delay(100);
    //Turn the same led off
    digitalWrite(gnd[i],HIGH);
    digitalWrite(power[j],LOW);
    delay(100);
   }
 }
}
```

Random Rain

For the sunshine umbrella code, I thought it would be nice for the light output to mimic rain, where the LEDs act like raindrops hitting the umbrella. But instead of getting wet, you get small bursts of light—as long as it is actually raining on the umbrella.

I chose to light up random LEDs when the sensors are activated in order to get a more natural feeling to the interaction. You can use the random() command to do random calculations.

```
random(int min, int max);
```

This command gives you a random number in the range that you declare with a minimum and maximum value, both int. Remember that this command gives you a random number between the two values supplied, so if you want the actual random number to be five, you would have to write:

```
random(0, 6);
```

The problem with computer-generated random numbers is that they are not very random. If you make a simple sketch that prints random values to your serial monitor, you find that every time you restart your Arduino board, the same sequence of values are printed and the only new value printed is a new random number, which will also be remembered in the sequence of values. You can try this out by printing five values and then restarting the Arduino; you will find that it prints the same five numbers again.

To solve this problem you have to add the command randomSeed() to your sketch and declare an analogRead() inside the brackets as follows:

```
randomSeed(analogRead(0));
```

For this, you need to use an analog pin where nothing is connected. The reason for this is to add another input to generate the random values. If you don't have something connected on an analog pin, you can still read values that change on them. This is because static electricity in the air affects these pins. This is perfect to use for generating random values because this effect occurs very randomly.

Now let's put everything together, as follows:

```
//Declare pins as power pins
int power[]={2,3,4,5,6};
//Declare pins as ground pins
int gnd[]={7,8,9,10};
//Declare first water sensor
int sensor1=A3;
//Declare second water sensor
int sensor2=A2;

void setup(){
  //Set power pins as outputs
  for(int i=0; i<5; i++){
    pinMode(power[i],OUTPUT);
  }
  //Set gnd pins as outputs and turn them high to block gnd
  for(int i=0; i<4; i++){
    pinMode(gnd[i],OUTPUT);
    digitalWrite(gnd[i],HIGH);
  }
  //Activate randomSeed to read values from analog pin 0
  randomSeed(analogRead(0));
}

void loop(){
  //Save status from sensor one
  int rainSense1 = analogRead(sensor1);
  //Save status from sensor two
  int rainSense2 = analogRead(sensor2);
  //If sensor one or two detects rain
```

```
      if(rainSense1 < 10 || rainSense2 < 10){
       //Run the random rain light
       randomRain();
      }
    }

    void randomRain(){
      //declare a random value between 0 and 5
      int gndRandom = random(0,5);
      //declare a random value between 0 and 6
      int powerRandom = random(0,6);
      //Activate gnd with the random value
      digitalWrite(gnd[gndRandom],LOW);
      //Activate power with the random value
      digitalWrite(power[powerRandom],HIGH);
      //Wait for some time
      delay(30);
      //Deactivate gnd with the same random value
      digitalWrite(gnd[gndRandom],HIGH);
      //Deactivate power with the same random value
      digitalWrite(power[powerRandom],LOW);
      //Wait a bit more
      delay(30);
    }
```

Pin Point Control

This last code example is included just to show you how a function can be made to control each LED individually—if it's ever needed. Do not be alarmed by the length of the code since most of it is repetition for all the LEDs. In fact, to make the code shorter would make it more complex, and it's a complexity that I felt was beyond the scope of the book.

```
//Declare power pins
int power[]={2,3,4,5,6};
//declare ground pins
int gnd[]={7,8,9,10};


void setup(){
 //Set all the power pins to outputs
 for(int i=0; i<5; i++){
  pinMode(power[i],OUTPUT);
 }
  //Set all the gnd pins to outputs and set the to high the block gnd
  for(int i=0; i<4; i++){
      pinMode(gnd[i],OUTPUT);
   digitalWrite(gnd[i],HIGH);
  }
}

void loop(){
    //Run the setLed function on led 2,3,12 and 20 in the matrix and use a delay
```

```
    //of half a second
    setLed(2,500);
    setLed(3,500);
    setLed(12,500);
    setLed(20,500);
}
//Declares the setLed function wth two parameters, one for the led in the
//matrix and one for the delay time
void setLed(int led, int time){
  //Depending on what value is stored in led switch to a case
  switch (led){
    //If led is 1 do everything until break
    case 1:
    flashLed(gnd[0],power[0],time);
    break;

    //If led is 2 do everything until break
    case 2:
    flashLed(gnd[0],power[1],time);
    break;

    //If led is 3 do everything until break
    case 3:
    flashLed(gnd[0],power[2],time);
    break;

    //If led is 4 do everything until break
    case 4:
    flashLed(gnd[0],power[3],time);
    break;

    //If led is 5 do everything until break
    case 5:
    flashLed(gnd[0],power[4],time);
    break;

    //If led is 6 do everything until break
    case 6:
    flashLed(gnd[1],power[0],time);
    break;

    //If led is 7 do everything until break
    case 7:
    flashLed(gnd[1],power[1],time);
    break;

    //If led is 8 do everything until break
    case 8:
    flashLed(gnd[1],power[2],time);
    break;

    //If led is 9 do everything until break
```

```
case 9:
flashLed(gnd[1],power[3],time);
break;

//If led is 10 do everything until break
case 10:
flashLed(gnd[1],power[4],time);
break;

//If led is 11 do everything until break
case 11:
flashLed(gnd[2],power[0],time);
break;

//If led is 12 do everything until break
case 12:
flashLed(gnd[2],power[1],time);
break;

//If led is 13 do everything until break
case 13:
flashLed(gnd[2],power[2],time);
break;

//If led is 14 do everything until break
case 14:
flashLed(gnd[2],power[3],time);
break;

//If led is 15 do everything until break
case 15:
flashLed(gnd[2],power[4],time);
break;

//If led is 16 do everything until break
case 16:
digitalWrite(gnd[3],LOW);
digitalWrite(power[0],HIGH);
delay(time);
digitalWrite(gnd[3],HIGH);
digitalWrite(power[0],LOW);
delay(time);
break;

//If led is 17 do everything until break
case 17:
flashLed(gnd[3],power[1],time);
break;

//If led is 18 do everything until break
case 18:
flashLed(gnd[3],power[2],time);
```

```
        break;

        //If led is 19 do everything until break
        case 19:
        flashLed(gnd[3],power[3],time);
        break;

        //If led is 20 do everything until break
        case 20:
        flashLed(gnd[3],power[4],time);
        break;
    }

}

void flashLed(int ground, int power, int delayTime){
    //Activate led
    digitalWrite(ground,LOW);
    digitalWrite(power,HIGH);
    //Wait for a bit
    delay(delayTime);
    //Turn the same led off
    digitalWrite(ground,HIGH);
    digitalWrite(power,LOW);
    //Wait a bit more
    delay(delayTime);
}
```

The solution implements the use of switch cases, which can be compared to using multiple if statements. There are 20 options in this example, which would lead to 20 if statements and a lot of extra code. Instead, we set out 20 cases and compare them to the LED that is declared using the setLed() function. If the LED matches a case, the code below the case statement will be executed until it reaches a break. In our example, inside every case statement is another function that handles the actual on-and-off switching, which you can find at the end of the code. The sketch is written this way so that we get a nice control command used inside the loop:

```
setLed(2,500);
```

This command in turn calls the setLed() function and enters case 2 since this is what is set as the first parameter.

```
case 2:
flashLed(gnd[0],power[1],time);
break;
```

Inside case 2 we call the flashLed() function; to do so, we set the parameter to the corresponding power and ground line for LED 2 and the amount of time that you want the LED on. Once flashLed() has turned the LED on and off, it will jump back to the case.

You find the break command after the flashLed() function. This command is used to indicate that it is the end of the case and it's time to jump out of the case statement.

You're controlling LEDs in this project, but most actuators can be set up in a matrix and controlled by multiplexing if needed.

Wrapping Up

A final touch is to make a holder to keep the battery and Arduino board in place, as shown in Figure 10-15, and cover the remaining connections with electrical tape.

Figure 10-15. The Arduino placed on to the 9V battery and fixed to the umbrella pole using a self-locking cable tie

In this project, we looked at how to use rain as a means of interaction to light up your rainy days. The core of the project was the matrix of LEDs, which you learned to control by multiplexing a signal. You also learned that water is not always deadly when it comes to electronics, but it can easily make some unwanted connections.

Once you have a basic understanding of how the code examples in this chapter work, I urge you to play around to see if you can come up with some new ones. A caution though: if you easily get dizzy or suffer from epilepsy, avoid a fast blinking speed with the LEDs. Running this chapter's first test code too fast made me dizzy.

For the next project, we continue to build upon the knowledge learned in this chapter with a dress that lights up from a sound beat.

CHAPTER 11

Beat Dress

The LED dress has become the "the little black dress" of wearables, so of course it's included in this book. To add a twist with some fun interaction, this dress will react to sound that will be calibrated to loud sounds like a drum beat in music. To stay true to the original inspiration, this project is based on a simple cut, little black dress—so that you can keep it business in the daytime and light up your nightlife after work.

This project is a progression on the methods and technology from the sunshine umbrella project. A more advanced technique of matrix construction will be introduced using conductive thread instead of wires. So if you haven't had a look at the previous chapter, I suggest you do so before you get started with this project.

Tool and Materials Needed

The following tools and materials are needed to create your beat dress:

- Sewing machine and sewing pins
- Pliers and a wire cutter
- Conductive thread
- Normal thread
- Fabric
- Arduino LilyPad
- LilyPad power supply
- 60 LEDs
- 220 ohm resistors
- Microphone kit/ADMP401

Getting Started

This project might be one of the most time-consuming in the entire book. It is what I like to define as "complex simplicity." Connecting one LED and writing a sketch to control it should be fairly easy if you followed the prior projects in this book. However, connecting and controlling 60 LEDs in a dress is a different story.

Don't let this scare you, but I urge you to take the time to study the schematic and construction process a few times before you get started in order to save time later on. You will not be connecting LEDs in a matrix with wires in this project like you did with the sunshine umbrella, but you will make a matrix using only conductive thread and fabric. The advantage with using wires is that the wires are isolated in plastic and you only have to make sure that the stripped connections do not cross one another. While making the matrix in this project, the entire dress will have 16 open connections that cannot come in contact with one another at any point.

This is not impossible, but the best tip I can give you is to make sure that you know where you are going before you start sewing. To get started with the matrix, we need the actual full shape of the dress. The matrix will be placed into the lining fabric and then an outer fabric will be placed over this, and the LEDs will be pushed through both fabrics and connected to the matrix.

The Little Dress Design

The beat dress could be made from any dress design really, but I recommend a design that is as simple as possible because when it's time to implement the matrix, you want to be able to make connections as straight as possible. The design presented in Figure 11-1 is only made from two pieces of fabric (and two additional ones for the lining fabric). Start by cutting the lining fabric into shape.

Cutting the Dress

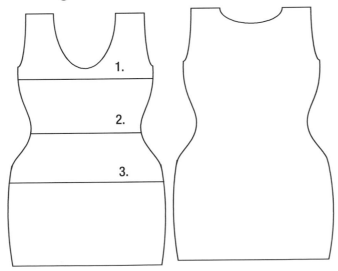

Figure 11-1. The little dress pattern

To make the pattern, start by measuring your chest, waist, hips, and the space in between. This will be the base for your pattern. Then draw your pattern around these measurements. The easiest way is to start by making half of the front pattern. To do so, divide all your measurements by four and draw the contours of the body from the center-front line. Be sure to add about 1 centimeter (0.4 inches) to the pattern for the seam allowance.

Note We divide by four because we want just half of the front (the front is the measurements divided by two), which we divide by two again to get half. This is a very rough pattern estimate, so take your time to adjust the pattern after your own measurements.

Then fold the lining fabric and cut out the pattern. You should have two matching sides. You can also use this pattern to cut the fabric for the back, but don't forget to raise the neckline.

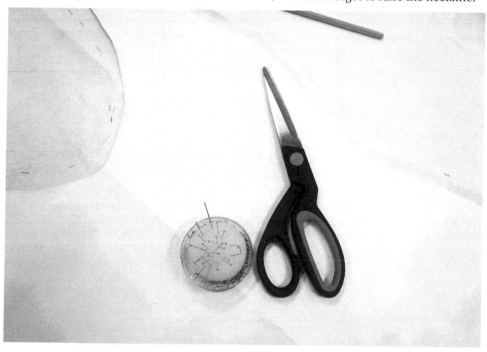

Figure 11-2. Do not forget to add 1 centimeter for the seam allowance.

Once you have the two pieces cut, it is time to sew them together along one of the sides up to the armpit. Do not sew the other side together yet. First, we must add the matrix.

Reenter the Matrix

I presented the theory behind the matrix and multiplexing in the sunshine umbrella project; it hasn't changed for this project. But this time around we will step it up a notch and the mission is to implement a matrix to control 60 LEDs. You will divide the matrix into a 10 × 6 grid, where you will have ten ground lines and six power lines.

Figure 11-3 shows an abstraction of the grid that needs to be implemented into the dress.

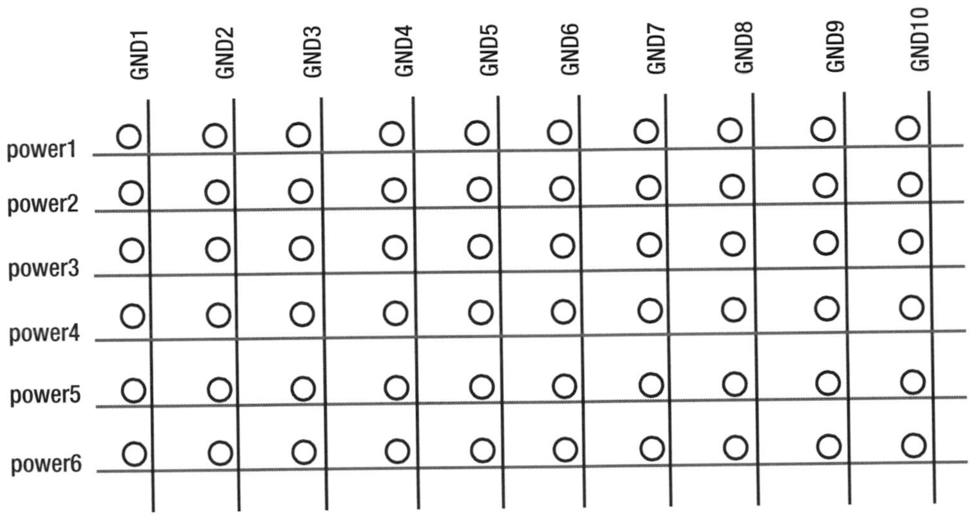

Figure 11-3. A 10×6 matrix

The idea is to divide the LEDs to have 30 on the front of the dress and 30 on the back. As you might remember from the umbrella project, the power and ground lines should not be broken and cannot come into contact with one another—or the matrix will not work.

This is why you have only sewn one side of the lining fabric together. We can make vertical and horizontal connections along the dress. To do this, you need to use a sewing machine with conductive thread as the bobbin thread. This should keep the conductive thread on only one side of the fabric (the spool thread will be on the other side). It might be a good idea to make a small test piece to see how this works and to get the hang of how the thing will work. I recommend using a spool thread that has a distinct color in contrast to the conductive thread so that you can easily spot if the thread ends up on the wrong side.

Once you feel comfortable stitching conductive thread with the sewing machine, you can get started marking the matrix on the lining fabric, as shown in Figure 11-4.

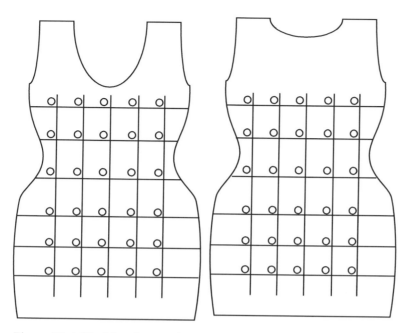

Figure 11-4. Marking the matrix connections

It's good to mark the placement of the LEDs as well so that you can find them later on when it is time to connect them. Once you have marked the matrix, it's time to sew the connections, as shown in Figure 11-5. Make sure that you use a highly conductive thread. You want as low a resistance as possible. To avoid making the dress thicker by adding another layer of fabric, there will be connections touching the body on the inside of the dress. This is completely safe since you will be running only 3.3 volts along the LEDs. But still, we want to make certain that the thread doesn't have more resistance than your body; if it does, the electricity will skip the LED and go into your body instead. But if you had a look at the beatbox hoodie project, you know that the body's resistance is very high, so using conductive thread with low to zero resistance will avoid this.

Figure 11-5. Conductive thread matrix

You have to make all the ground connections on one side of the fabric and the power connections on the opposite side. To keep it simple, I suggest you start by making all the horizontal lines on one side and then all the vertical ones on the opposite side before you start with the connection, back towards where you will place your Arduino or LilyPad board. Figure 11-5 shows where you sew all the power lines on one side of the fabric; you flip the fabric over to sew the ground lines. In other words, it is a good idea to have the matrix in place so that you can calculate where to make the connections back to the Arduino board (as shown in Figure 11-6), which is placed at the bottom hem. The spacing between the lines will also be the spacing in between your LEDs, and this really depends on what you prefer and the dress size. When I made a size 8 dress, I used spacing of about 8 centimeters (3 inches) between the lines to get good coverage. The LEDs do not need to be put in a straight line, however, if you don't want them to be—as long as the LEDs can reach both the ground and power line.

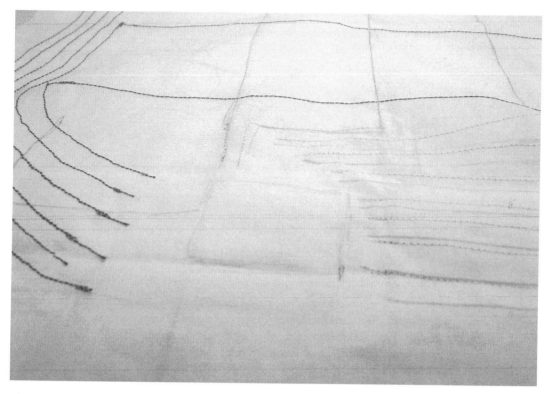

Figure 11-6. Making the Arduino/LilyPad connections

The last step at this stage is to make the connections from the matrix back to where you will place the Arduino/LilyPad board. I found it best not to cover the dress all the way to the button hem, but leave about 15 centimeters of free space where the board can be placed. This project can be made with either a standard Arduino LilyPad or an Arduino Pro Mini. Both have pros and cons when it comes to this project. Since it's a tight dress design, the smaller form factor of the Pro Mini makes the design a bit nicer; but since you will be using most of the pins on the board, the wider spacing on the pin holes of the LilyPad makes it easier to separate the connections. I ended up using the LilyPad for this project, but the choice is yours.

217

Dress Stitching and LED Poking

Once the matrix is in place, it is time to move on to stitching up the dress, starting at the side and then along the shoulder straps, as shown in Figure 11-7. Don't forget to leave holes for the arms.

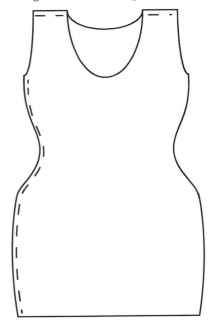

Figure 11-7. *Stitching up the lining fabric*

At this point it also a good idea to hem the arms and along the neck opening. Fold the edges about 1 centimeter and stitch around the openings, as shown in Figure 11-8. Make sure you make the fold the right way around and that the right side of the fabric is facing the inside of the dress. The lining fabric will be covered with the outer fabric, so you want the stitching facing the outside on the lining fabric.

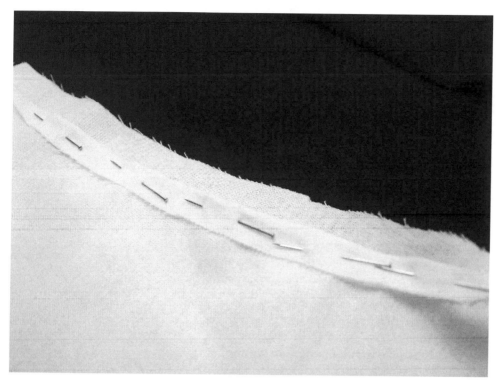

Figure 11-8. Folding and stitching the edges

You can leave the bottom hem for now since you will need access to the front of the lining fabric while adding the LEDs and programming the Pro Mini/LilyPad.

Then it's time to repeat the entire process for the outer fabric, but without implementing a matrix into that fabric. It is a good idea to make the covering dress piece slightly bigger, adding about 2 centimeters (0.8 inches) since the dress lining needs to fit inside it together with all the LEDs, as shown in Figure 11-9.

Figure 11-9. The dress with lining fabric; the matrix is on the inside

Once you have the outer dress cut and stitched, insert the lining dress. Now it is time to add the LEDs. Connecting the LEDs is not hard, but requires a bit of craftsmanship and time. The idea is that the LEDs will hold both fabrics together and, as a last step, the arms and neck opening will be stitched together. Do not do this now since you will need to be able to reach between the layers while adding the LEDs. If you are using a different pattern, make sure you have access to the entire area between the fabrics once you start adding LEDs. Be sure to start adding LEDs from the middle if you have two openings; or if your pattern only has one opening between the layers, start with placing the LEDs that are the furthest from the opening.

The idea is that the LEDs will be visible on the outside of the dress, like small pearls, and to attach them you simply poke them through the dress. But the tricky part is that you need to connect the LED legs to the matrix.

Start by taking a look inside your dress to find your LED markings and figure out the position on the outer fabric. Then take an LED and poke both legs straight through the outer fabric, as shown in Figure 11-10.

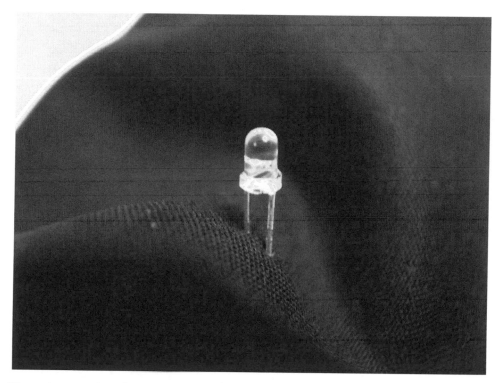

Figure 11-10. Poking both LED legs through the outer fabric

Be sure to start from an upper corner on either the front or back of the dress, and work down the five vertical lines. The next step is pushing one of the LEDs through the lining fabric; and once this is done, the two fabrics can't be separated. You want to make sure you have access to all the LED points.

Next, you have to find the spot where you have marked the LEDs inside the dress between the fabrics. Once you find it, bend one of the LED legs so that it lines up with the exposed connection on that side of the lining fabric, in between the lining and the outer fabric, as shown in Figure 11-11. If you have the ground conductive thread lines on this side, bend the shorter leg; if you have your power connections exposed on this side, bend the longer leg.

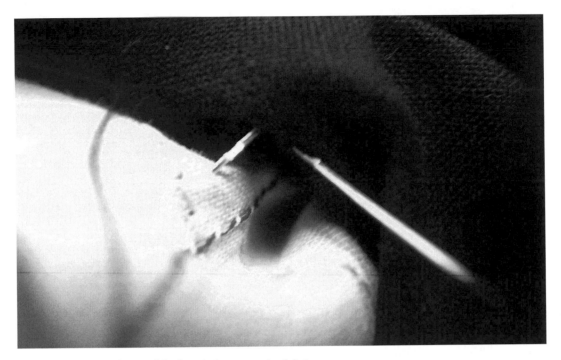

Figure 11-11. Bend one of the legs in between the fabrics

I found it easier to just leave the leg bent at this point and then poke the remaining leg through the lining fabric. Try to hold the LED and leg in place as you find the remaining leg on the inside of the dress. Again, bend the leg so it lines up with the conductive thread line exposed on the other side. At this point you need pliers and a cutter.

Start by cutting off half the leg since you do not want it to be too long; then bend the leg with the help of the pliers to make a small hook. The hook on the leg helps you attach the LED leg in between the conductive thread and lining fabric, as shown in Figure 11-12.

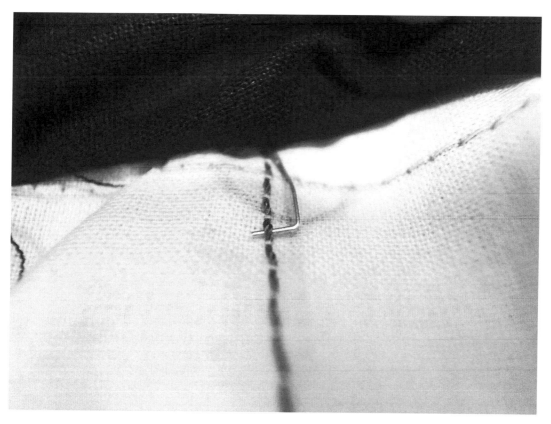

Figure 11-12. Hooking the LED to the conductive thread

Once the LED leg is hooked under the thread, squeeze the leg around the thread using your pliers. Be sure to make it nice and tight to make a good connection. Then do the same for the LED leg in between both fabrics. Take some time to also make sure that the leg has no contact with the other side of the fabric, that the thread has not been broken, and that the leg is really held in place, as shown in Figure 11-13. Because when you have done it once, it's is time to do it 59 times more, and if one of the legs slips away, it might be very hard getting access to that spot on the dress if it is in the middle of the matrix.

As I said at the beginning of this chapter, this might be the most time-consuming project in the entire book since adding the LEDs takes a lot of time and some finesse. But trust me when I say, it will be worth your while once you see the dress light up for the first time.

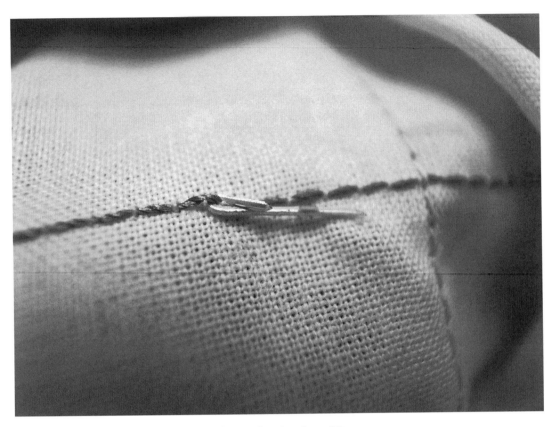

Figure 11-13. Securing the LED leg to the conductive thread line

Hooking Up the Arduino and Microphone

As soon as all the LEDs are in place, it is time to connect everything to the Pro Mini/LilyPad and add the microphone. Once again I will stick with the ADMP401 microphone circuit since I really like its very small form factor. If you choose to use another microphone circuit, you might need to modify the schematic accordingly.

■ **Note** It is very easy for loose conductive threads to cause a short circuit on your LilyPad, so make sure that you check twice that all the connections are separated.

Most wearable projects only use a few pins since wearable devices usually have very specific functionality and interactions. This is true for the beat dress, but because of the large number of LEDs, you will use most pins available; so planning how to connect everything is important. The schematic is shown in Figure 11-14. You will need to make some connections to the board from opposite sides of the lining fabric.

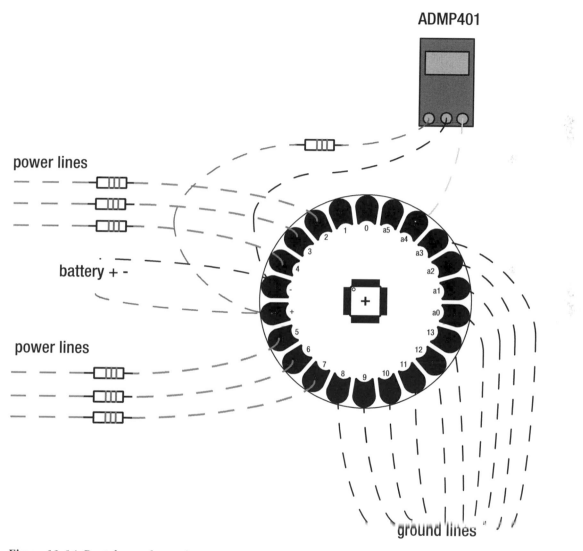

Figure 11-14. Beat dress schematic

Before making the final connection on the power lines from the matrix, you need to add a 220 ohm resistor for each power line. The ADMP401 microphone is only powered at around 3.3 volts, which is a lower voltage than what the LilyPad Power supply provides, so you will need to add another resistor on the power thread to the ADMP. Using a 220 ohm resistor will bring the voltage down to about 3.3 volts, which is what you want.

To avoid getting tangled with the LilyPad and to be able to sit down in the dress, I recommend putting the LilyPad in the front of the dress between the fabrics. Once all the necessary connections are made, it's time to test that the dress works.

Writing the Code

At this point, it might be nice to check that all the LEDs are connected properly. To do this, use the following example code that will loop all the LEDs one by one:

```
//Declare the power lines array
int power[]={2,3,4,5,6,7};
//Declare the ground lines array
int gnd[]={8,9,10,11,12,13,14,15,16,17};

void setup(){
//Set all power lines as outputs
  for(int i=0; i<6; i++){
    pinMode(power[i],OUTPUT);
  }
//Set all gnd lines as outputs and turn them high to block ground
  for(int i=0; i<10; i++){
      pinMode(gnd[i],OUTPUT);
      digitalWrite(gnd[i],HIGH);
  }
}

void loop(){
    //Loop through all the power line
    for(int i=0; i<6;i++){
        //For all power line loop through all the ten ground lines
        for(int j=0; j<10;j++){
            //Open up a ground port and turn power line on
            digitalWrite(gnd[j],LOW);
            digitalWrite(power[i],HIGH);
            //Wait for some time
            delay(500);
            //Close the same ground port and turn power line off
            digitalWrite(gnd[j],HIGH);
            digitalWrite(power[i],LOW);

        }
    }
}
```

Try the code out. If any of the LEDs do not turn on, check the connections; but hopefully everything will work on the first try. The code example implements two for loops, where the first one loops each power line. For each power line, every ground line is looped once, which turns all the LEDs on and off in one row and then switches to a new power line.

At some point it will be useful to figure out which LED is the first one in your array since this will be good to know later on when we try to control the pattern. To do this, you can either follow the first power and ground line (which are pin 2 and pin 8) declared in your code via the LilyPad connection back to the LED; or you could just write a simple sketch that turns power up pin 2 and opens ground on pin 8, and the LED will turn on. But first let's try the dress out with some crazy random patterns controlled by sound.

Lightning Beat

Before you get started, it's a good idea to check the kind of values your microphone is giving in case you need to modify the following sketch so that it fits with your microphone values.

```
int sound=18;

void setup(){
  //Start serial communication
  Serial.begin(9600);
  pinMode(18, INPUT);
 }

void loop(){
  //Print the microphone value
  Serial.println(analogRead(sound));
  delay(200);
}
```

The following code expands on the prior test code. Here you will implement the sound detection and additional functions for random patterns to display on the dress.

```
//Declare the power lines array
int power[]={2,3,4,5,6,7};
//Declare the gnd lines array
int gnd[]={8,9,10,11,12,13,14,15,16,17};
//Declare the microphone input
int sound=18;

void setup(){
  //Start serial communication
  Serial.begin(9600);
  //Set all the power lines as outputs
  for(int i=0; i<6; i++){
    pinMode(power[i],OUTPUT);
  }
  //Set all the gnd lines as outputs and turn them high to block gnd
  for(int i=0; i<10; i++){
    pinMode(gnd[i],OUTPUT);
    digitalWrite(gnd[i],HIGH);
  }
  //Activate a random seed on analog pin 4
  randomSeed(analogRead(4));
}

void loop(){
  //Print the microphone value
  Serial.println(analogRead(sound));
  //If the microphone value is smaller than 460 or bigger then 530
```

```
  while(analogRead(sound)<460||analogRead(sound)>530){
    //Run pattern two. This sketch includes 2 more patterns and you can switch
    //this pattern for either pattern1() or pattern3().
    pattern2();
  }
}

//Function for pattern one which is the test pattern
void pattern1(){
    for(int i=0; i<6;i++){
        for(int j=0; j<10;j++){
            digitalWrite(gnd[j],LOW);
            digitalWrite(power[i],HIGH);
            delay(2);
            digitalWrite(gnd[j],HIGH);
            digitalWrite(power[i],LOW);
            delay(2);
        }
    }
}

//Function for pattern two which lights up a random LED for a short while
void pattern2(){
  int r1=random(0,11);
  int r2=random(0,7);
  digitalWrite(gnd[r1],LOW);
  digitalWrite(power[r2],HIGH);
  delay(2);
  digitalWrite(gnd[r1],HIGH);
  digitalWrite(power[r2],LOW);
  delay(2);
}

//Function for pattern three which lights up three random LEDs for a short while
void pattern3(){
  digitalWrite(gnd[random(0,11)],LOW);
  digitalWrite(power[random(0,7)],HIGH);
  digitalWrite(gnd[random(0,11)],LOW);
  digitalWrite(power[random(0,7)],HIGH);
  digitalWrite(gnd[random(0,11)],LOW);
  digitalWrite(power[random(0,7)],HIGH);
  delay(2);
  digitalWrite(gnd[random(0,11)],HIGH);
  digitalWrite(power[random(0,7)],LOW);
  digitalWrite(gnd[random(0,11)],LOW);
  digitalWrite(power[random(0,7)],HIGH);
  digitalWrite(gnd[random(0,11)],LOW);
  digitalWrite(power[random(0,7)],HIGH);
  delay(2);
}
```

When it comes to the analog sensor, the value range from your microphone might be different from the one I used; this is why serial communication is initiated in the sketch, so that you can check your value range. As long as sound is detected within the range of the while loop, the sketch will run one of the pattern functions, depending on which one you put in the loop. The first one is the test code. The second one blinks one random LED very fast. The third one blinks three random lights.

The idea behind the third pattern was to blink three random lights, but I realized that I made a mistake once I uploaded to the dress. The third pattern turns on three random LEDs, but my mistake was that it turns off three random LEDs and not the same ones that are turned on. But I kept it this way since this is a classic example of "art by accident." The third pattern lights up random segments of LEDs and keeps them on until a new sound is detected, which looks very cool.

Remember that you probably have to modify the threshold in your while loop. The bigger the range in the while loop, the less sensitive the dress will be to sound. My recommendation is to set the values fairly high and put on some music with heavy beats in it, and watch how the dress interacts with the music. I have to say, it's a beautiful thing.

What is "high" depends on the values from your microphone, which might be different from the one I used. You can quickly check this out using the short sketch at the beginning of this section, and play music while reading the values.

Dress Texting

The last sketch illustrates how to use the dress as a text display. As a matter of fact, you can display anything that fits within a 6 × 5 pixel screen size. This is assuming you have followed the pattern for the LEDs in this project where the LEDs have been placed in line with one another because half the LEDs are in the front of the dress and the other half in the back of the dress in a rectangular grid.

To save patterns, you can implement an array where you store the state of every LED. In the following code example you will find an array called screen, which has 60 positions for all the LEDs. A 0 indicates an inactive LED and a 1 indicates an active LED. The goal is to loop through all LEDs and cross reference to the screen array. If it's indicated in the array that a LED at a certain position is active (set to 1), then this LED will be turned on and off. If the LED is set to 0, the LED will remain off. This is all done with very short delays to give the illusion that more than one LED is on at a time.

```
//Declare the power pins
int power[]={2,3,4,5,6,7};
//Declare the ground pins
int gnd[]={8,9,10,11,12,13,14,15,16,17};
/*Declare the pattern. The first 5 positions are for the first row on the back of the dress
and the next 5 are for the first row on the front. The next 5 positions are for the second row
on the back and so on. The spaces in the array has no effect on the program but is implemented
so you can visually separate the front LEDs from the back. The left column is for all LEDs on
the back of the dress and the right column is for the front. If you want to change the pattern
merely change the 0 to 1. Another good thing is that we can visually design a pattern. If you
look closely at the array below you should be able to see that the 1s form an A and a T*/

int screen[]={
1,1,1,1,1, 1,1,1,1,1,
1,1,0,1,1, 1,1,1,1,1,
1,1,0,1,1, 0,0,1,0,0,
1,1,1,1,1, 0,0,1,0,0,
1,1,0,1,1, 0,0,1,0,0,
1,1,0,1,1, 0,0,1,0,0,
//back       front
```

```
};

void setup(){
 //Set all power pins to outputs
 for(int i=0; i<6; i++){
  pinMode(power[i],OUTPUT);
 }
 //Set all ground pins to outputs and turn them high to block gnd
 for(int i=0; i<10; i++){
   pinMode(gnd[i],OUTPUT);
   digitalWrite(gnd[i],HIGH);
 }
}

void loop(){
 //Start counting the LED loops. After all LEDs have been looped the
 //counter will be reset.
 int activeLed=0;
 //Loop through the power pins
 for(int i=0; i<6;i++){
  //For each power pin loop, loop through all the gnd pins
  for(int j=0; j<10;j++){
   //If this LED position is set to active in the screen array
   if(screen[activeLed]==1){
    //Turn this LED on and off with a short delay
    digitalWrite(gnd[j],LOW);
    digitalWrite(power[i],HIGH);
    delayMicroseconds(10);
    digitalWrite(gnd[j],HIGH);
    digitalWrite(power[i],LOW);
    delayMicroseconds(10);
   }
   //For each LED loop add one to the counter
   activeLed++;
  }
 }
}
```

This sketch illustrates the core mechanics of implementing a program to add controlling possibilities to each LED. This will display a static image on the dress, which is the letter A on the back and the letter T on the front. By combining the sound activating part from the previous example, and adding more letters in new arrays, you can make the dress spell different things or make a small animation.

Once you have made it this far, you should have a good enough understanding of your dress matrix and the code so that you can continue developing cool new patterns.

Wrapping Up

The last step is to stitch up the bottom hem of the dress. I suggest leaving a small hole and attach some Velcro so that you can access your Arduino/LilyPad board for reprogramming and to access the batteries. If Velcro does not fit with your design, you could make the outer fabric a bit longer and skip attaching the bottom hem lining. Once you're done, you are ready to light up the night!

Even if the dress can be worn without adding an extra lining fabric, I recommend covering up the LED legs on the inside with *flizelin* or interlining so that when you go dancing in the dress, you don't scratch yourself on the legs if they come loose.

This project should put both your sewing and electronics skills to the test. It is essential that you understand the circuitry in this project before you get started since one wrong thread might render the project useless until you can find the short circuit. Hopefully you have also learned how to plan your wearable project since, in one sense, making a wearable project is much harder than a standard physical object because you have to calculate how it will be worn as well as work. But still, making an LED dress is a lot of fun, and if you stick with it, the reward is usually greater than anticipated.

With this project, you also learned more advanced programming techniques. The sketches in this chapter don't implement any new commands, but this proves the point that more advanced programming does not imply that you have to learn new things. You just have to rethink the things you know.

This project also demonstrated the basics of how most modern displays work using matrix connections and multiplexing signals, even if only at a very low resolution. Even in this age of high definition screens everywhere you look, an LED dress can still impress if you ask me.

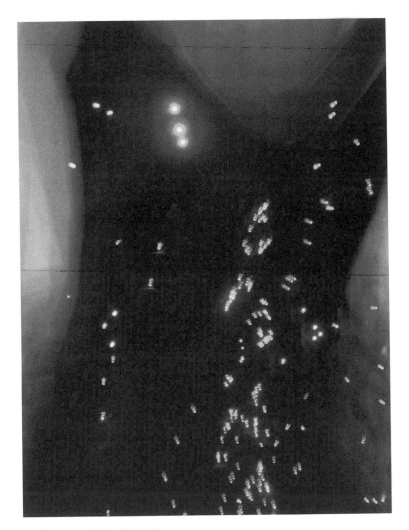

Figure 11-15. The final dress

CHAPTER 12

Shape Memory Flower

Making things move in wearable objects is always a tricky issue since creating movement from electricity usually requires some sort of motor. It is true that you can find very small motors like the ones used as vibrators inside mobile phones, but if you are looking for movement that is noticeable by sight, you probably need something bigger. There are materials, however, that can create movement without taking up too much space. One of those materials is shape memory alloy, which we will use to create a moving fabric flower. Constructing small things with shape memory alloy can be tricky, so this project focuses on how to make use of it on a smaller scale; and once you have understood the basics, you can start developing projects on a larger scale or implement the flower into a garment of your choice.

Materials and Tools Needed

The following materials and tools are needed to create your shape memory flower:

- IRFZ24 transistor (or a transistor that handles more than 2 volts and 1 ampere)
- Shape memory alloy wire
- Alligator clips
- LilyPad Pro Simple
- Battery connector clip
- 9V battery
- 3V coin cell battery
- LDR (mini photocell)
- Wire
- Fabric, multiple colors
- Normal button
- Small magnet (preferably a rare earth magnet)
- Crimp beads

Shape Memory Alloy

Shape memory alloy (SMA) is also known as nitinol, which is a metal composed of nickel and titanium. SMA is usually used in mechanical components like mechanical arms and leavers. It looks like ordinary metal wire and works the same way, but with one special feature: it remembers its original position. You can form it into any shape you want and when the wire is heated, it returns to its original position. To set a new original position, you need to heat the wire to 500°C (930°F) and keep it in that position for 5 minutes. The amount of heat that is needed to make it move depends on the SMA wire, but it usually is between 70°C and 90°C (158°F to 194°F). The only downside to SMA wire is that it is very expensive compared to normal metal wire. The good thing is that you usually don't need that much when it comes to wearables. In fact, SMA wire that is too long might become an issue since it needs a lot of power and might drain your battery too quickly.

Generating Heat

You can use any heating source you want to active SMA wire, such as hot water or a hair dryer, but in this project we will use electricity. Electric heating refers to the process of converting electricity into heat. You are probably already familiar with this concept from the use of electronic appliances like toasters or the seat heating in a car. You will find some sort of electrical resistor inside electronic heaters. A resistor can be made from a large variety of materials, but the point is that it is a material that is conductive but limits the flow of electrons.

Without getting too technical, the flow of electrons is limited because they collide inside the resistor and when they do, they vibrate a bit. It is these small vibrations that create heat in the material. The effect is similar to "rope burns" when rubbing any material very fast. If you do it slowly, nothing happens; but if you do it quickly, you can feel the material heat from the friction.

The same principle applies to the SMA wire: if you apply electricity to the wire, it heats up. High voltage and amperes make it heat up even faster, which makes the SMA wire return to its original position faster.

Testing the Wire

You can make a small test of the SMA wire without any programming and very little wiring. You just need two alligator clips, a 9V battery, and some SMA wire. Figure 12-1 shows how to connect the wire. You simply connect each end of the SMA wire to one side of each crocodile clip and the other two sides to the battery.

Start by bending and twisting the wire into any shape you desire.

Figure 12-1. *SMA wire connected to a 9V battery*

In Figure 12-1, I'm using a piece of SMA 20 gauge (0.8mm or 0.03in.) wire with the original position set to a spring. Later on in this chapter we will also cover how you can "reprogram" the original position of SMA wire.

Once the clips are connected to the battery and the wire, the wire starts to heat up. This takes a few seconds, but you should be able to see how the wire slowly starts to move towards the original position.

After a few seconds more, the wire has reached its original position, as shown in Figure 12-2, and you can disconnect it from the battery. If you leave it connected, the wire will stay in its original position, but will continue to generate heat. So always make sure to let SMA wire cool before you grab it. Also, you don't want contact with the SMA wire while it is powered because it is an open connection.

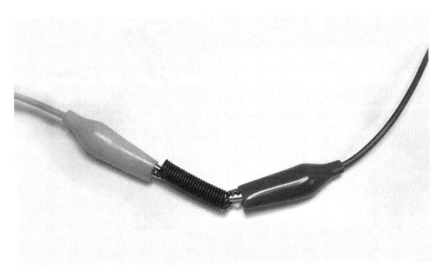

Figure 12-2. The SMA wire when it has reached the original position

It is a good idea to measure the time it takes for the wire to reach its original position because you will need to keep track of this time later on while writing the sketch for controlling it. It's hard to make exact calculations on this without testing because it depends on the length and thickness of your wire. The safest way is to test it yourself.

Creating the Flower

This project is not based on an entire garment but merely on a flower that can be fixed as a brooch on a garment. I say "fixed" because the idea is to hide the LilyPad and battery pack somewhere so that you get the magical effect of a fabric flower that moves.

This tutorial shows you how to make the most of a limited piece of SMA wire since it's very expensive, but you could use multiple SMA wires to make all the petals move around. I used SMA wire in combination with magnets to hold the flower together in a bud; when the flower is activated, it pops open.

Start by taking two pieces of fabric and lay them on top of one another. Mark a flower pattern on top of the first fabric. Use the length of the SMA wire you have as measurements for the length of the flower. The length of the wire should almost cover the diameter of the design (one petal tip to the other across the center). Be sure to make the shape of the flower a little bigger than the final shape you want since it will be turned inside out. Once your pattern is done, stitch along the outline all the way around the flower. You can do this by hand or using a sewing machine. You should end up with something similar to Figure 12-3.

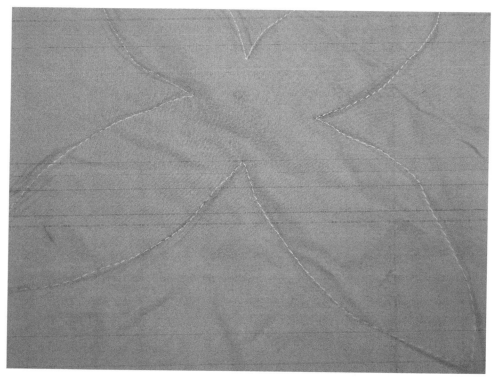

Figure 12-3. Stitching the flower pattern

Once you have stitched the flower, cut the flower out of the fabric along side the stitching. Once the flower is free, cut a hole in the fabric, which will be the back side of your flower, and turn the flower inside out from the hole, as shown in Figure 12-4. Repeat the entire process depending on the number of layers of petals you want, but don't make too many since you want to be able to fold all the petals together while still making room for the two magnets to attach through all the layers. For my flower, I made one additional layer in another color, making it eight petals in total.

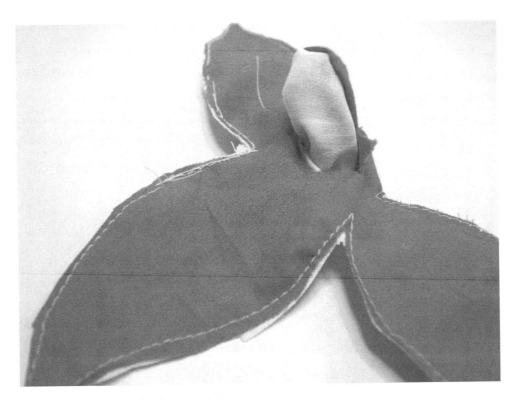

Figure 12-4. Turning the flower inside out

The next step is to prepare the SMA wire. I recommend using soft electrical wire to connect electricity through the SMA wire. As shown in Figure 12-5, soft wire consists of multiple thin metal strands inside the plastic casing, making it a bit more flexible than the normal wire, which is usually a single solid core.

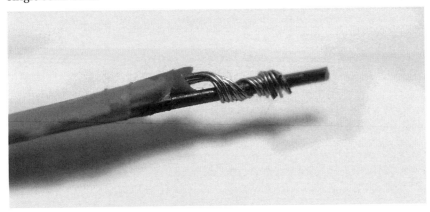

Figure 12-5. Attaching normal wire to the SMA wire

The tricky thing with SMA wire is that it can not be soldered because titanium has a very high resistance to heat. So you can use crimp beads to squeeze the wire and SMA wire together. A cheaper option is to place the normal wire along the SMA wire and hold it in place with some sticky tape. Then roll the stripped part of the normal wire around the SMA wire, as shown in Figure 12-5, and solder the normal wire. The solder will not attach to the SMA wire, but it will still help to make a snug connection between the wires. The reason for not using conductive threads to do this is simply because the SMA wires move around; and after a lot of testing, I haven't found a decent way to keep SMA wire from escaping conductive thread.

The next step is to place the SMA wire inside your flower, as shown in Figure 12-6. The idea is to use an SMA wire with the original position set to a straight line. To fit the wire through the hole on the back side you probably need to bend it a bit to make it fit. Make sure that the wire is placed so each end of the wire ends up in a petal opposite another.

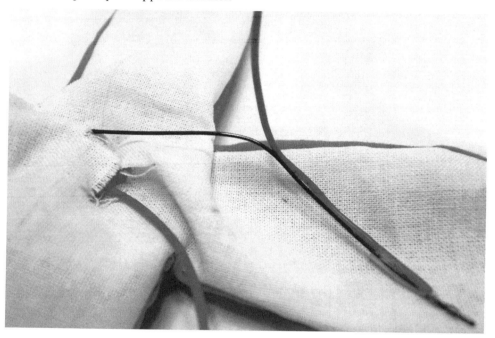

Figure 12-6. Placing the SMA wire inside the flower

The next step is to place the other layers of petals, depending on how many petals you want, behind the flower with the SMA, as shown in Figure 12-7. You need to make a hole in the additional flower to fit the soft wires.

To hold the flowers together, use a normal button and stitch it in the middle of the flower. Be sure to stitch through both fabrics, as also shown in Figure 12-7. Make a few thread loops around the SMA wire while stitching the button because this will help to hold the SMA wire in the middle. Do not worry about the SMA wire moving from side to side; you want a little bit of room for it to move around. Also, because it gets very hot, you don't want the fabric too snug around the SMA. Again, do not fear that the flower will catch fire. As long as do you don't heat it for too long after it has reached it original position, this should not be a problem.

Figure 12-7. Place the button in the middle of the flower

The last step at this stage is to add two magnets to the flower: one glued on top of the button and one at the end of a petal, as shown in Figure 12-8. It doesn't matter which leaf it is as long as you place it at the end. The magnets will hold the petals once you fold the flower together. Then, when you apply power to the SMA wire, it will eventually push the magnet apart and the flower will pop open. Now you are ready to try the button.

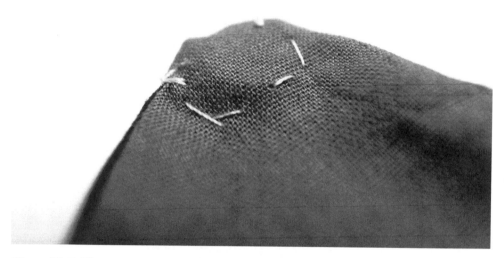

Figure 12-8. Place one magnet on the very tip of a flower petal

Fold the petals of the flower like in Figure 12-9. Start by folding the two petals with the SMA wire over the button with the magnet. Then you fold all other petals except the one with the other magnet, which you leave for last. This petal will hold the rest in place.

The idea behind this method is to save you from adding SMA wire to all the petals to make the entire thing move. If you now connect the soft wire to the 9V battery, after some time the flower slowly starts to move a bit. But the SMA wire is trapped under the magnets and the rest of the petals. Eventually enough pressure will build up in the SMA wire to separate the magnets and push the rest of the petals away, and the flower will pop open.

I used rare earth magnets, which are very strong, to keep the petals in place since folding the flower adds up to a lot of fabric layers. Normal magnets might work if you use fewer petals.

The next step is connecting the flower to a LilyPad Simple and adding some interaction.

Figure 12-9. *The magnets hold the flower together*

Connecting the Flower to a LilyPad

Since the flower needs a bit more electricity than can be provided by the LilyPad, you will need to add an additional power source in the form of a 9V battery. You will use a transistor to control the power that activates the flower. To make things a bit more interesting, I have added a light sensor (LDR) to the circuit in Figure 12-10. The idea is that with the LDR we can measure light and when we decide that it is light enough, we will activate the flower so it will "bloom."

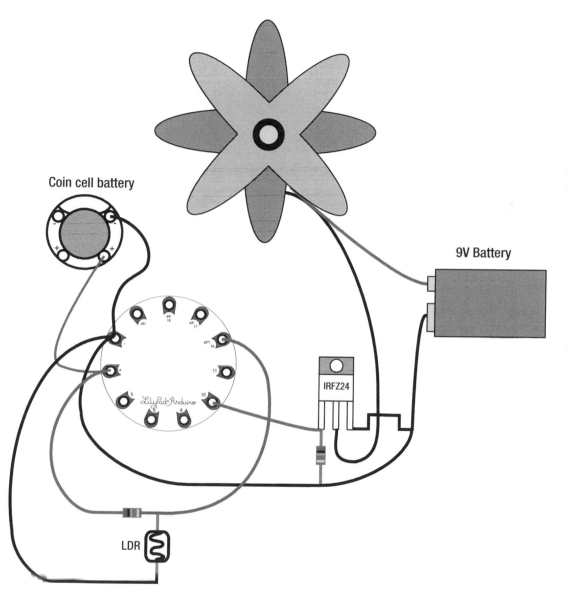

Figure 12-10. The shape memory flower circuit

One of the wires from the flower is connected straight to the positive of the 9V battery. It does not matter which end of the memory wire you connect. The other end of the wire is then connected to the middle leg (drain) of the transistor. It's an IRFZ24, the same transistor used for the solar-powered glow-in-the-dark bag. This is a very good transistor because it handles heat quite well. The right leg (source) of the transistor is then connected to the negative end of the battery.

243

The left leg (gate) of the transistor is connected both to a digital pin on the LilyPad and a 1K resistor, which in turn is connected to both the GND of the LilyPad and the battery. This is because without a shared ground connection, the LilyPad will not be able to activate the transistor. The resistor is used as a pull down resistor in this case, where it keeps the signal pin of the transistor low when there is no power on the digital pin from the LilyPad. This is to prevent the transistor from latching on, which means that even if the signal is turned off, the power running through the transistor from the flower back to the 9V battery keeps the connection open. With a pull down resistor, the signal pin is forced to off if there is no electricity from the digital pin.

The LDR is connected to the coin cell battery pack through a 10K resistor, and in the same connection it is connected to an analog pin. The opposite side of the LDR is then connected to ground.

Before you start to implement the circuit into a garment, it might be a good idea to test everything on a breadboard while testing with software. The problem here is that the LilyPad is great for sewing into fabrics, but not as handy for trying out circuits on a breadboard. I recommend using a standard Arduino board to do this. Figure 12-11 shows you how to set up everything on a breadboard.

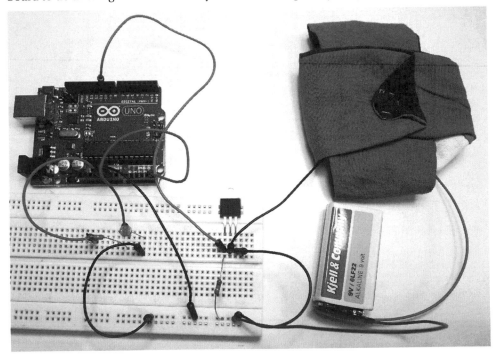

Figure 12-11. Testing the connections on a breadboard

While testing the circuit on a breadboard, you do not need the coin cell battery. The standard Arduino will be powered from the USB cable, so you can connect the LDR to the 5V pin. Remember, however, to calibrate your code if you later switch to a LilyPad board because the lower voltage from a 3V coin cell battery will give you a different value range from the LDR.

Programming the Flower

To start, you can check that the SMA flower is connected properly through the transistor by using the following example code:

```
//Declare pin 10 as flower
int flower=10;


void setup(){
  //Set the flower pin to be used as a output
  pinMode(flower,OUTPUT);
}

void loop(){
 //Turn the flower pin high
 digitalWrite(flower,HIGH);
 //Wait for 10 seconds
 delay(10000);
 //Turn the flower pin off
 digitalWrite(flower,LOW);
 //Wait for 30 seconds
 delay(30000);
}
```

This code will turn the flower pin high for 10 seconds to activate the transistor, which in turn completes the connection between the SMA wire and the 9V battery. With a fresh battery and approximately 10 centimeters (4 inches) of SMA wire, 10 seconds was enough to pop the flower open and for the wire to reach its original position. Depending on your wire, you might have to modify this time. Then the transistor is turned off and kept off for 30 seconds to give the SMA wire time to cool and to give you time to fold up the flower again. As before, the time might need to be modified depending on your wire and how fast you can fold the flower.

Next we will implement the code for reading the light state for the LDR, and use this information to decide when to activate the flower. We will also implement the use of Booleans in the next code example; let's take a moment to clarify their use.

Using Booleans

A Boolean is a datatype like integers and characters, but in contrast to these two types, which we have used for most of the sketches in this book, Booleans can only store two different values (which we touched on briefly in Chapter 3). The two values are true or false, which refers to the logical condition where a state of some sort is either true or false. Booleans are also used in logic philosophy. I can claim, for example, the statement:

It is snowing outside.

This statement is either true or false; it depends on if it's actually snowing outside. Now you might ask what logic philosophy has to do with programming, which is a fair question. You see, most programming languages build upon the same rules as logical philosophy. In programming we also make claims and predictions about things, which we then evaluate. For example:

```
if(lightSensor>350){
  //do something
}
```

This code is an `if` statement, which is a logical question that can be evaluated by connecting a sensor to an Arduino. We can then check if this statement is true or not. If it is true, this information might also be useful for other reasons inside your sketch; thus, you should store the answer to the logical question in a variable.

In the next code example, we implement the LDR data and there is a certain state we want to keep track of; that is, we want to know when we have left the SMA wire on for more than 10 seconds. After 10 seconds we want to turn it off and keep it off for some time; this is when a Boolean comes in handy. So, there are two things we need to keep track of:

- Whether or not the SMA wire is turned on
- The length of time the SMA wire has been on

Once the SMA wire has been on for 10 seconds, we can store a Boolean variable as `true` and use the Boolean every time we need to know if the wire has been on for more then 10 seconds. Once enough time has passed for the wire to cool down, we will switch it back to `false`.

It's no problem to turn on the wire for 10 seconds and then turn it off, but the Arduino doesn't remember the number of times it has turned it on. This project has a very physical problem related to it; the SMA wire gets very hot if kept on too long, which is why we turn it off for a minimum of 30 seconds.

To declare a Boolean is not anywhere near as hard as understanding why they are good to use. You simply declare them as any other variable type.

```
boolean myState = true;
```

The only difference is that Booleans can only be stored as `true` or `false`. To help you understand Booleans a little better, let's put them into context inside a sketch.

Adding the Light Sensor

This code example implements an LDR, which you can place close to the flower. When light shines on the LDR for enough time, the SMA flower is activated. This example code also implements a safety mechanism so that you can't turn the SMA flower on for more than 10 seconds at a time. If 10 seconds have passed, the flower will be turned off for 30 seconds to give the SMA wire some time to cool off.

```
//Declare pin number 10 as flower
int flower=10;
//Declare analog pin number 5 as LDR
int ldr=5;
//Declare a variable to store the time limit for the SMA wire
long heatLimit;
//Declare a boolean variable to tell we it's ok to turn the SMA wire on and
//set it as true from the start
boolean onOk = true;

void setup(){
  //Declare flower as a OUTPUT
  pinMode(flower,OUTPUT);
  Serial.begin(9600);
  heatLimit = 10000+millis();
```

```
}

void loop(){
  //Check how long since the Arduino was turned on and store the time
  long timeOn=millis();
  //Turn the flower off
  digitalWrite(flower,LOW);
  //Check and store the value from the LDR
  int ldrValue=analogRead(ldr);
  //While the ldr value is below 500 and onOK is true
  while(ldrValue<500 && onOk){
    //Check if the value goes above 500
    ldrValue=analogRead(ldr);
    //Keep the flower pin high
    digitalWrite(flower,HIGH);
    //Check the time and if has passed the heat limit
    if(millis()>heatLimit){
      //Set onOk to be false
      onOk=false;
    }
  }
  //If the onOk is not true
  if(!onOk){
    //Turn the flower pin off
    digitalWrite(flower,LOW);
    //wait for one minute
    delay(30000);
    //reset the heat limit to the current time plus ten seconds
    heatLimit = 10000+millis();
    //Set onOk back to true
    onOk=true;
  }
}
```

The first thing done inside the loop is to set the timeOn variable to the time passed since the Arduino was switched on. The information is needed later when we want to check if 10 seconds have passed since the SMA wire was turned on. The next step is to read and store the values from the LDR. Then we use this information as an end condition for the while loop. Again, you might have a different value range, so you might need to modify this value depending on which threshold you prefer for the amount of light needed to activate the flower. The while loop also has a second end condition that needs to be met for it to end: the onOk variable needs to be true. The onOk is set to be true when declared so the first time the loop runs, it enters the while loop when the LDR value is smaller the 500.

Inside the while loop, the flower pin is turned on, which starts heating the SMA wire. There is also an if statement that checks the amount of time the Arduino has been on and compares this to the time when the loop was entered, plus the time limit for heating the flower, which is stored in heatLimit. If the Arduino clocks into the loop at 15,000 milliseconds and the time limit is 10,000, the if statement will be true when the current time from the millis() function passes 25,000 milliseconds. Once it does this, the onOk variable is set to false because 10 seconds have passed since the SMA wire was turned on. If the onOk is set to false, it breaks the while loop and we continue on down inside the sketch.

After the while loop, there is an if statement that states:

```
if(!onOk)
```

This is the same as saying "if the onOk variable is not true." The ! sign is used to indicate the negative of something or, in other words, the opposite. The if statement needs to be stated as a logical question.

Computers are logical but not rational, so I understand if this might seem confusing to you. To write an if sentence like the previous one would be the same as if you wrote the following:

```
if(onOk == false)
```

In fact, you don't really need to use Booleans at all because the same operation could be done by using an integer variable that only stores a 0 and a 1. But again, as you get more advanced in your programming and your sketches start developing in size, I think you will see how using 0s and 1s can complicate the understanding of the sketch.

Learning programming is similar to learning spoken languages. To get better at communicating, you need to develop your vocabulary. In both cases, the more you words you know, the more efficient and elegant your pronunciation will be.

The ten-second rule might need to be modified depending on the length and thickness of your SMA wire. The SMA wire needs constant power for some time before it has reached its original positions or popped the flower open. But this code is set up so you can flash the LDR on and, in turn, the SMA wire on and off for short periods of time. If you do this for more than 10 seconds, however, the one-minute pause will still activate, even if the flower is not open. This is because the SMA wire, as I said before, gets very hot and we don't want to take any chances of burning something.

Reprogramming the Wire

The original position of SMA wire can be "reprogrammed." It is easy in theory and requires no actual programming. All you need to do is to set the SMA wire to any position you like and heat it to 150°C (302°F) for 5 minutes and it will lose its first position and adapt to the current position. The tricky part is that the SMA wire will try to find its original position at 70°C (158°F), and will keep on doing so until it eventually snaps into the new position. The hotter the wire gets, the faster it will move. But this also means that the wire will get hotter as long as you are powering it; that's why we add time for the wire to cool off. The length of time it takes until your wire has reached the original position depends on the length and thickness of the wire. These things can be hard to calculate, so I suggest you simply power the wire you have and measure the time it takes for it to reach the original position, as well has how long it takes to cool down.

It wasn't until I tried reprogramming SMA wire that I found out how surprisingly strong SMA is. Forget trying to do this with normal sticky tape. You will need a more sturdy construction. Figure 12-12 demonstrates a solution that is fairly easy to set up; it uses a piece of wood and some screws.

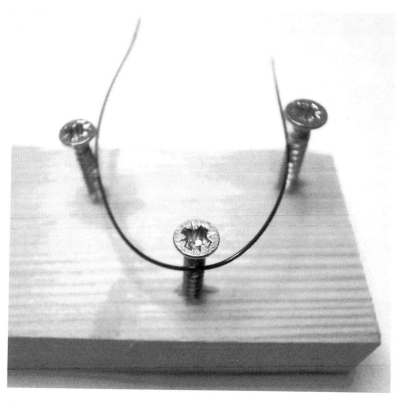

Figure 12-12. Reprogramming the SMA wire

I recommend using a heat gun to heat the wire. Keep moving it around to make sure you cover the entire wire with heat. Five minutes is an approximation, so you might need some trial and error before you get it right. But once you do, your wire should have a new original position and you can bend it any way you want. Once electricity is applied, it will find its way back to the new shape.

By using multiple wires with different positions, you can make the flower move back and forth creatively.

Wrapping Up

In this chapter you learned about the functionality of SMA wire. SMA wire is a lot of fun to play around with, but keep in mind that it generates heat—so always keep it at a distance from sensitive components and direct contact with your skin. The chapter also introduced you to the theory of how heat can be generated from electricity. Using electricity to generate heat, however, is very inefficient, and for this reason, in some countries there are laws preventing electric heating of homes. This is simply because you need a lot of electricity to generate heat. If you tried making the flower, you know that it drains the battery very quickly. Unfortunately, the best source of electricity is batteries when it comes to wearables.

The next chapter is based on another glowing dress, but this time around you will use another form of lighting: EL light. The cool thing with EL light is that it is not only manufactured in flat panels, but also as long wires that glow in different colors.

Figure 12-13. The finished flower

EL Wire Dress

It is hard to deny that LED dresses look cool, but designing with LEDs might seem a bit limited because if LEDs are placed too far from the microcontroller, construction often becomes more complex. Even with highly conductive thread, the length of the thread becomes an issue if you use threads that are too long because the thread can't carry the current needed to power the LEDs. Making long connections in wearables is also always a problem because it adds to the chances of the connections breaking.

In this project, we will focus on another dress that lights up, but instead of using LEDs, we will use EL wire. EL wire follows the same principles as the EL panels used in the solar-powered glow-in-the-dark project. EL wire offers a different range of creative freedoms than the use of LEDs and creates a different feel to your creation.

We will learn how to move beyond LilyPads and standard Arduinos, and use a board called an EL sequencer, by SparkFun, which is specially designed to power and control EL wire. The project also introduces alternative construction methods in implementing electronics into garments.

Materials and Tools Needed

The following materials and tools are needed to create your EL wire dress:

- EL sequencer
- 9V battery clip
- 12V inverter
- 4 EL wires, 3 meters each
- Fabric
- Velcro
- FTDI basic serial to USB converter or USB serial light converter
- 3.7 LiPo battery
- 6-pin male pin headers
- Male DC connector
- Eyelets and punch

- Sewing elastic approximately 0.5 centimeters (0.2 inches)

EL Wire

EL wire is short for *electroluminescent wire*, which consists of a thin, copper core coated with phosphor. When an alternating current is applied to it, it glows. EL wire is used in vehicles, decoration, safety signs, toys, and more. What makes EL wire special is that it produces a 360-degree light source; it is also flexible. Most EL wires operate between 20 and 220 volts, but the optimum operating rage is around 120 volts.

Figure 13-1 shows what's on the inside of the EL wire. In the center, you find copper core, which is covered with phosphor. The phosphor is then wrapped with a very fine copper wire. This is covered with a see-through protective sleeve. The last layer is the PVC, which gives the EL wire its color. When electricity is applied to the copper core and the fine copper wire, electrons jump from one side to the other; and when they do, they activate the phosphor, which makes it glow.

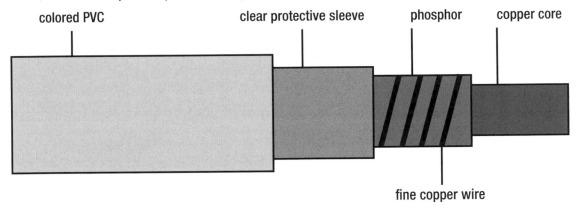

Figure 13-1. EL wire parts

EL wire can be cut in any length you want, but beware that it is very tricky to solder connectors because they need to be attached to the very thin copper wire and the core in the center without touching one another. We will use 3m EL wire, which can be purchased with pre-soldered connectors.

Later on when you power up the EL wire for the first time, note that the inverter will make noise; there is nothing wrong with it, so don't be afraid—this is perfectly normal (see Chapter 6 for more on EL inverters). EL wire works at 200Hz to 1000Hz, which means that the inverter is switching on and off very fast. This is known as oscillating; and it's this oscillating of the power that generates the nice glow.

The Dress Design

The inspiration for this project actually came from the fabric satin. Satin is a weaving technique the uses a minimal amount of interlacing fibers and is made from materials like nylon, polyester, and silk. By using very fine fibers and a minimal amount of interlacing, it is possible to produce very thin and smooth textiles such as satin. It's usually recognized by its glossy surface.

The problem with thin materials like satin when it comes to wearables is that it is hard to use any electronics with them since they are quite sensitive, and it's very easy to rip holes in the material. So the idea behind this dress is to divide it into two major parts, where both parts will be merely wrapped together instead of being attached together. One part is the dress itself and the other part is all of the electronics, which will be mounted into a belt worn under the dress. At the end of the project, both parts will be tied together with the EL wire.

Start by cutting three, 80 × 80 centimeter (31 × 31 inch) pieces of fabric according to Figure 13-2. This dress pattern is made to fit most body types, so the fabric cut size should fit all.

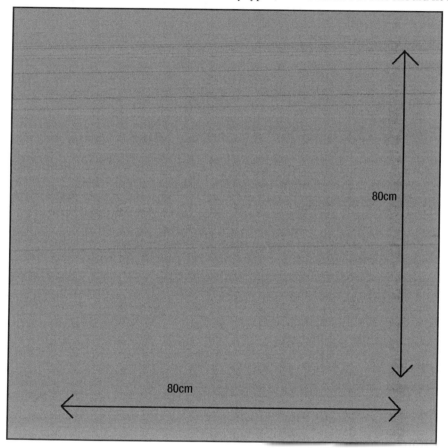

Figure 13-2. The base of the dress consists of three square pieces.

Once you have cut the pieces, it is time to sew them together. Start by sewing two of the pieces together along one of the seams, leaving approximately 20 centimeters (8 inches) at the top, as shown on the left in Figure 13-3. Then fold the last piece diagonally to make a triangle and sew two of the edges together with the other pieces, also shown in Figure 13-3, again leaving 20 centimeters (8 inches) at the top. This should leave a hole at the top once the three pieces are sewn together.

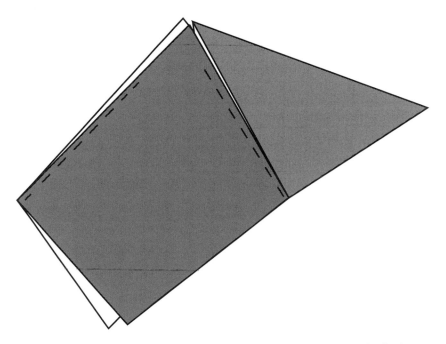

Figure 13-3. Sewing the pieces together, leaving 20 centimeters (8 inches) or so open at the top

If the three pieces are sewn together correctly, it should leave you with three triangular shapes, as shown in Figure 13-4. Two will be facing the front of the dress and one facing the back of the dress. At this stage, you can fold the under edges and stitch the hems. If you are using satin to make this dress, it might be a bit tricky since satin is very slippery; so take your time.

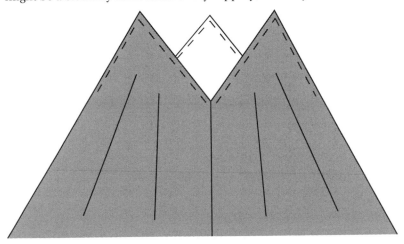

Figure 13-4. Stitching the top edges of the dress

After stitching the top edges of the dress, you might be wondering how the dress will be strapped to the body. This is where the EL wire will come into the picture at a later stage. To hold the EL wire in place with the dress, we will attach elastic loops to the dress, through which we can thread the EL wire at a later stage.

Figure 13-5 shows two loops placed at the points at the top of the dress. Cut approximately 4 centimeters (1.5 inches) of elastic and fold it in half. All the prior stitching can be done by using a sewing machine, but I found it very hard to stitch the elastic to satin with a machine; so I recommend doing this by hand. You can place as many elastic loops in the dress as you want, but I found that two are really needed at the triangular tips of the dress and it doesn't hurt to have one at the bottom of the V in the front and the Vs in the back. The idea behind the dress is that you can be creative in how the EL wire will hold up the dress by cross stitching all over the dress with these loops.

Figure 13-5. *Adding the elastic loops to the top corners of the dress*

All the electronics will be placed inside the dress, so you will need to make an opening for the EL wires. To do this you can simply use eyelets. I recommend placing them on the back of the dress along with the electronics since it is the easiest place to hide them, as shown in Figure 13-6. Most eyelets come with the simple tools needed to snap them into the fabric if you do not own a dedicated tool for this. But before snapping them in place, I recommend overlaying the inside of the dress with some stiffener or a small piece of more rugged fabric so the eyelets don't rip a hole in the dress.

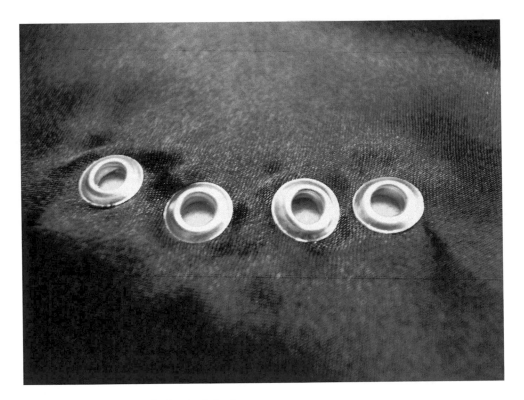

Figure 13-6. Eyelets on the back of the dress

Place the eyelets on the center back of the dress. Be sure to choose eyelets that are big enough to fit the EL wire through. The eyelets shown in Figure 13-6 have a 0.5cm (1/5in) opening through which you can squeeze the 4.6mm- (0.18in-) thick EL wire (equivalent to 5-gauge wire). You could also use bigger eyelets if you want more than one cable in each eyelet.

The last part of this stage is to fold and stitch the bottom edges of the dress—and the base construction of the dress is done. We can now move on to prepare the belt that will hold the electronics in place.

Making the Electronic Belt

Sometimes it might be hard to sew electronics into the fabric, as in the case of satin. Even though some electronics can be sewn into fabric, components like batteries might still be too heavy to hold in place in the actual garment. In these situations, designing a belt might come in handy.

This belt design is a fairly easy one. You just need a single piece of fabric. I recommend using a cotton fabric since cotton is usually quite sturdy, but you could use any fabric you like. Start by cutting the fabric.

The measurements in Figure 13-7 are relative, but you should add about 20 centimeters (8 inches) to your waist size.

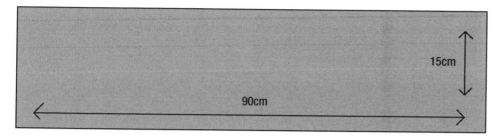

Figure 13-7. Belt pattern

The next step is to add elastic to the horizontal edges so that the belt is held in place around your waist. To do this, simply cut a piece of elastic approximately 10 centimeters (4 inches) shorter than your waist size. To make sure this is not too tight, try it out around your waist before cutting it.

Then place the elastic at one end of the fabric, fold the horizontal edge over the elastic, and secure it with pins, as shown in Figure 13-8.

Figure 13-8. Placing the elastic in the belt

Keep folding until you've almost reached the end of the elastic. Then it's time to stitch the fold using a sewing machine. Make sure you only stitch into the fabric and not the elastic since it needs to be able to move around inside the fold. Also, be sure to stretch the elastic all the way to the outer end of the belt and hold it in place with pins. Once you have stitched the fold, you can make a few stitches into the elastic at each end of the belt to secure it. Then repeat the entire thing for the opposite horizontal edge. You could also use a zigzag stitch to hold the elastic in place and then make the fold.

The next step is to mark onto the belt the placement of all your components. Place all the components on the belt like in Figure 13-9 and mark each side of every component with a pen.

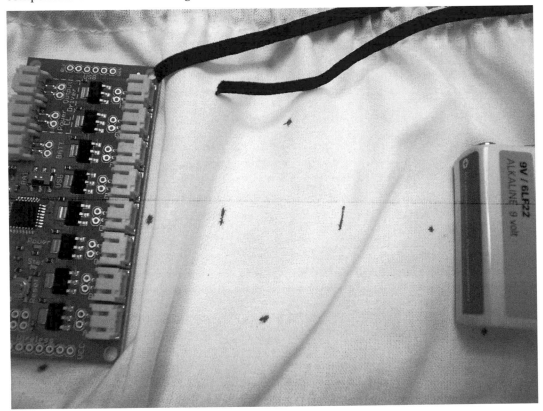

Figure 13-9. Marking the placement of the components

The placement of the components on the belt should be on the part that faces the back of the dress. It doesn't really matter where you place them as long as the cables reach where they need to be connected. The EL sequencer should be able to connect to the EL inverter; and the 3.7V LiPo battery and the EL inverter should be able to connect to the 9V battery. Be sure to leave enough space for the EL wire connection to the EL sequencer.

Once you have made your markings, start cutting pieces of elastic, which you will use to hold the components in place. The idea is to make a cross over each component using elastic. Make them slightly shorter than what is needed to cover each component so that they stretch over the components a bit.

Once you have all the elastic pieces, stitch the ends of the elastic bands to your markings. Once you are done, try fitting the components in place, as shown in Figure 13-10.

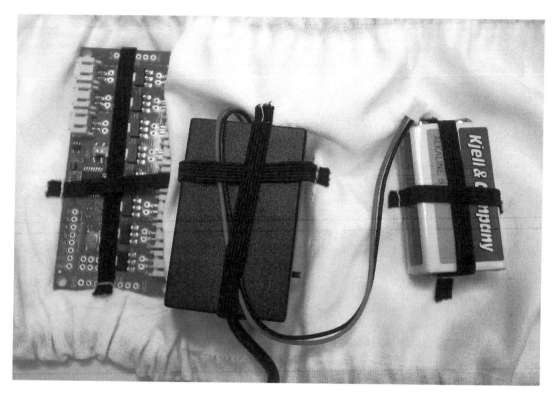

Figure 13-10. The components placed in the belt

When everything fits, the last step is to add some Velcro to the edges of the belt so the belt holds in place around your waist, as shown in Figure 13-11. I recommend using wide pieces of Velcro so that you can tighten the belt if needed.

Figure 13-11. Adding Velcro to the belt

Be sure to place the Velcro on opposite sides of the edges of the belt so that one overlaps the other when closed. You are done with the stitching part of this project once the belt is done, so let's have a look at the components and how to connect them.

EL Components

As you might have noticed, we will not be using an Arduino for this project; instead, we will use something called the *EL sequencer*, which is an ATMega-based control board specially designed to control EL wire or EL panels.

■ **Note** ATMega is the same microcontroller used on the Arduino board. This means that the EL sequencer can be programmed the same way as a normal Arduino board.

Recall that EL wire is not powered by DC but with high-voltage AC electricity. That is why we will need to include a 12V inverter in this project. The 12V inverter is a little black box (see Figure 13-12) where you connect DC electricity, and AC electricity comes out on the other side. It's the same thing used for the solar-power glow-in-the-dark bag project; but in this project, the inverter takes a larger input voltage. This is also why this inverter is a bit bigger than the 3V inverter used in the bag project. The reason for the bigger 12V inverter in this project is so that you can use a bigger battery—because EL wire needs quite a lot of power.

You can't use normal transistors to control AC power since they can only control DC power; but there is a component similar to a transistor called a TRIAC (triode for alternating current), which is used to control the power of the EL wire on the EL sequencer. TRIACs can conduct current in either direction, whereas transistors can only conduct current in one direction.

Figure 13-12. *The EL sequencer, a 12V inverter, and a 9V battery*

In situations where additional hardware is needed, some people (and companies) design boards that can be placed on top of the standard Arduino board. These boards are known as "shields" or "piggyback boards," which add more capability to the Arduino board.

For the use of EL wire, there is a board called EL Escudo, but the problem with this board is that it needs the standard Arduino board; but when it comes to making wearable devices, it is not very practical. Fortunately, there is the EL sequencer, which has a smaller form factor and integrated ATMega chip.

But before we have a closer look at the EL sequencer, I want to warn you to never touch the TRIAC while the board is powered. Figure 13-13 shows a close-up of two TRIACs on the EL sequencer.

Figure 13-13. A close-up of TRIACs on the EL sequencer

When working with electronics you are constantly dealing with open connections like the ones on the TRIACs; but the thing with these TRIACs is that when powered, they have 110 volts running through them. It will probably not hurt you if you come in contact with them, but speaking from experience, it is not a pleasurable feeling to receive a shock from them. This can easily be avoided by covering the TRIACs with some electrical tape, but make sure to keep your fingers away from the TRIACs while the board is powered and avoid connecting EL wires while it is powered.

You don't need to worry about any shocks when powering the EL sequencer from the USB port. The USB port is not able to power the EL wire, but only power the ATMega part of the board. To do this and ensure that your board works, try connecting the USB to serial converter with a USB cable to your computer, as shown in Figure 13-14.

Figure 13-14. USB to serial connector

The EL sequencer is sold without male pin headers soldered to the board. Male pin headers are metal pins used for connecting electronic components. The opposite connecter is known as a female connecter, like the pins on the standard Arduino board. The FTDI serial converter comes with female connectors soldered to the board. When making wearables, you want to avoid male pin headers on your components if not connected at all times since they have a tendency to get tangled into fabrics or scratch your skin. So in this case, you can just stick them into the USB converter temporarily to connect to the EL sequencer and make sure that the small green LED on the EL sequencer lights up. Once the code is uploaded, you can then unplug the male pin headers.

You can solder the male pin headers straight onto the EL sequencer if you want, but I would avoid it since it's easy to scratch yourself once wearing the board on your back. If you don't solder the pin headers to the board, you might need to hold the FTDI converter in place while you upload your code.

Adding Power to the Sequencer

The EL sequencer is made to be used with a 3V inverter; but with some minor modifications to the board schematic, it can be used with a 12V inverter in order to power the EL wire. The actual EL sequencer can only be powered between 3 volts and 4.2 volts.

Figure 13-15 shows the 3V inverter connected to the POWER and OUTPUT connector and the LiPo battery is connected to BAT. The inverter receives power from the battery through the POWER socket, then inverts it and outputs AC power back to the socket, also named OUTPUT.

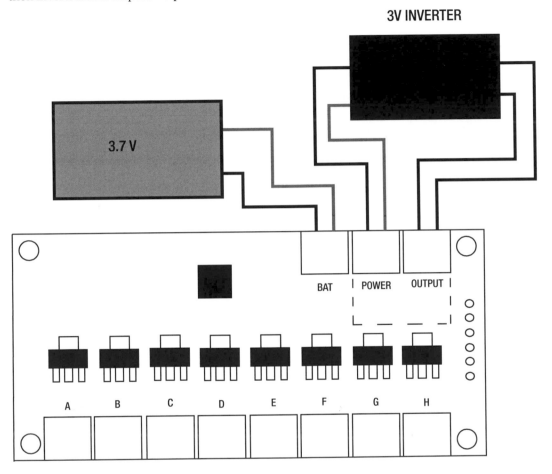

Figure 13-15. *Connecting a 3V inverter to the EL sequencer*

For our project, we will need to make a small modification and connect the power sources a bit differently, as shown in Figure 13-16.

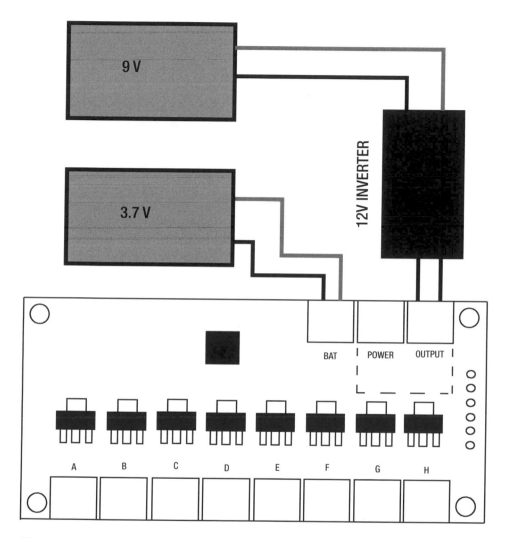

Figure 13-16. Powering the EL Sequencer with the 12V inverter

There is only one problem and that is that the OUTPUT doesn't share ground with the rest of the board. When using a 3V inverter, the ground is shared through the inverter between POWER and OUTPUT; but if we use the set up in Figure 13-16, there is nothing connected to the POWER socket. The good new is that this is an easy fix—and the basic principle of hacking.

■ **Note** A hacker is not a criminal that hacks into your computer and steals all your information. A true hacker is someone that modifies technology to fit her or his needs.

To make the hack that makes the setup in Figure 13-16 work, simply solder a connection between the two ground connections on POWER and OUTPUT, as shown in Figure 13-17.

Figure 13-17. Soldering a connection between the grounds

Use a small piece of wire to solder the connection, but don't turn your soldering iron off just yet. If it so happens (as with the 12V inverter I used for this book) that your inverter comes with a female DC jack, you might need to make a connector for the battery. All you need is a male DC plug and a 9V battery clip, as shown in Figure 13-18.

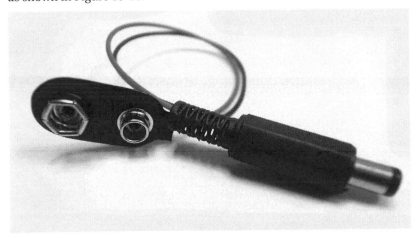

Figure 13-18. A 9V battery connector with male DC connector

Battery clips come with pre-mounted cable, but you will need to solder them to the DC connector. To do this, unscrew the plastic casing from the metal connector and you will find something like Figure 13-19.

The shorter metal piece is the positive side and the longer piece is the ground. The wire on the battery clips are usually color-coded red and black, which you know by now stands for power and ground. So simply solder the red wire to the short metal piece and the black wire to the long piece.

■ **Caution** Make sure to pull the wires through the plastic casing before you solder the cables since you will not be able to put it on afterwards. This is a mistake I have made many times.

Once you are done soldering, cover one of them with some electrical tape so that they don't come in contact by accident once the plastic casing is twisted on.

Figure 13-19. Soldering the DC connector

Once the DC jack is soldered, you have an entire plug-and-play system where all the components on the connector are merely held in place, not stitched, so this dress can actually be washed with ease compared to the beat dress.

But before we connect everything with the dress, let's take a look at how you program the EL wires.

Programming the Dress

When programming the EL sequencer, you do not need to power the board with a battery since it will be powered through the USB connection; however, if you want to try out the EL wire, you will need a battery to power it. Figure 13-20 shows you how to set everything up using the 12V inverter and a 9V battery. The EL sequencer has an onboard switch that says USB and BAT. To program the board, you need to set it to USB and disconnect the inverter. Once the sketch is uploaded, you will need to switch it back to BAT. Since there is a risk of getting shocked, I recommend always unplugging the battery and inverter when you upload your sketches. Once the code is uploaded, you can disconnect the FTDI converter, connect the inverter and battery, and switch to BAT, staying clear of the TRIACs. I know it's a bit of a hassle, but trust me, it beats getting a nasty shock.

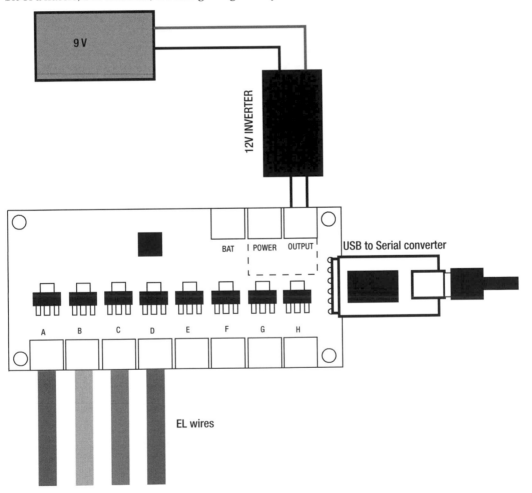

Figure 13-20. Test connections

The connecters named A through H are where you connect the EL wires. There are eight connectors available, but for this project, we will only use four. The reason I chose four is that the EL wires are 3 meters long, and 12 meters of EL wire is plenty; but if you feel that it is not enough, you have the option to add 12 meters more.

Test Sketch

Let's start with something simple to make sure all four wires work as they should. Controlling EL wire with the EL sequencer is no different from turning on and off LEDs. The only difference is that you are turning on 110 volts instead of 5 volts. Even though the connectors are marked A through H, they connect to pins 2 through 9.

```
//Declare pin 2 as A
#define A   2
//Declare pin 3 as B
#define B   3
//Declare pin 4 as C
#define C   4
//Declare pin 5 as D
#define D   5


void setup(){
  //Declare all pins as OUTPUT
  pinMode(A, OUTPUT);
  pinMode(B, OUTPUT);
  pinMode(C, OUTPUT);
  pinMode(D, OUTPUT);
}

void loop(){
  //Turn all the pins HIGH
  digitalWrite(A, HIGH);
  digitalWrite(B, HIGH);
  digitalWrite(C, HIGH);
  digitalWrite(D, HIGH);
  //Wait for a bit
  delay(2000);

  digitalWrite(A, LOW);
  digitalWrite(B, LOW);
  digitalWrite(C, LOW);
  digitalWrite(D, LOW);
  //Wait some more
  delay(500);

}
```

This code example simply turns the EL wires on and off. Before you try it out with your EL wire, make sure you have turned on your EL inverter. Some EL inverters have an on and off switch on them and some have additional modes in the same switch where you can set it to blink by itself; set it to full on mode on the inverter so you can control it from the EL sequencer.

Now you might wonder why we don't skip the EL sequencer and just use the EL inverter to make the EL wire blink. Well, to be honest, if you only want the dress to constantly blink or be fully on all the time, you could skip the EL sequencer. But if you want to connect more than one EL wire, it gets very messy; and if you want more advanced blinking, you need the EL sequencer.

The following example shows how you individually control each wire to have all four switch on and off one by one.

```
//Declare pin 2 as A
#define A  2
//Declare pin 3 as B
#define B  3
//Declare pin 4 as C
#define C  4
//Declare pin 5 as D
#define D  5


void setup(){
  //Declare all pins as OUTPUT
  pinMode(A, OUTPUT);
  pinMode(B, OUTPUT);
  pinMode(C, OUTPUT);
  pinMode(D, OUTPUT);
}

void loop(){
  //Turn all the pins on and off one by one
  digitalWrite(A, HIGH);
  delay(2000);
  digitalWrite(A, LOW);
  delay(500);
  digitalWrite(B, HIGH);
  delay(2000);
  digitalWrite(B, LOW);
  delay(500);
  digitalWrite(C, HIGH);
  delay(2000);
  digitalWrite(C, LOW);
  delay(500);
  digitalWrite(D, HIGH);
  delay(2000);
  digitalWrite(D, LOW);
  delay(500);
}
```

One thing that is new to this sketch is the declaration of the variables for the pins. They are not declared as integers this time around, but are declared using define. If you define a variable like this

```
#define D  5
```

you have declared the variable as a static variable, which means that it cannot be changed. If you declare variables as an int or a char, they are declared as dynamic variables, which means that the value stored in them can be changed at a later stage. The reason for using define is that it saves a bit of memory space since the computer knows the variable size and it will not change. If you declare it as a dynamic variable, the computer doesn't know what you might store later, so it makes the space in the variable very big—just in case you want to save a big number in it.

Random Blinking

As I mentioned in Chapter 10, if you print from an analog pin without anything connected to the pin, you will still receive values that jump around a bit. Recall that this is because of static electricity in the air, which affects the pin even when nothing is connected. Static electricity is perfect for using as a variable for generating a random number. The following sketch introduces randomness to the blinking:

```
//Declare a variable to store the random number
int randomNbr=0;

void setup() {
  //Start serial communication
  Serial.begin(9600);
  //Uses analog noise on a analog pin as base for generating random numbers
  randomSeed(analogRead(0));
}

void loop() {
  //Generate a random number and stor it into randomNbr
  randomNbr=random(5,20);
  //Print the random number
  Serial.println(randomNbr);
  //Wait for a bit
  delay(500);
}
```

So, the random seed gives the random() command a new starting point for generating random numbers every time the Arduino is reset. This provides random numbers that are more arbitrary.

Adding Randomness to the Blinking

The following sketch introduces a bit of randomness to the blinking where random EL wires are lit for a random amount of time:

```
//Declare an array to store all the wires
int wire[]={2,3,4,5};
//Declare a variable to store a random pin
int randomPin=0;
//Declare a variable to store a random time
int randomTime=0;

void setup(){
  //Loop all positions of the array
  for(int i=0; i<5; i++){
```

```
    //Declare all wires as OUTPUTs
    pinMode(wire[i],OUTPUT);
  }
  //Start the random seed and use analog pin 0
  randomSeed(analogRead(0));
}

void loop(){
  //Generate a random pin to turn on and off
  randomPin=random(0,5);
  //Generate a random on and off time
  randomTime=random(100,500);
  //Turn random pin high
  digitalWrite(wire[randomPin],HIGH);
  //Delay a random time
  delay(randomTime);
  //Turn the same pin low
  digitalWrite(wire[randomPin],LOW);
  //Delay with the same random time
  delay(randomTime);
}
```

Note that you have to generate the random time and pin before you turn each EL wire on and off, so the same wire that is turned on will be turned off. The EL sequencer can power all of them at the same time, so if you want a different effect with a random number of wires on at the same time, you can do as follows:

```
int wire[]={2,3,4,5};
int randomPin=0;
int randomTime=0;

void setup(){
  for(int i=0; i<5; i++){
    pinMode(wire[i],OUTPUT);
  }
  randomSeed(analogRead(0));}

void loop(){
  digitalWrite(wire[random(0,5)],HIGH);
  delay(random(100,500));
  digitalWrite(wire[random(0,5)],LOW);
  delay(random(100,500));
}
```

The difference between this example code and the previous one is that the random pin and time is generated inside the commands instead of being generated and stored in variables. This will turn a random number of wires randomly on and off instead of just one random wire.

Fading the Wires with PWM

On the standard board, there are pins that have a tilde sign (~) next to them. These pins are also called PWM pins, which stands for *pulse width modulation*. As you know by now, if you turn a digital pin on, it goes from 0 volts to 5 volts; but it does not do this instantly. It takes a bit of time until it gets all the way to 5 volts, even if it's very little time. It's faster than any human can notice, but not faster than the Arduino.

A PWM pin on the Arduino has a special function that can switch it on and off very fast; even faster than the time it takes for the pin to fully charge to 5 volts. This means that these pins can switch off before the voltage has reached 5 volts and then on again. If you then switch a pin on and off repeatedly at a very high speed, you can control the voltage, depending on the length of time that you leave it on. This is how the analogWrite() command works: it controls the voltage of a pin by cutting the power at different voltage levels and turning it on again to keep it at a certain level. This is how you would fade the light of a LED, for example.

Turning the wires on and off in random patterns looks pretty cool, but you might want to fade them as well. This creates a problem, however, since EL wires store electricity, which remains for a bit after the electricity has been turned off. In this case, we are talking microseconds, but even this short time creates a problem with the analog write command. As I noted, to fade LEDs we use the PWM pins with the analog write function to control the intensity of the LEDs.

So if EL wire is charged with a load of electricity, they can stay on for a little longer after the pin has been turned off, and the analog write function will not work so well.

This said, the analog write command still works for fading the EL wire, but it is not as smooth a fade as you get with LEDs. The EL wire will probably flicker a bit.

But if you ask me, these complications should be embraced. You probably can get around the flicker with some advanced coding or additional components, but sometimes I think you should embrace when things do not work out as expected. When I set out to make this example, I expected I could fade the wire as I would an LED; but when I saw the weird flickering, I actually liked it and decided to incorporate it into the design of the sketch rather than preventing it because this is one thing that separates EL from LED light. To get the same effect with LED as naturally happens with the EL wire would be very hard. In a sense, this is what this book is about: to learn the tools and materials, and how they act and react so you can make them your own materials for designing wearables.

The final code example for this project combines the parts for prior sketch examples into an example that I think shows the beauty of randomness. Since not all of the connectors on the EL sequencer are PWM, you might need to move some of the EL wires. The connectors that are PWM are B, D, E, and H.

```
//Declare an array to store the wires
int wire[]={3,5,6,9};
//Variable to hold random number for activating pins
int randomPin=0;
//Variable to hold random time
int randomTime=0;
//Variable to hold random loop
int randomLoop=0;

void setup(){
  //Loop through the array
  for(int i=0; i<5; i++){
    //Declare all pins as OUTPUTS
    pinMode(wire[i],OUTPUT);
  }
  //Start a random seed and use analog pin 0
```

```
    randomSeed(analogRead(0));}
void loop(){
  //Loop through a random amount which will control the intensity of the EL //wires
  for(int i=0; i<random(255); i++){
    //Set the intensity of a random El wire
    analogWrite(wire[random(0,5)],i);
    //Delay 10 milliseconds so we can see the fading
    delay(10);
  }
  //Wait a random time once the EL has faded up
  delay(random(0,1000));
  //Loop through a random amount which will control the intensity of the EL //wires
  for(int i=random(255); i>0; i--){
    //Decrease the intensity of a random El wire
    analogWrite(wire[random(0,5)],i);
    //Delay 10 milliseconds so we can see the fading
    delay(10);
  }
  //Turn all of the EL wires off
  for(int i=0; i<5; i++){
    digitalWrite(wire[i],LOW);
  }
  //Wait for a random amount of time
  delay(random(0,1000));
}
```

This sketch will basically fade the EL wires up and down at random intervals, which gives the entire thing a very electric feeling.

Finalizing the Dress

The last step to finalizing the dress is to literally wrap up the dress. Start by mounting all the electronics to the belt and around your waist. Then pull the EL wires through the eyelets, as shown in Figure 13-21, and start wrapping. There is no correct way to wrap the EL wires really, but the design was made for you to be as creative as you want. The idea is that the EL wires will work as straps for the dress, so the easiest way is to start with the supporting structure looping the EL wire through the elastic loops.

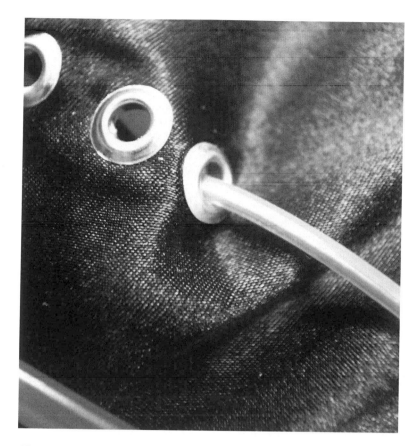

Figure 13-21. *Pull the EL wires through the eyelets*

The dress design might not be the most practical, and you might need a friend to help you, but trust me when I say you will not go unnoticed wearing this dress. Figure 13-22 shows how the dress might look in daylight.

Figure 13-22. The dress in daylight

Unfortunately, you can't really see the glow in direct sunlight, but as soon as it is dark, you notice the neon-like glow, as shown in Figure 13-23.

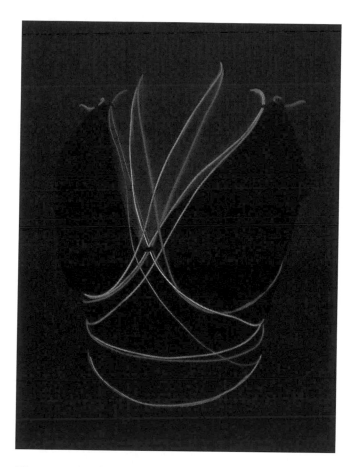

Figure 13-23. The dress in the dark

Wrapping Up

In this chapter, you were introduced to a specialized alternative to standard Arduino boards. Both the standard Arduino board and the LilyPad are general-purpose boards, even if the LilyPad is made especially for wearables. You can find these special types of boards by browsing the Internet. They are created for a specialized area of use, but are still compatible with the Arduino IDE and programming language.

The chapter also introduced a different method in the construction of wearables, showing that sometimes it is best to separate a project into parts than build everything into one piece. We also looked at more-advanced options for dealing with randomness in programming.

If you have done all the projects in this book and reached this point, you should feel comfortable working with electronics and textiles. You have hopefully started to generate some ideas about creations of your own. Once you have come this far, you might be interested in minimizing and optimizing your project—which will be the next and last topic of this book. In the final chapter, we will focus on how to make things tiny.

CHAPTER 14

Making Things Tiny

In this last chapter, we will dig deeper into the IDE (integrated development environment) of the Arduino and focus on how to make your own "bare bones" microcontroller board. When it comes to wearables, size matters. As I have said before, the Arduino standard board is the best microcontroller I have found for making rapid prototypes with electronics. The LilyPad is great for when you have reached the point of making things wearable. But then there is the point where you want to finalize your project and leave things in place. These boards might be an unnecessary cost because you probably won't use the entire functionality of the board.

So in this chapter we will introduce the use of a microcontroller called the ATtiny. As the name suggests, this microcontroller is very small. What makes it a good option is that it is inexpensive. It is also compatible with the Arduino programming language and can be programmed through the IDE.

You will also learn more about the inner workings of the IDE, as well as how to modify your IDE by adding libraries to it.

Materials and Tools Needed

You will need the following materials and tools for this project:

- Arduino Uno board

- ATtiny25/45/85

- Wires

- Conductive ink

- LEDs

- $10\mu F$ capacitor

- Conductive thread

- 1 kilohm resistors

- 200 ohm resistors

- 1 megohm resistor

- Fabric

- 8 ohm speaker

- 3V LilyPad coin cell battery holder

- 2 × 1.5V AA batteries

- AA battery pack

- Header pins

- Transparent overhead paper

- Glue

The ATtiny

ATtiny is a collective name for a set of microcontrollers from Atmel, the same company that manufactures the ATmega used for the Arduino boards. The limitation to these microcontrollers is that they don't have full support of all the functions of the Arduino board and they have much less memory; but the benefit is that some ATtinys are very small in size and some can even be powered as low as 1.8 volts. Yet even though they are tiny, they pack a lot of punch.

This chapter focuses on the ATtiny25, ATtiny45, and ATtiny85; the differences between these chips are memory space and price. Usually the price does not differ that much, but if you want my suggestion, you should buy either the ATtiny45 or the ATtiny85 because the ATtiny25's small memory might become a problem if you make your sketches too big.

Like most microcontrollers and other electronic components, all three chips come in different form factors. The form factor we will use is known as a DIP, which stands for *dual in line package*, an electronic device package. Figure 14-1 shows an ATtiny45 DIP format. It, the ATtiny25, and the ATtiny85 each have eight legs.

Figure 14-1. DIP ATtiny with 8-pin DIP

The original design of the DIP was created by Bryant Rogers in 1964. It was designed with a rectangular shape to make it easier to pack. Not all DIPs have eight legs; they come in a range of numbers—like the ATmega chip on the standard Arduino board, which has 28 legs. In electronic equipment, you often find these chips mounted in a socket (like the Arduino in Figure 14-2) or soldered to the circuit board.

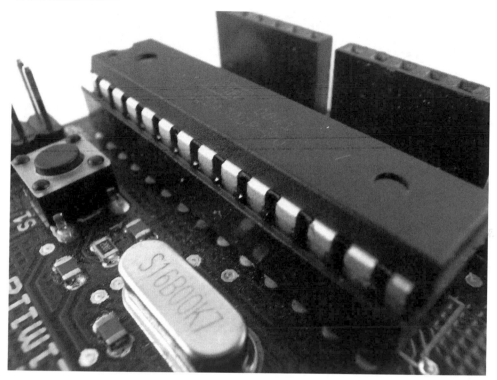

Figure 14-2. DIP ATmega328 mounted in a socket

The other form factor of these microcontrollers is known as SMT or *surface-mounted technology*, where the component is mounted to the surface of the circuit board instead of through a hole connection. DIPs are surface-mounted technology; the legs of the component go through the circuit board and the component is soldered on the other side. The benefit of using SMT components is that they are often smaller than DIP, but require machines to solder them. Figure 14-3 shows a surface-mounted ATmega chip, which can be found on the LilyPad.

Figure 14-3. The surface-mounted ATmega328 on the LilyPad

The DIP ATtinys are tiny enough for this chapter and probably most projects that need one.

The Arduino IDE does not support the ATtiny by default, but you can enable it to program an ATtiny by adding a library to the IDE.

Libraries and Programming the ATtiny

There are tons of cool stuff you can do with the Arduino, and even if the Arduino team consists of very clever people, it is hard for them to think of all its possibilities. Conversely, there are other clever people that also know a bit about electronics and have figured out how to make a lot of these cool things happen. To make these cool things happen, you might need to change either the Arduino board or the Arduino IDE to add functionality that was not there from the beginning.

The nice thing about the Arduino is that it is open source, which means that you are free to make any changes you want to the hardware and software to fit your needs. In many cases, these things might be very difficult for most people to figure out by themselves. This is where we strike to the core of open source. People working with open source believe in sharing knowledge and, in a more practical sense, the sharing of code. In a way, it is very similar to the ideas behind the craft of sewing, where patterns and techniques are shared between people. So in the same sense that someone might lend you a pattern for a dress, there are people that will lend you their code.

When someone has figured out how to do something with the Arduino that could not be done by default or is very complicated, he or she makes it a library to share with other people. In essence, a library is a folder with code in it; and to be able to program ATtinys from the Arduino IDE, we need to modify it by including a library that will add this support.

Adding a Library

This chapter covers the use of Arduino-Tiny, which is a set of ATtiny "cores" for the Arduino platform created by David A. Mellis, Renè Bohne, R. Wiersma, Mark Sproul, Alessandro Saporetti, and Brian Cook. To start, you will need to download the zip file containing the library, which is at http://code.google.com/p/arduino-tiny/.

Once you have downloaded the folder, you will need to figure out where your sketch folder is stored on your computer. The easiest way of doing this is to start your Arduino IDE and open File Preferences. The Preferences window, like the one shown in Figure 14-4, should display your sketch folder location.

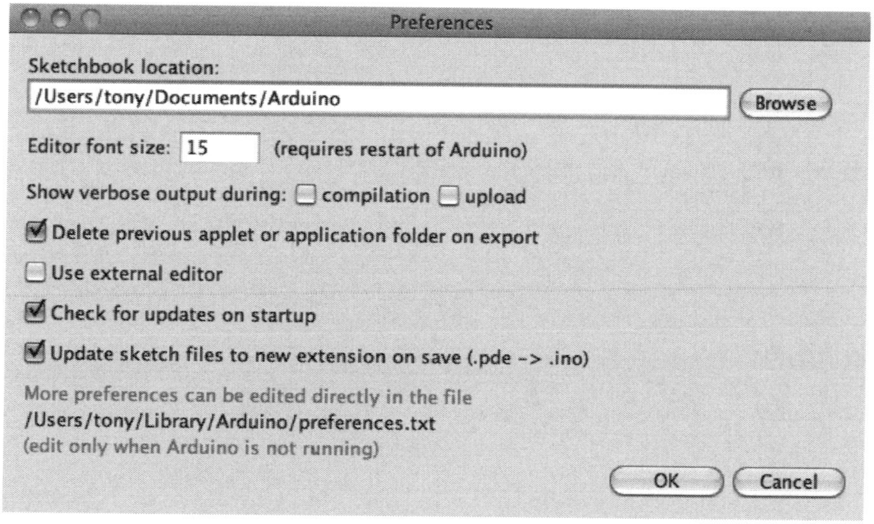

Figure 14-4. Locating your sketch folder

On my computer, the Arduino sketch folder is located in /Users/tony/Documents/Arduino. Inside your Arduino folder, you will find all your saved sketches. Create a new folder here called hardware.

After creating the hardware folder, unzip the zip file you downloaded and place the folders named tiny and tools inside the hardware folder, and you are done. If you have your IDE open, you will need to close it and open it again. The next time you open up the IDE, the tiny library (which includes the cores needed to program the ATtinys) will be available.

A core library is a set of code and functions for a particular microprocessor. By default, core libraries are included in the IDE for ATmega processors since this is what is used on the Arduino boards. But "libraries" also refers to prewritten code that is made into a function that can be called from your sketch. You might end up with a long piece of code when writing the code for controlling a complex component like an LCD screen. So instead of writing the code every time you want to use a LCD screen, you can make it into a library with functions, put away the code, and then call these functions from the sketch.

283

Tiny Speed

The tiny library adds the cores needed to program ATtiny chips. To check that the library is installed correctly, open your Tools Board menu. You should find that the list has gotten longer. The following list of boards should be present:

- ATtiny84 @ 16 MHz (external crystal; 4.3 V BOD)

- ATtiny84 @ 8 MHz (internal oscillator; BOD disabled)

- ATtiny84 @ 1 MHz (internal oscillator; BOD disabled)

- ATtiny85 @ 16 MHz (external crystal; 4.3 V BOD)

- ATtiny85 @ 16 MHz (internal PLL; 4.3 V BOD)

- ATtiny85 @ 8 MHz (internal oscillator; BOD disabled)

- ATtiny85 @ 1 MHz (internal oscillator; BOD disabled)

- ATtiny45 @ 8 MHz

- ATtiny45 @ 1 MHz

- ATtiny85 @ 128 KHz (watchdog oscillator; 1.8 V BOD)

- ATtiny25 @ 8 MHz

- ATtiny25 @ 1 MHz

- ATtiny4313 @ 8 MHz

- ATtiny4313 @ 1 MHz

- ATtiny2313 @ 8 MHz

- ATtiny2313 @ 1 MHz

As you can see, there are a few options when it comes to ATtiny processors; but for this chapter we will only focus on the ATtiny25, ATtiny45, or ATtiny85. There are even different options among the same processor, in which you can choose either 1MHz, 8 MHz, or even 16MHz for the ATtiny85.

These numbers refer to the clock speed of the microcontroller: all processors need to be able to keep track of time, or they will not function. In a sketch you tell the microprocessor what to do, but to be able to do it, it needs to be able to keep track of time for the processor to know when it is time to do something. The ATtiny has an internal clock inside the actual chip that can run at either 1MHz or 8MHz. There are also external clocks that use oscillator crystals to boost them to 16MHz. Without getting too technical, these clocks take an electrical input, and then they output this electricity by oscillating it up and down at a steady rate; the processor is able to tell time from this oscillation.

This is why a 1.5GHz computer is faster than a 1GHz computer—because the first computer can slice time smaller than the other computer, which also means it can process programs faster. Today most laptops operate at 2GHz (2,000,000,000Hz) and more, so 8MHz (8,000,000Hz) might not sound that impressive. But laptops need to keep track of a whole lot of stuff inside your computer, such as keeping track of your keyboard, mouse, and screen, as well as operating a bunch of programs at the same time. Yet when it comes to making wearables, you usually just want to keep track of some input and some output; in that case, 8MHz is usually enough. You can add an external clock to the ATtiny to make it work at 16MHz, but I think this defeats the purpose of this chapter since we are trying to make things as tiny as possible. So we will stick with the internal clock and run things at 8MHz.

Programming the ATtiny

To program the ATtiny you need an ISP, which stands for *in-system programmer*. You can buy an ISP like the USBtinyISP or the AVRISP mkII, which connects via USB to your computer; or better yet, you can program a normal Arduino board into an ISP.

The process is simple and the only thing you have to do is upload the Arduino ISP as any other sketch to your Arduino Uno board. The sketch can be found in File ➤ Examples ➤ ArduinoISP. Once the ArduinoISP sketch is on the board, you need to hook up the ATtiny chip to the Arduino board using a breadboard and some jumper wires.

Figure 14-5 shows the pin layout of the ATtiny.

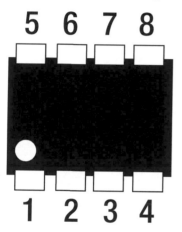

Figure 14-5. ATtiny pin layout

Most DIP chips look identical from both sides with the exception of a small dot in one of the corners. The dot always indicates pin 1 and then they follow in canonical order, with the numbering on the opposite side. The pins functions in Figure 14-5 are as follows:

1. RESET
2. Analog input 3
3. Analog input 2
4. GND
5. VCC
6. Analog input 1
7. Digital pin 1 (PWM)
8. Digital pin 0 (PWM)

VCC and GND are power and ground. The RESET is used to reset the ATtiny. The rest are programmable pins; their numbering refers to the pin numbering you use inside your sketch.

To program the chip, place the ATtiny over the middle break of the breadboard and connect the wires according to the schematic in Figure 14-6. To clarify the connection that needs to be made, the Arduino should connect to the ATtiny as follows:

- ATtiny 1 to Arduino 10
- ATtiny 4 to Arduino GND
- ATtiny 5 to Arduino 5V
- ATtiny 6 to Arduino 13
- ATtiny 7 to Arduino 12
- ATtiny 8 to Arduino 11

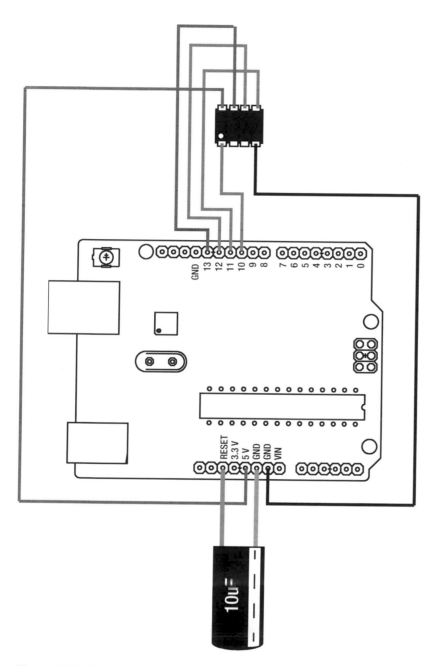

Figure 14-6. How to connect the ATtiny to a standard Arduino board

Pins 2 and 3 on the ATtiny are not connected for programming it. In Figure 14-6 you will also find an additional component, which is needed to program the chip; it is a 10µF capacitor connected to the Arduino RESET pin and GND. This is used to prevent the Arduino from resetting itself while uploading the sketch for the ATtiny. You need to look on the side of the capacitor to tell which leg of the capacitor needs to be connected. The GND leg side is marked with a white strip with negative (–) signs on it.

The next step is to upload a simple sketch that checks that everything works.

```
void setup() {
  //Set pin number 0 on the Attiny to a OUTPUT
  pinMode(0, OUTPUT);
}

void loop() {
//Turn pin number 0 HIGH
  digitalWrite(0, HIGH);    // set the LED on
//Wait for a bit
  delay(2000);                  // wait for a second
//Turn pin number 0 LOW
  digitalWrite(0, LOW);    // set the LED off
//Wait for a bit
  delay(2000);                  // wait for a second
}
```

Before you try to upload the code, make sure you have set the right board type under Tools Board to ATtinyXX @ 8MHz. You also have to select the Arduino as ISP under Tools Programmer Arduino as ISP. By default the ATtiny is set to work at 1MHz, so if this is the first time you've programmed a chip, you need to press Tools Burn | Bootloader. This will not actually burn a bootloader on the ATtiny since it does not use one, but it will set it to operate at 8MHz because some of the functions in Arduino code need to run at a higher speed than 1MHz. If all goes well, the IDE should read "Done burning boot loader" above the black window in the IDE; but it will also give you an error message telling you the following:

```
avrdude: please define PAGEL and BS2 signals in the configuration file for part ATtiny25
```

Don't worry. This is normal. The next step is to press Upload to upload the actual sketch. This will also generate the same error message, but again, it is nothing to worry about.

To tell that the sketch is on the ATtiny and that it is in fact working, you will need to connect a LED, like shown in Figure 14-7, to pin 8, which is given the name 0 in the code. All the pins on the ATtiny are renamed in the code to help keep track of which one is which. 0 and 1 are digital pins and the analog pins are named 1, 2, and 3.

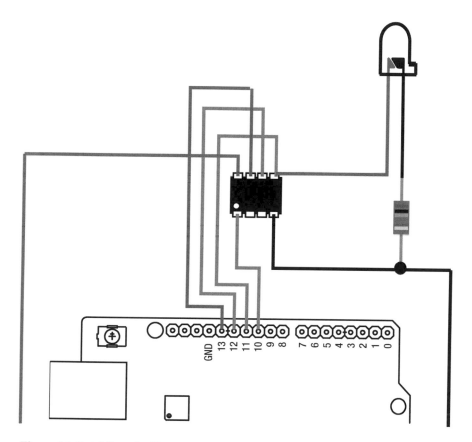

Figure 14-7. Adding the LED

You will also need to add a 220 ohm resistor for the LED. If everything goes according to plan, the LED should start blinking.

The Tiny Chip That Could

Not all the commands that work with the Arduino will work with the ATtiny, but it still has the basic functionality that is needed for most projects. The following are the commands that do work.

- analogRead()
- analogWrite()
- delay()
- delayMicroseconds()
- digitalWrite()

- digitalRead()

- millis()

- micros()

- pinMode()

- pulseIn()

- shiftOut()

If you read all the prior chapters in this book, you should be familiar with most of the commands; yet two of them haven't been used thus far. They are the shiftOut() and pulseIn() commands. pulseIn() is used to calculate the time of a pulse, which is electricity going on and off. The pulseIn() command can, for example, be used to calculate the length of time a button is pushed. The shiftOut() is used to send byte data from the ATtiny to another microcontroller, like another ATtiny or an Arduino board.

When you upload sketches to the ATtiny, you need to disconnect any additional components besides the connection wires found in Figure 14-7; additional components might interfere with the uploading of the code.

Three Tiny Projects

To show where an ATtiny might come in handy, I will present three short and tiny projects. They're tiny in both size and code; however, manufacturing these projects might not be a tiny task. A general rule of thumb when it comes to wearables, or any electronics for that matter, is that the smaller the project, the harder it is to manufacture.

The first one is yet another bracelet, the second is an angry toy rabbit, and the last one is truly a wearable electronics project by definition.

Skin Sound Bracelet

In this project, we will use skin as an analog input. Since skin conducts electricity, we can use it as an input for the ATtiny. We will use the value range from the reading to generate sounds. The idea is to pass electricity from one arm to the other through the body to get a larger range of values. This would also work between two or more people, where their bodies act as resistors.

When it comes to dealing with ATtiny, the process of making a project has problems similar to any wearable project, but these problems are often amplified. As a result, you have to program the ATtiny before you make anything else. You need your sketch on the ATtiny because it will be very hard to program it once it is placed into the garment. With wearables in general, even when made with Arduino boards, you have the same problem because once they are in place inside a garment, they can be tricky to reach for reprogramming. So I recommend hooking up the entire circuit on a breadboard to test everything before we get started with the bracelet. Figure 14-8 shows a schematic of the entire circuit and connection to the Arduino.

Besides the set up for programming the ATtiny, you will need a small 8 ohm speaker, a 1 megohm resistor, and additional wires. The two wires to the left in the schematic that are not connected to anything at the ends are the actual sensor. These two wires will connect to your body; and while testing, you can simply grab them with your hands.

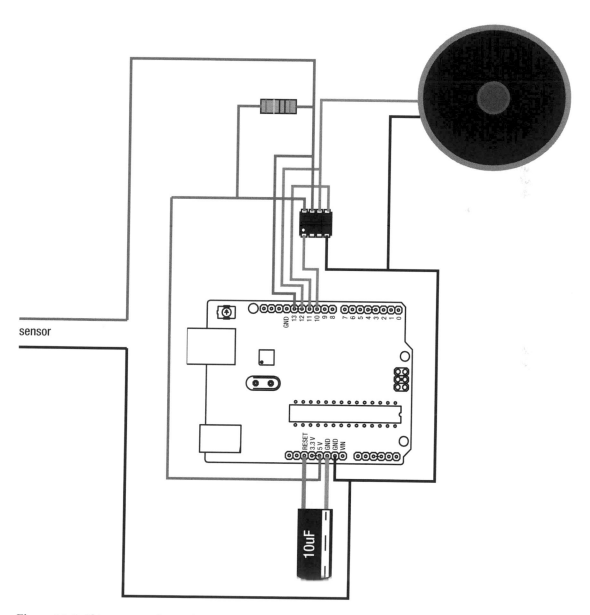

Figure 14-8. Skin sensor schematic

Programming the Bracelet

The code is fairly simple. You read the resistance in your body through an analog pin, and then use the value as a delay for generating tones.

```
//Declare digital pin 1 as speaker
int speaker=1;
//Declare analog pin 1 as skinSensor
int skinSensor=1;

void setup() {
  //Set speaker as a OUTPUT
  pinMode(speaker, OUTPUT);
}

void loop() {
  //Declare a temporary variable and store the values from the sensor
  int skinValue=analogRead(skinSensor);
  //If the value is below 200
  if(skinValue<200){
    //Make a few loops to keep the tone
    for(int i =0; i<30; i++){
      //Set speaker HIGH
      digitalWrite(speaker, HIGH);
      //Wait for a bit
      delayMicroseconds(skinValue *3);
      //Set speaker LOW
      digitalWrite(speaker, LOW);
      //Wait for a bit
      delayMicroseconds(skinValue *3);
    }
  }
}
```

The threshold in the if statement worked according to my body size, so you might want to change this. When the two sensor wires are not touched, the analog pin should read values around 1000; when you touch them, the value should be lower. Inside the if statement, the code for generating the tone is looped a couple of times to make the sound a bit nicer. The delay is also multiplied by three to make the tone range bigger. If you want an even bigger range, you can multiply it with a bigger number. A nicer solution to this to this would be to use the map() function, but unfortunately this command is not supported by the ATtiny. Another problem is that you can't communicate the analog value back to the serial monitor, so you could say that you are coding a bit in the dark.

Instead of complicating things, I suggest a bit of trial and error by uploading sketches to the ATtiny every time you change a value and test it until you get it right. Since the previous sketch is short, it should not take too long until you have figured out a threshold that works with your body. The goal is that the speaker should not sound when you are not touching the wires.

The next step is making the bracelet.

Making the Bracelet

The schematic in Figure 14-9 shows how everything needs to be connected on the bracelet. You don't need to follow this schematic exactly, but you will need to make sure that none of the connections come in contact with one another. What you will need for the actual bracelet is the speaker, the ATtiny, the resistor, and a 3V LilyPad coin cell holder.

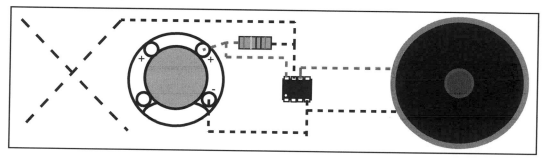

Figure 14-9. Placement of the components

As you might note in Figure 14-9, the ground connection is missing from where it was shown in Figure 14-8. This is where your body will be used instead. When you touch the connection, which is made of conductive thread (the cross in Figure 14-9), you complete the circuit through your body back to the ground connection.

Start by cutting a piece of fabric that fits around your wrist and make it as wide as your speaker, assuming that you are not using a speaker smaller than any other component. Also, cut two strips of elastic approximately 4 centimeters (1.5 inches) shorter than the fabric, as shown in Figure 14-10.

Figure 14-10. Fabric and elastic for the bracelet

Next, stitch the elastic strips to both ends of the fabric and stretch them over the full horizontal length. The elastic is for making sure that the bracelet fits snuggly around your wrist because parts of it need to have good contact with your skin.

The next step is attaching the components to the bracelet and stitching the connections using conductive thread. In some cases, I like to show off the technology, and in this project I think it's really cool to show as much as possible since it adds a nice "wow" factor. So to attach the ATtiny, simply push the legs straight through the fabric, as shown in Figure 14-11.

Figure 14-11. Attaching the ATtiny

To secure the ATtiny in place, bend inward the legs that you will not be using. Leave the legs you will use until it is time to connect the thread connections. The technique I find best for attaching the conductive thread is making a knot around the leg and then squeezing down the leg of the ATtiny. Another trick I use to make the connections more secure and help prevent the thread from fraying at the connections with the leg is to paint it with a bit of conductive paint, as shown in Figure 14-12. Since there is not a lot of space between the legs of the ATtiny, you don't want the conductive thread to move too much since it might come in contact with the leg next to it. When the conductive paint dries, it helps to keep the thread in place.

Figure 14-12. *Paint the end connections with conductive ink to make them more secure.*

Instead of using conductive paint, you could also use super glue; but you have to make sure you have good contact between the conductive thread and the ATtiny leg before you apply. It is a good idea to have a multimeter close by so that you can test every connection and check that it has no short circuits anywhere.

The speaker I used had no good areas for sewing it in place, so I just glued it to the bracelet using super glue.

The cross in Figure 14-9 is the touch pad made of conductive thread, which should be on the front of the bracelet. Be sure to make it as big as possible so that you get a good contact area for the skin.

The last step is to cover everything on the inside of the bracelet with another piece of fabric—except the ground stitches, which you want exposed against the skin on the inside or the sensor will not work. I made an extra ground line in the elastic, the length of half my wrist, to make sure I get good connections, as shown in Figure 14-13.

Figure 14-13. The extended ground connection between the battery and the ATtiny made with conductive thread into the elastic that connects to the skin

Your skin sound bracelet should be done. Now pop in a 3V coin cell battery in the battery holder and find out what your body sounds like. When you touch the cross on the bracelet with the opposite hand, the bracelet should start making some funky sounds.

The Angry Rabbit

The second tiny project is a fun little stuffed toy. The idea is that when you squeeze the belly of the rabbit, it gets angry. It indicates this by flashing its red eyes. For this project, we need to construct a pressure sensor. Making a pressure sensor is very easy and you can make it very cheaply. All you need is a piece of conductive foam. When you buy electronics, they usually come packaged in foam that is conductive to protect them from static electricity. This foam is perfect for building sensors. To make a pressure sensor, you only need to stick two wires into each end of the foam and add glue to the sides and the wire, and you are basically done (see Figure 14-14).

Figure 14-14. Pressure sensor made from conductive foam

Before we get started with the ATtiny circuit, try out the sensor with an Arduino board according to the schematic shown in Figure 14-15.

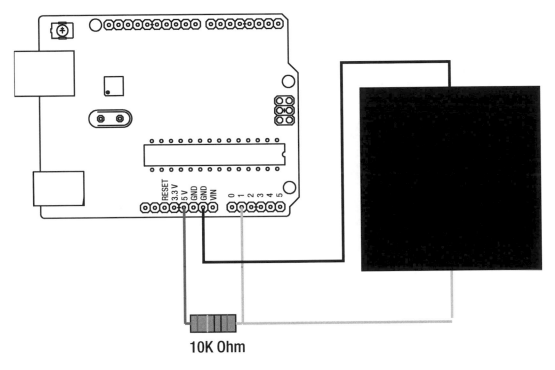

10K Ohm

Figure 14-15. Pressure sensor made from conductive foam

You need to add a resistor connected to 5 volts to make a reference value. The value of the resistor depends on the size of your conductive foam. The foam piece I used is similar in size to the one in Figure 14-15, if you compare it to the Arduino board. In this case, a 10 megohm resistor gave me a nice value range.

Next, try out the pressure sensor with the following code, which will print the values from the sensor back to the monitor:

```
//Set pressureSensor to analog pin 0
int pressureSensor = 1;

void setup() {
  //Start serial communication at 9600 baud
  Serial.begin(9600);
}

void loop() {
  //Declare a temporary variable and store the value from the sensor
  int pressureValue = analogRead(pressureSensor);
  //Print the value
  Serial.println(pressureValue);
  //Wait for a bit
  delay(100);
}
```

The sensor I made gave me a reading around 1000 when the sensor was not touched; when I put pressure on the foam, the value dropped all the way down to around 300. If you are not getting a good range of values from your piece of foam, try to gradually increase the resistance of the resistor used in Figure 14-14. With the value from the foam in relation to time, we will be able to calculate how long and how hard someone is squeezing the rabbit.

There is a problem, however. When we switch over to powering the ATtiny with batteries, the analog readings might change a bit. So while working with the ATtiny, try out your circuits as much as possible with an Arduino board, and once you have the basic functionality of what you want to achieve, switch over and test your circuit with the ATtiny.

You are not actually using the pressure data in this project; you are using the sensor like a button because you are basically looking for an on/off state in the code. The pressure sensor is just a quicker way of making a large push button compared to gluing two pieces of conductive materials to a piece of non-conductive foam with a hole in it.

The Angry Rabbit Code

The following sketch has the basic functionality of the way I intended my angry rabbit to work. When you squeeze the pressure sensor, the LEDs start to fade up and down. If you continue to squeeze the sensor, they continue to fade faster and faster until they go into a blinking mode to indicate that the rabbit is very unhappy. This sketch also implements a timer in which five seconds have to pass to let the rabbit calm down, which is when the LEDs start over from a fading state. If you squeeze the rabbit during the cool down time, it will jump to the angry state you left it in during the prior squeeze.

```
//Declare analog pin 1 as pressureSensor
int pressureSensor = 1;
//Declare digital pin 0 as eye1
int eye1= 0;
//Declare digital pin 1 as eye2
int eye2= 1;
//Variable for delaying each fade step
int angryTime=10;
//Declare variable for timer
int coolDownTime;

void setup() {
  //Declare eye1 as OUTPUT
  pinMode(eye1,OUTPUT);
  //Declare eye2 as OUTPUT
  pinMode(eye2,OUTPUT);
}

void loop() {
  //Start counting the time
  int time=millis();
  //If angryTime is down to 1 and time has passed the coolDownTime
  if(angryTime==1 && time> coolDownTime){
    //Reset angryTime to 10
    angryTime=10;
  }
  //While the pressureSensor is below 400 loop over and over agin
  while(analogRead(pressureSensor)<400){
```

299

```
      //Reset the coolDowntime to current time plus five seconds
      coolDownTime=millis()+5000;
      //If angryTime is bigger than one
      if(angryTime>1){
        //Loop from 0 to 255
        for(int i =0; i<255; i++){
          //Increase the light with one every time
          analogWrite(eye1,i);
          analogWrite(eye2,i);
          //Wait for a bit
          delay(angryTime);
        }
        //Loop from 255 down to 0
        for(int i =255; i>0; i--){
          //Decrease the light with one every time
          analogWrite(eye1,i);
          analogWrite(eye2,i);
          //Wait for a bit
          delay(angryTime);
        }
      }
      //Decrease angry time by 2 for every loop
      angryTime-=2;
      //If angry time is smaller or equals to 1
      if(angryTime<=1){
        //Keep angryTime at !
        angryTime=1;
        //Turn on eye1
        digitalWrite(eye1,HIGH);
        //Turn off eye2
        digitalWrite(eye2,LOW);
        //Wait for a bit
        delay(100);
        //Turn off eye1
        digitalWrite(eye1,LOW);
        //Turn on eye2
        digitalWrite(eye2,HIGH);
        //Wait for a bit
        delay(100);
      }
    }
    //Outside the while loop make sure the LEDs stay off
    digitalWrite(eye1,LOW);
    digitalWrite(eye2,LOW);
}
```

You probably need to try this code with your ATtiny and the circuit setup found in Figure 14-15. You should be able to set up the circuit with the wire connections needed to program it from the Arduino found in Figure 14-16. The only thing you might have a problem with is the threshold for the while loop. So the way to do it is to upload the sketch, then disconnect the power from the Arduino, and power the ATtiny from the battery pack. If the LEDs are on when you are not putting pressure on the sensor, the threshold is too big. If they don't go on while putting pressure on the sensor, then the threshold is too small. You might need to lower or raise the threshold a few times until you get it right. Remember that you have to disconnect the LEDs every time you upload a sketch to the ATtiny.

Constructing the Angry Rabbit

The following figure shows how to make the circuit for the angry rabbit; but before you get started, you need the final sketch on the chip, found in the previous section of this chapter. Once you have everything working on a breadboard, you can get started with the rabbit.

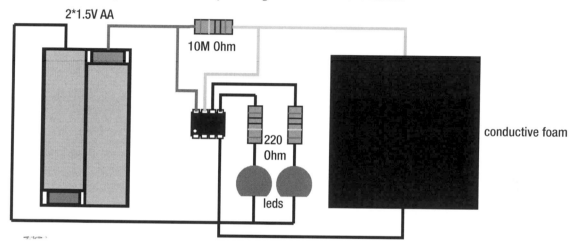

Figure 14-16. The angry rabbit circuit

This project does not include a design pattern because the final base design of my rabbit is only made from two pieces of fabric, as shown in Figure 14-18. Instead, the idea is to solder all components together straight onto the ATtiny chip so that the only part that needs to be mounted into the fabric are the LED eyes and the pressure sensor. The ATtiny is then glued straight to an AA battery pack, which I recommend for this project. As long as the circuit and battery fit, you can make any stuffed animal or creature; it doesn't need to be a rabbit.

Start with drawing your rabbit (or other animal) design onto a piece of fabric. If you want any other details using other fabrics, this is the time to add them. The next step is to poke the LEDs through the side that will be the front of the fabric. On the inside, twist the LED legs with your pliers, as in previous projects, and solder the wires to both the negative and the positive legs.

The next step is to solder all other components and connections shown in Figure 14-16 straight to the ATtiny (see Figure 14-17). Be sure not to heat the ATtiny legs for too long, or you might end up burning the chip.

Figure 14-17. Soldering all connections straight to the ATtiny

The resistors can be soldered straight to the ATtiny legs where needed, and then you just add cables on the other side. Use a helping hand to hold the ATtiny steady while soldering. Once all connections have been made, you can glue the ATtiny to the battery connector and cover it with electrical or normal sticky tape, which will help prevent short circuits.

Use textile glue to attach the pressure sensor any place you desire. Don't put it too close to the LEDs, however, because you want to avoid squeezing in that area.

Once your electronics are in place, place another piece of fabric facing the front of the rabbit and stitch the outline of your design. Leave enough room to turn the rabbit inside out so that the electronics make their way to the inside.

The last step is to fill the rabbit with stuffing, put batteries in the battery pack, and make the rabbit angry, as shown in Figure 14-18.

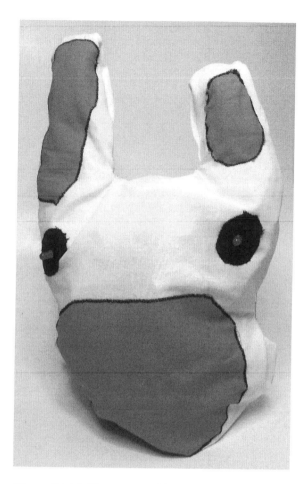

Figure 14-18. The angry rabbit

Tiny Boards

The third tiny project, the final project of the book, shows how to make your own Arduino-compatible board using only an ATtiny, conductive paint, and transparent overhead paper. Conductive paint is nice to use for securing connections like in the skin sound bracelet project; but you can also use it for making straight connections. Bare Conductive (www.bareconductive.com) is a company that makes conductive material and produces a nontoxic conductive paint that is perfect for experimenting. The paint is water-based; there is no need to worry about messing up your connections because the paint can be washed away with water. As a side note, however, if you do get it on fabric, the fabric might need a good washing. It is a good idea to try it out on a cheaper material that is easy to wash if needed. I like transparent overhead paper since it washes easily and helps you to keep track of your traces.

The project simply shows how to add male pin connectors to the ATtiny so that you can plug it straight to an Arduino board. You might not be able to use it as a functional prototyping board since the design is a bit fragile, but it is a good exercise in circuit design. The only real difference from the board you will make and a manufactured board like the Arduino or the LilyPad is that they are made by machines in different materials. When you reach this far, however, you probably understand the basics of printed circuit boards. The next step is to start using professional software tools for your designs.

If you truly want to "wear" your electronics, you can even paint the circuit onto your skin. Bare Conductive has a conductive paint made especially for use on skin. But before we get ahead of ourselves, let's have a look at how it can be done on a piece of plastic.

Making the Board

To make your own ATtiny "board," start by lining up the row of male pin headers to one of the edges of the transparent plastic sheet. Make sure the short pin headers are pressed against the plastic sheet. Then add a little bit of super glue to the two pins at the edges, making sure they stick to the plastic sheet. Wait for a few seconds to let the glue dry.

To attach the ATtiny, make eight small holes into the sheet for the ATtiny's legs. Leave some space between the placement of the ATtiny and the male pin connectors. Before you get started with the conductive paint, it might be a good idea to mark your traces with a pen so you can make sure everything goes in the right place and that all the traces have enough room. Figure 14-19 shows the traces needed to program the ATtiny—except for the 5V connector since this is placed on the other side of the Arduino board.

Figure 14-19. Marking the traces onto the overhead

In Figure 14-19, it looks like one of the traces goes through the rest, but it is actually marked on the other side of the overhead. Once you put the ATtiny in place, bend the legs as shown in Figure 14-19. The legs of the ATtiny are poked through the plastic sheet and are then bent outwards from the chip to hold it in place. This also enables making a dual-layer board. It is also a technique used in manufacturing PCB; when there is no room for making an entire circuit on a single side, you add another layer so connections can cross one another on opposite sides of the PCB. Normal computers have as many as 16 layers or more.

In Figure 14-20 you see the traces that need to be made, as well as two pads that will work as the ground and power connection so that you can connect a battery once you are done programming your board.

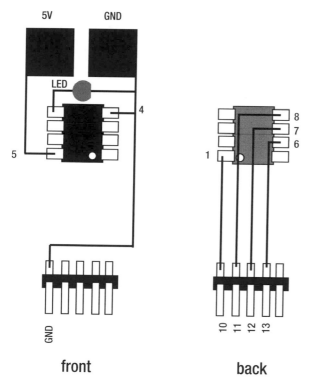

Figure 14-20. ATtiny board traces

Figure 14-20 shows the traces for the front and back that need to be made. I also added a LED connected to digital pin 0 of the ATtiny and the GND connection so we can tell if it's actually working. Once you have them marked out, it's time to start painting. Be sure that none of the traces of conductive paint comes in contact with each other. This is why it's nice to use transparent overheads to play around with; it is easy to spot if any of the traces come in contact with one another. If they do, don't worry. You can just leave the paint to dry. When it is dry, it gets hard, and then you can use a small screwdriver to scrape the traces clean of one another. Even if you make a complete mess out of things, it's no problem because you can clean everything off the overhead with some water and paper towel, and start over again.

Once the painted traces have dried, you can check the connections with a multimeter from end to end. If there is no connection, the trace might be broken and you will need to paint it some more.

Connecting the Board

Once you are done, it's time to try out your homemade board with a sketch. We began this book with a blinking LED sketch; I find it fitting to end it with one as well. If you have gone through all the projects in the book, you probably know how to make it yourself.

To program your board, simply plug it into your Arduino board between the GND pin to pin 10, and use a crocodile clip to connect the power pad to 5V (as shown in Figure 14-21)—and don't forget the 10µF capacitor while uploading your sketch.

Figure 14-21. Uploading the final sketch

Wrapping Up

In this chapter, I introduced the concept of going beyond off-the-shelf components. The ATtiny microprocessors were used for customizing and minimizing your projects. I also introduced ways you can modify the Arduino IDE to extend its functionality.

The Arduino programming language and board, as well as the LilyPad, are truly great tools for making wearable electronics projects. They serve a huge range of potential needs. Yet it is impossible for the people behind these great inventions to anticipate every single need their users might have. This is the beauty of open source—you are not limited to what the creators of these tools have made possible. Open-source tools invite anyone to build upon the progress of others and make tools fit others' needs.

The three tiny projects in this chapter demonstrate that once you have reached the point where you know exactly what it is you want to do, there are other options to making your creations as wearable as possible.

If you have managed all the projects in this book and you feel that you have a good grasp on how they work, then it is time for you to face the next project on your own.

Index